BOY SCOUTS of AMERICA®

A CENTENNIAL HISTORY

BOY SCOUTS of AMERICA®

A CENTENNIAL HISTORY

BY CHUCK WILLS

ON THIS PAGE Ernest Thompson Seton draws a crowd around the Boy Scouts of America rock, engraved with the organization's initials and 1911.

CONTENTS

FOREWORD

The year was 1910, and a Chicago publisher—gentlemanly in his appearance yet passionate about his vision—incorporated the Boy Scouts of America. His name was W. D. Boyce, and on February 8, under the laws of the District of Columbia, his inspired dream of creating an organization that would cultivate and harness the highest ideals and aspirations for the nation's young boys started a century of service to America.

Like many ideas that endure, this vision was inspired by life experiences that left indelible impressions. Specifically, in 1909, Boyce was lost in a dense London fog. A boy came to his aid and guided him to his destination. When Boyce offered a tip, the boy refused it, explaining that he was a Boy Scout and could not accept money for doing a good turn. Intrigued, Boyce set out to learn about the Boy Scouts and its founder, Robert Baden-Powell.

Baden-Powell had become a military hero during his service in the Boer War in South Africa. Upon his return to England after the war, he was surprised to learn that a manual he had written for soldiers about tracking and survival had become popular with British boys. Building upon the manual's outdoor skills and his own ideas about citizenship and positive living, Baden-Powell developed what became the Boy Scouts.

Boyce took what he learned back to the United States. Other Americans were already working with boys through their own character-building and outdoor groups, including Ernest Thompson Seton with his Woodcraft Indians and Daniel Carter Beard with his Sons of Daniel Boone. James E. West, who was later to become the first Chief Scout Executive, worked for the YMCA and other youth-support organizations.

LEFT (top) A Joseph Csatari painting celebrates the World Scouting 100th Anniversary. (bottom) The noble traditions of Scouting continue with a new generation.

Collectively, these men are recognized as the founding fathers of the Boy Scouts of America. The product of their vision, talents, experiences, and determination lives on today. It lives on through the images and stories captured on the following pages and has remained fundamentally unchanged and relevant through the decades. Officially, its purpose is presented this way:

"The mission of the Boy Scouts of America is to prepare young people to make ethical and moral choices over their lifetimes by instilling in them the values of the Scout Oath and Law."

This powerful statement crystallizes the volunteerism, the sacrifices, the dreams, the aspirations, the patriotism, and the collective essence of our truly American story over the past century. Our nation has always been anchored in the ideas of service, community, and purpose; and synonymous to this, by way of the Scouting programs that develop them, is the sustaining power of values and morals in the lives of individuals.

We are Robert Baden-Powell, Ernest Thompson Seton, Daniel Carter Beard, William D. Boyce, James E. West; we are the Boy Scouts of America. The more than 110 million alumni who have been and who are now part of our movement represent our centennial history and the highest ideals our shared vision has instilled in them.

So as we approach the year 2010 and the 100-year anniversary of the Boy Scouts of America, our relevance to young boys in our society remains strong. This milestone and the contents of this wonderfully illustrated book, *Boy Scouts of America: A Centennial History*, represent our journey—a journey ignited by the vision of our founding fathers, nurtured by our volunteers, and enjoyed by millions of young people. It is a journey that is inextricably linked to the American story.

In this spirit, let us all celebrate our glorious past while we look with excitement and anticipation into our unlimited future.

JOHN GOTTSCHALK
President

TICO A. PEREZ
National commissioner

RANDALL STEPHENSON
National chairman

ROBERT J. MAZZUCA
Chief Scout Executive

"To the Unknown Scout Whose Faithfulness in the Performance of the Daily Good Turn Brought the Scout Movement to the United States of America."

INSCRIPTION OF THE BUFFALO STATUE DEDICATED TO THE UNKNOWN SCOUT, GILWELL PARK, 1926

LEFT A Norman Rockwell painting inspired by the "Unknown Scout" assisting W. D. Boyce across a foggy London street. The boy helped Boyce by performing a "good turn," without expecting any sort of reward.

PART ONE

THE BIRTH OF THE BOY SCOUTS

c. 1898–1920

One day in August 1909, a wealthy American newspaper and magazine publisher, W. D. Boyce, set out on foot for a business meeting in London. The city—a metropolis still largely heated by coal and lit by gas—was in the midst of one of its legendary "pea-soup" fogs. The fog was so thick that Boyce hesitated before crossing the street.

At that moment a boy "about ten or twelve years old, I think" (as Boyce recalled two decades later) appeared out of the gloom, a lantern in his hand. The boy offered to guide Boyce across the street, and the grateful American took him up on the offer. When they reached the other side in safety, Boyce reached into his pocket for a coin. But the boy refused Boyce's tip. He was a Boy Scout, he explained, and he was simply doing a "good turn." "I was interested," Boyce later wrote, "and asked him about his organization."

Boyce never learned the boy's name. To this day the lad with the lantern is revered in the lore of Scouting as the "Unknown Scout." But the eventual result of this random meeting on a foggy London day was the founding of the most successful and enduring youth movement in the history of the United States—the Boy Scouts of America.

SETTING THE STAGE FOR THE SCOUTS

As America entered the 20th century, three distinct but related movements—concern over the physical, moral, and citizenship development of American boys; an appreciation of the importance of contact with nature in a rapidly urbanizing society; and a growing interest in American Indian culture—began converging to create the Boy Scouts of America.

At the turn of the century, America was rapidly changing from a nation of farmers and artisans to one of factory hands and office workers. The country's transition to an urbanized, industrialized society worried some Americans. Certainly, there was widespread pride in the nation's growth and accomplishments. But there was also a sense that some valuable things were being lost in this transition—particularly where the moral, physical, and spiritual development of boys and young men was concerned.

An American who was around fifty years of age at the turn of the 20th century lived in a nation that had been transformed since his or her childhood. America's population had soared from barely 23 million in 1850 to more than 76 million in 1900, in part because of a tide of immigration that surged in the 1890s and would peak in 1907, when 1.25 million new

Americans entered the country. There were forty-five stars on the American flag when the new century began; three more—representing the new states of Oklahoma, Arizona, and New Mexico—would be added by 1912. In a famous lecture givwen in 1893, historian Frederick Jackson Turner proclaimed "the end of the frontier"—the vanishing of the line between settled and unsettled land in the West.

The products of the nation's mills and mines, factories and workshops, forests and fields, now made it an economic powerhouse that rivaled and soon exceeded Great Britain, then the world's greatest industrial nation. In 1900, for example, one American corporation—U.S. Steel—produced more of the metal than all of Britain's steel mills combined.

America's industrial might was made possible not only by its great natural resources and its growing labor force, but also by huge advances in technology. In the last decades of the 19th century, those advances were the wonder of the world—and they changed daily life in America profoundly. Homes that were once lit by whale-oil lamps were now illuminated by Thomas Edison's electric lights. Families could gather in their parlors to listen to, say, the great opera singer Enrico Caruso on another of Edison's inventions—the phonograph. If the family lived in a community that offered the service, they might invite the neighbors over using Alexander Graham Bell's invention—the telephone. If they chose instead to go out, they could take in the silent, black-and-white, flickering but fascinating entertainment that would soon become known as "the movies"—another product of Edison's New Jersey laboratory. Henry Ford's Model T—"the car that put America on wheels"—would not appear until 1908, but "horseless carriages" were already a common sight on city streets.

Throughout much of the 19th century most Americans had made their living from the land. Every family member—male or female, young or old—had to contribute their labor. A boy was expected to help his father in the fields as soon as he was physically able. On frontier homesteads, boys learned outdoor skills—hunting, tracking, fishing, trapping, and foraging for wild foodstuffs—from an early age. In these circumstances, living an active, outdoor life was a matter of necessity, not choice: The family needed food on the table. And in an era before electricity and the automobile, learning to ride a horse, to feed and care for domestic animals, and to use an ax and other implements were part of growing up. Later generations would be spared

this labor, but many of the boys who grew to manhood in this era would later recall just how fun, and fulfilling, their rural boyhoods had been.

As the 19th century drew to a close and more and more Americans moved to towns and cities to take wage-earning jobs, things changed for a lot of American boys. Many no longer worked side by side with their fathers, expecting to one day take over the family farm or workshop and to live with their families until they married and began families of their own. Growing numbers of young men—clerks, mechanics, and factory workers—began living relatively solitary lives in urban boardinghouses, where they might fall prey to drinking, gambling, or other temptations.

And as the nation industrialized, many boys (and girls, for that matter) were pretty much deprived of a childhood altogether. Laws against child labor lay in the future; around 1900, for example, 25,000 American boys did backbreaking work in the nation's coal mines alone. Many child laborers were the children of immigrants, which raised another concern: How could children growing up in these grinding conditions learn to become good American citizens?

By the turn of the century there was already a wide variety of organizations devoted to providing wholesome recreation, moral guidance, and citizenship training for boys and young men. Nineteenth-century America being a churchgoing and mostly Protestant nation, many of these groups were affiliated with various Protestant churches. Besides the groups associated with specific churches, there was also the non-denominational Young Men's Christian Association (YMCA). Founded in Britain in 1844, the YMCA came to America in the early 1850s, and a half century later the organization played a major role in the establishment of the Boy Scouts on both sides of the Atlantic. Another British-bred organization, the Boys' Brigade, combined religious instruction with military drill, while America's home-grown anti-alcohol movement sponsored youth groups like the Church Temperance League.

Besides worries about the moral health of America's boys and young men, there was also concern, as the 20th century dawned, over the toll that America's growth had taken on the land itself, and on the wild creatures that lived on it. In the mid-19th century, for example, huge herds of buffalo (or, more properly, the American bison) roamed the Great Plains of the

ABOVE (left) Allegorical print showing aspects of frontier life, with vignettes of activities such as surveying, mining, and hunting, 1881. (right) Family in front of their farm in Nebraska, 1886.

West. By the late 1880s, their numbers had been thinned to a few thousand as hunters shot them for their meat, their hides, or for sport. The buffalo, at least, escaped extinction. The passenger pigeon wasn't so lucky. The birds—whose migrating flocks numbered in the billions and darkened the skies for days in their passing—were slaughtered so relentlessly (often just for fertilizer) that the last living specimen died in an Ohio zoo in 1914. Meanwhile, the drive to wring ever more wealth from the land—in the form of crops, timber, coal, or minerals—put some of the nation's most beautiful wilderness areas in danger.

Congress established the nation's first national park—Yellowstone, in Wyoming—in 1872, but it wasn't until around the turn of the 20th century that a movement for conservation and preservation of America's natural resources gathered strength, fueled by the writings of naturalists such as John Muir (1838–1914) and John Burroughs (1837–1921). President Theodore Roosevelt—an avid naturalist and outdoorsman himself—was a strong supporter of conservation efforts.

Plains—had been crushed by overwhelming military force by 1890. (And, in the case of the Sioux, by the slaughter of the buffalo herds on which they depended for their traditional way of life.) As the 20th century dawned, the Indian population in the West had dwindled to a couple of hundred thousand people living in extreme poverty on reservations.

Ironically, even before the Indians ceased to be a threat to settlement, white Americans had admired many aspects of American Indian culture—their physical hardiness, their skill in living in harmony with nature, and the values by which they lived their lives. American Indian society, for example, was in many ways more "free and equal" than that of white America. When the great Sioux leader Sitting Bull (c. 1831–1890) visited cities in the 1880s, he was shocked by the gap between rich and poor. Among his people, everyone ate well when a hunt was successful, regardless of who actually brought in the game.

The mainstream view of American Indian life at the turn of the 20th century may have been a bit romanticized and

Besides worries about the moral health of America's boys and young men, there was also concern, as the 20th century dawned, over the toll that America's growth had taken on the land itself.

There were differences between conservationists and preservationists—the former wanted to make sure natural resources would be available for economic development in the future, while the latter wanted to safeguard wilderness areas from development of any kind. But even though conservation sometimes trumped preservation, the movement as a whole led many Americans to appreciate the spiritual value of contact with nature—something that the philosopher Henry David Thoreau (1817–1862) had expressed decades earlier when he wrote that "In wildness is the preservation of the world."

Some Americans also sought to preserve the legacy of the nation's original inhabitants: the American Indians.

From colonial times onward, most white Americans considered the Indians "savages" and an obstacle to settlement. By the end of the 19th century, though, the Indians were no longer a threat to the progress of "civilization." The last Indian nations to seriously resist the tide of white settlement—the Apaches of the southwestern deserts and the Sioux of the Great

simplistic—but at least there was a rising awareness that much of that life was admirable and worthy of emulation. At the same time, as more and more Americans left the country behind for the city, the heritage of the white pioneers who had settled the West (at the expense of the American Indian) also became enshrined in America's consciousness.

Two men—Daniel Carter Beard (1850–1941) and Ernest Thompson Seton (1860–1946)—would play leading roles in weaving these parallel American strands together, within the wider tapestry of the worldwide movement created by a British general named Robert Stephenson Smyth Baden-Powell (1857–1941).

DANIEL CARTER BEARD AND THE SONS OF DANIEL BOONE

Daniel Carter Beard was born in Ohio in 1850, and his family moved to Kentucky shortly after the Civil War broke out in 1861. The eleven-year-old boy became the "man of the house" when his father—a portrait painter—joined the Union Army. When he wasn't helping his mother or caring for his younger sisters, he roamed the nearby woods with a gang of friends, pretending to be pioneers in the spirit of Daniel Boone, the frontiersman who'd spearheaded Kentucky's settlement a century earlier.

Dan inherited his father's artistic talent, but he trained as an engineer and worked as a surveyor for a map publisher before turning his hand to art full time. The story goes that Beard was visiting his brother in New York City in 1878 when a magazine publisher happened to see a sketch of a fish that Beard had made on one of his surveying trips. The publisher offered Beard $25 for the sketch. Beard accepted, gave his notice at the map company, and enrolled at the city's Art Students League to get some formal training. For the rest of his life he made his living as an illustrator, editor, and writer.

For a time Beard made a good living indeed. He had a wonderful eye for nature and a lively visual style. Over the next few years he won commissions from *St. Nicholas*, *Youth's Companion*, and other leading children's magazines. His first book, *The American Boy's Handy Book*, appeared in 1882. In print ever since, the *Handy Book* was a do-it-yourself guide to outdoor fun and woodcraft skills; organized by seasonal activities, it showed boys how to do everything from camp out in a tent to how to perform "basic taxidermy."

In 1889, Mark Twain hired Beard to do the illustrations for his novel *A Connecticut Yankee in King Arthur's Court*. Twain (the pen name of Samuel Clemens) was one of the most popular American writers of the time, having already published classics like *The Adventures of Tom Sawyer* and *Adventures of Huckleberry Finn*.

Getting Twain's nod as an illustrator should have been a big career boost. But while Twain liked Beard's illustrations, some powerful Americans did not. Beard had a keen social conscience and he held some ideas that were radical by the standards of the time: For example, he was a staunch supporter of economist Henry George, who promoted an economic system based on a single tax on land as a way of leveling the playing field. Under George's plan, people who did not own land would not be subject to taxes at all.

ABOVE (top) Photograph of Daniel Carter Beard in his element, wearing outdoor gear in the midst of a forest. (bottom) The original cover of Beard's first book, depicting boys engaged in a number of adventurous activities.

Constitution of the
Sons of Daniel Boone

Article I.

T HE NAME of this Association is THE SONS OF DANIEL BOONE. The name of this Fort is

Fort Brownville, *No. 219.*

Article II.

OBJECTS.

The objects of this Association are, the elevation of sport; the encouragement of all healthy, wholesome *outdoor* recreation and fun; the promotion of true manliness; the preservation of our native wild plants, birds and beasts, and the study of woodcraft, of the lives and exploits of American pioneers and of the natural history of the country.

Article III.

THE OFFICERS.

The officers of this Fort shall be a President, with the title of Daniel Boone; a Secretary, with the title of Davy Crockett; a Treasurer, with the title of Kit Carson; a Librarian, with the title of Audubon; the Keeper of the Tally Gun, with the title of Simon Kenton; a Forester, with the title of Johnny Appleseed; a Founder, and as many lively boys as possible with the title of Scouts.

Dan. Beard is the Founder and Presiding Officer over all the Councils, and the only boy over twenty-one having a voice in the Councils.

All the other officers shall be elected by ballot, for term of one year, at the annual meeting of the Fort.

Article IV.

DUTIES.

The duties of Daniel Boone, Davy Crockett and Carson shall be those usual to the offices of Preside Secretary and Treasurer.

Daniel Boone. Daniel Boone shall preside at all Co cils of the Fort and attend to the other duties usua the office of President.

Davy Crockett. Davy Crockett shall write all offi letters and keep the minutes of the meetings of the Cou

Kit Carson. Kit Carson shall keep the funds of Fort, accounting to the President and Council for moneys received and paid, and perform the other du usual to a Treasurer.

Audubon. Audubon shall subscribe for one copy the *Woman's Home Companion* for the use of the F and shall take charge of the files of the magazine a other literature belonging to the Fort.

Simon Kenton. It shall be the duty of Simon Ken to keep the Fort's tally-gun and to make the notche its stock in the presence of the Council when so direc by Daniel Boone.

Johnny Appleseed. It shall be the duty of Johnny Appleseed to act as Peace Maker in the camp, in the field and on the playground, to prevent or adjust all quarrels among the Scouts, and to decide any disputes that may arise during athletic contests or games. He shall also act as umpire, judge or referee at the games, and be the presiding officer at the tree-planting on Arbor Day.

Founder. It shall be the privilege of the Founder to act as general adviser to all Sons of Daniel Boone.

Scouts. It shall be the duty of the Scouts to be jolly good fellows and to aid their officers on all occasions so as to make a success of the Association in general and of their own Fort in particular.

Article V.

MEMBERS AND HONORARY MEMBERS.

Any boy under twenty-one years of age, of good moral character, may become an active member. Any "boy" over twenty-one who is a subscriber to the *Woman's Home Companion* may be elected an Honorary Member, but can take no part in the business of the society, except as an adviser; and an Honorary Member's advice or suggestions may, or may not, be acted upon, as the Fort decides.

Article VI.

BALLOT.

The ballot for membership shall be secret. 2 black balls shall be necessary to debar a candidate from becoming a member of the Fort.

Article VII.

ORDER OF BUSINESS.

The order of business shall be as follows:
(1) Roll call by Davy Crockett.
(2) Bringing in the Gun by Simon Kenton.

(The gun-keeper, Simon Kenton, escorted by the Secretary, Davy Crockett, carries the gun to its accustomed resting-place in the meeting-room, while all the members stand.)

(3) Committee reports.
(4) Old Business.
(5) New Business.

(Under the two latter heads, Committees may be appointed, discussions held, and

timber, but use dead or imperfect trees, and best to preserve the forests. I realize that, besides being of immense value to my country, they are the retreat of all forest-loving beasts and birds.

(5) I realize that a good woodsman is careful with fire, and I will never carelessly permit fire to run in the woods.

(6) I will never allow a fire-arm, even though it be unloaded, to point at any person, nor will I allow it to point at any animal I do not wish to kill.

(7) In all my conduct I will remember that I am a loyal SON OF DANIEL BOONE and will never willingly bring discredit upon the organization.

This shall be Considered the Official Charter of Fort **Brown**, *No. 219.* of the Sons of Daniel Boone, when Signed and Sealed by the Founder.

Dan Beard
Founder.

Dated, *February 11,* 19*07.*

NOTE! Fill in the blanks with the name of the Fort, the number of black balls necessary to exclude a candidate, and the amount of dues. Each Fort decides for itself the number of black balls necessary to defeat a candidate for membership, also what dues, if any, are required to run the Fort.

When *A Connecticut Yankee* was published, some of the wealthy and powerful noted that Beard's drawings of the book's villainous characters bore more than a passing resemblance to leading political and business figures. Beard's publishing commissions became fewer and farther between.

When Beard first arrived in New York, he'd been horrified by the sight of newsboys sleeping on the street. It was a stark contrast to the healthy outdoor life he'd enjoyed as a boy in Ohio and Kentucky. So as the 19th century turned into the 20th, Beard channeled his talents and energy into creating a national boys' movement inspired by the nation's frontier heritage and the new interest in conservation.

The movement took form in 1905 in the pages of *Recreation* magazine, which Beard edited, and it was called the Sons of Daniel Boone. (Later, legal disputes over the ownership of the name led Beard to rename the group the Boy Pioneers.) In Beard's words, the Sons of Daniel Boone was aimed at "The elevation of sport, the support of all that tends to healthy, wholesome manliness; the study of woodcraft, outdoor recreation, and fun, and serious work for the making of laws prohibiting the sale of game, and the preservation of our native wild plants, birds, and beasts." As the movement's name implied, Beard's main inspiration came not from American Indian culture but the example of the pioneers he called "Knights in buckskin."

The Sons' organizational unit was a "fort," which was supposed to include four "stockades" of eight boys each. Stockade leaders were known by ceremonial names such as Kit Carson, Johnny Appleseed, and Davy Crockett. (The fort leader, of course, was Daniel Boone.) The Sons was fairly loosely organized so total membership between 1905 and 1910 isn't known. Estimates range from 2,000 to 20,000.

ERNEST THOMPSON SETON

Seton was born in England in 1860 and immigrated to Canada with his family six years later. As a boy, he had a difficult relationship with his father—something that would later lead him to change his name (he was born Ernest Evan Thompson). To escape his troubled home life, Seton spent as much time as he could in the woods around his family's Ontario farm, closely observing animal, plant, and bird life.

Young Seton proved to have a remarkable talent for capturing wildlife in drawings and paintings—a talent he refined at the Royal Academy in London and later at the Art Students League in New York City, where he first met another nature-loving artist, Daniel Carter Beard. Travels in the wilds of western Canada led to the publication of his first book, *Mammals of Manitoba*, in 1886.

Over the next few years Seton became a highly regarded and sought-after writer and artist, especially after he published *Wild Animals I Have Known* in 1898. The book's success allowed him to purchase a country estate in Cos Cob, Connecticut, which he named Wyndygoul.

Seton was a complicated and charismatic man. Journalist Lincoln Steffens described him "[as] tall, handsome, poet-like, he was animal-like, too. I suppose 'child-like' is the word most people would use to describe the animal sense he had for springs, trees and shady nooks." He socialized with many of the leading literary, business, and political figures of the time, but

LEFT (foreground) One of the many nature drawings Ernest Thompson Seton sketched in his childhood, showing a hunting dog's bounty by a blazing campfire. (background) Beard's outdoorsman manifesto: the Constitution of the Sons of Daniel Boone, signed by Beard himself. **ABOVE** Seton at fourteen years old, dressed in a bow tie and suit for a formal portrait.

he continued to slip away into the wilds, where he found not only new material for his "animal stories" but spiritual renewal.

Like so many leading figures of the day, Seton worried about the impact changes in American society were having on the nation's manhood as more and more boys grew up in towns and cities, cut off from nature and ignorant of the skills that he called the "woodcraft idea." Seton railed against the "money grubbing, machine politics, degrading sports . . . town life of the worst kind that [has] turned such a large proportion of our robust, manly, self-reliant boyhood into a nation of flat-chested cigarette smokers, with shaky nerves and doubtful vitality."

To combat these evils Seton held up the example of the traditional Indian way of life. He particularly admired the great Shawnee leader Tecumseh, who had tried to form a coalition of American Indian nations to resist the rising tide of white settlement in the early 19th century. In Seton's words: "No one now questions the broad statement that Tecumseh was a great athlete, a great hunter, a great leader, clean, manly, strong, unsordid, courteous, fearless, kindly, gentle with his strength, dignified, silent and friendly. . . ." Several of the points of the BSA's Scout Law—which calls on Scouts to be, among other things, "friendly, kind, clean, and brave"—clearly have parallels with Seton's description of Tecumseh.

Seton first put the woodcraft idea into practice in 1902 in Cos Cob after a gang of local boys—angry that Seton had fenced in some land on which they liked to roam—tore down part of the fence. Instead of going to the police or to their parents, Seton invited the boys to "come up to the Indian Village on my place" when the local school closed for spring break.

Forty-two boys, aged ten to sixteen, took Seton up on his offer. Proclaiming himself their medicine man, he announced that they were a tribe, and he had them elect their own leaders to a tribal council. Over the next few days, the boys learned how to track animals and identify birds, "hunted" a deer made from a burlap sack, swam, canoed in the estate's lake, and gathered every night in front of a "council fire." In front of the crackling logs, Seton regaled them with tales of Indian life and folklore.

Seton described the success of his "Indian village" in a series of articles in the *Ladies' Home Journal* magazine. The articles—later expanded by Seton into a book, *The Birch-Bark Roll of the Woodcraft Indians*—laid the foundation of a new boys' movement, devoted to "the promotion of interests in out-of-door life and woodcraft, the preservation of wild life and landscape and the promotion of good fellowship among its members. The plan aims to give the young people something to do, something to think about and something to enjoy in the woods, with a view always to character building, for manhood, not scholarship, is the first aim of education." In July 1902, the first organized tribe of Woodcraft Indians started up in Summit, New Jersey.

ABOVE (left) One of Ernest Thompspn Seton's early wildlife art pieces. (right) A young Ernest Thompson Seton.

Ernest Thompson Seton's Boys

A DEPARTMENT FOR BOYS

By the Author of "Wild Animals I Have Known"

"Freezing"

"FREEZING" seems a good subject for November, only I do not mean that kind of freeze. I mean the kind that Molly Cottontail taught Rag to do; the kind you must learn to do if you wish to see much of the wild animals about your home. "Freezing" is standing perfectly still, as still as though frozen — because, when the wind prevents them from smelling, it is movement more than anything else that betrays the animals to each other.

If you see or hear something in the woods, remain perfectly still and you will learn far more than if you went blundering forward to find out.

Nearly all animals practice "freezing" to an extent that will surprise you when you come to look for it. If you wish to see a good example at home drag something that looks like a Mouse at the end of a string and watch the Cat. In a moment she will turn rigid while she takes her observation. Another case, even more remarkable, is that which produced the Pointer and Setter Dogs. A clever sportsman observed that certain Dogs "froze" for an unusually long time when they discovered their prey, and taking advantage of this he selected those that paused longest and from them raised a breed which "froze" or "pointed" until they were told to go on and put the game up.

You have often heard a Tree Frog croaking in some small tree and have gone there expecting to find him, and though you knew just about where to look you could not find him no matter how you searched. The reason was that he knew how to "freeze." As soon as he saw or heard you coming he ceased blowing out his throat and croaking ; then lying flat on the bark that he is so like in color he defied you to find him.

ANOTHER good example that I have often seen is offered by the common American Bittern. When he finds himself cornered in the marsh he stands as straight and still as a post. His striped brown feathers help him to look like a bunch of dry reeds, and there he stays till the danger is past or till he is sure he cannot escape by that trick.

One of the most unexpected cases of "freezing" I ever saw was given by my own plow Oxen in Manitoba some years ago. They were turned out at noon each day to graze for two hours in a rough, brushy pasture field. I soon found that they would hide in the thickest bushes as soon as they saw me coming, and give a great deal of trouble and cause much loss of time before they could be found and brought back to work. They became so clever at hiding that I put a bell on the leader and for a few days this worked well. He would hide as usual, but either his jaws or the turning of his head would cause a little "tang" from the bell which led me to his hiding-place. But in a few days he learned how to keep the bell quiet. The old fellow on seeing me afar, or probably guessing that I would soon come, would lie down in a thick place and lay his head flat down, like a young Deer ; thus the bell was underneath and silent. I walked several hours one day before I found him, and then the discovery was due to his shining horns which stood up through low bushes.

But one day when I went after the Oxen I neither saw nor heard them. I walked about in the pasture which was a good many acres ; went into all the likely bushes and climbed a tree to look for those gleaming white horns. But no, nothing was in sight. I had searched here and there for two hours, and was standing on a high stump looking again when the thought struck me that they must be hiding somewhere near ; the red Ox was probably watching me closely, and carefully holding the bell under. So I let off an awful yell—"Get up out of this, you red rascal. Hi—Hi—Hi "—and instantly in a thicket close to me there was a great uproar and out dashed my two trusant Oxen. They had been hiding and watching me, and now, as I hoped, they supposed that they were discovered, the game was up, and off they ran. From this time I was careful to keep my over-cunning helpers each at the end of a long rope when they grazed.

ONE day as I went through the woods I came on a Deer ; he was walking about sixty yards away, but he saw me just as I saw him. At the same moment we both "froze" and stood gazing, each waiting for the other to make the first move.

I waited three or four minutes at least, but he did not stir. Then it occurred to me to time him. I very slowly slid my hand up to my watch and then stood as before, the Deer still watching me.

"AS LONG AS THE DEER'S HEADS WERE DOWN GRAZING I RAN TOWARD THEM"

One minute — two minutes — five minutes went by and still the Deer did not move. I began to wonder if I had not made a mistake after all and watched a stump that had somewhat the form of a Deer. Then I thought, "No, I saw him walk there." Six minutes — eight minutes — ten minutes passed, and still the Deer stood.

"It is not possible," I said to myself ; "no Deer would stand like that for ten minutes. And yet there he is. He was plainly a Deer when he went there." I waited another minute ; still no move. "I'll give him five minutes more, and if there is no move then I shall know I have been fooled by a stump." Eleven and a half minutes, not counting the time before my watch was out, and there was a change, for it was a Deer that had been so intently watching me all the time, and it so happened that he now decided that he had been fooled by a stump. He shifted his pose, turned to graze, and I had won the game of "freeze." I brought my camera slowly up and snapped it, but the light was too poor to get a picture. The Deer now saw me move, and he bounded away.

MANY years ago, when I used to carry a rifle instead of a camera, I was passing through a thick swamp in the Upper Assiniboin, looking for something for dinner. As I came out on a glade I heard the "Quit, Quit, Quit" of an old Partridge, warning her young ones to hide. I heard a number of "whirrs," for the young were now well grown, and I caught a fleeting glimpse of flying birds. All went from sight except one, the old one. She stood on a fallen log and uttered once or twice the warning note ; then all was still.

The young did not need the mother now and I did, so I raised my rifle and fired without any

MOLLY COTTONTAIL IS A GOOD "FREEZER"

effect. Then I sent another ball whirring over her head, and the only result was to convince myself that I had been firing at an old knot. At the same time I heard the warning that an old Partridge utters to her brood when she means "Hurry up now. I can't keep this up much longer."

I walked up within fifteen yards of this deceptive knot that I had fired at twice, and not until then did the mother Partridge cease playing her perilous game of "freeze" and dash away in the opposite direction from that taken by the young ones. She had simply played the old game and done it so well as to mislead me. It was dangerous play, but my hasty shooting had been her safety.

THERE is another way of "freezing" that hunters often turn to account. The last time I tried this was a few years ago when I lived in France. I was walking with a friend on the outskirts of the Forest of Fontainebleau, and we came to a wide open plain, in the middle of which were two Red Deer feeding. They are very shy and would have run had they seen us, but we were in cover.

I said to my friend : "Do you want to see me walk up within one hundred feet of those Deer ?"

He replied : "Yes, I should like very much to see you, for it is not possible."

"You stay here," said I, "and you will see me do it. They will not run till I get within one

A SETTER "FREEZING"

hundred yards of them and they won't do that as long as I do nothing suspicious. I am going toward them now, but whenever you see them watching me suspiciously you whistle, and the Deer will see me stop and will settle down every few seconds and then go on grazing. I remained as still as the stones around me. The Deer would watch me closely for a few seconds; up most as I moved toward them, I would move the very moment the Deer began grazing, and becoming suspicious I settled to the ground. So I worked up close to one of them, and just as the chance came which had been waiting, you stood up. I snorted, gave a jump and went off with my friend who had watched the whole thing.

MOLLY would have told Rag that he did not know what to do in the case of a hunter in the Western country. Molly would have said : "Now Molly Cottontail would have smelled the sharp nose of an enemy and would have kept herself unseen. Molly would have told Rag how to 'freeze' if ever he should be so unlucky as to meet a Cheyenne."

Last July I went with some cowboys after a lot of Steers that had strayed away, near the Cheyenne River. We came suddenly upon them, and they dashed away in the thickest of the brush. His little calf could not keep up and so cried "pa" most piteously. The mother looked backward and forward, and gave her young one a last kick of encouragement. Then as we found nothing of the calf I saw a big fox among the brush and, telling the boys to let them run, I started off alone and before he got out of sight.

I had been some distance away. On hearing the uproar I came back toward my own campfire, and as I did so my Indian guide pointed to a Cottontail twenty-five feet away from my tent. The Indian—

THE little Cottontail Rabbit in the brush did not wait to see that could not do a thing. "Hold on," I said. He understood and we held back. The Cottontail took alarm and gave a shrill whistle and like a statue. The Cottontail, going to run, but not yet ; I waited twenty or thirty seconds more and got up, and as I did the boys—

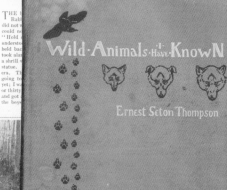

savages have been and came before a man "Get out of this," I said. "Go quick," I replied. The little Cottontail—

Molly put in ten feet to the right and we hope the second almost, and before the chase was well begun it was over ; her cotton tuft disappeared under a log ; she was safe in the pile of wood.

15

The Woodcraft movement's basic principles and organization had a big impact on the development of the Boy Scouts of America. Here are some major parallels:

First, while each tribe had adult leaders, their role was to teach and advise; the boys would lead themselves.

Second, it was non-competitive; boys won advancement at their own pace and according to their abilities, not by outdoing one another. (Seton was a particular foe of organized team sports for boys.)

Third, Woodcraft had a system of reward and recognition for achievement. Learning a new skill—basic first aid, for example—earned a boy a "coup." This took the form of an "Eagle feather" (actually from a turkey) to add to his headdress, which was based on the traditional headgear of Plains Indian warriors. (Boys without headdresses would get a colored bead—"wampum"—to add to a jacket or sash.)

Fourth, each tribe was organized into "bands" of three to ten boys, with each band identified by a "totem"—an animal, bird, or plant—much like the patrol system later adopted by the Boy Scouts.

Woodcraft tribes sprang up across the nation. The movement was loosely organized and Seton handled a lot of its business personally, so accurate membership numbers aren't known, but according to Seton's biographer H. Allen Anderson, there may have been as many as 200,000 braves by 1910. The braves included city boys, too; Seton worked with urban reformers to adapt Woodcraft to places like New York City, including "roof camping" atop tenements.

Seton continued to hold camps at "Standing Rock Village" on his Cos Cob estate. Julian Salomon, who camped there around 1908, recalled the experience many years later:

> Seton lived on one side of the lake and the camp was on the other, and he'd come over almost every morning. . . . The rest of the day we were by ourselves, and the older kids ran the camp. They were fifteen, sixteen, seventeen years old and had been coming there a long while. They'd take us younger kids on a nature hike, do some work around the camp, or build a bough bed or practice an Indian dance. . . . Seton had this great love of nature—birds, plants, trees—and in a very subtle way he inspired kids to gain the same kind of knowledge. It was a great thrill to know what a bluejay was or to tell the difference between a white-throated sparrow and an ordinary sparrow.

Thanks to Seton's continuing popularity as a writer and artist, the Woodcraft Indians got a lot of attention, even in the highest national circles. In July 1906, naturalist John Burroughs wrote to President Theodore Roosevelt:

> Seton has got hold of a big thing in his boys' Indian camp. . . . I have been there once and

am much impressed with it all, and with good results to the boys that are sure to follow from this scheme. All the boy's wild energy and love of deviltry are turned to new channels, and he is taught woodcraft and natural history and Indian lore in a most fascinating way. I really think it well worthy of your attention and encouragement.

In that very same month, Seton sent a letter and a copy of *The Birch-Bark Roll* to General Robert Baden-Powell, who was in the midst of forming an organization called the Boy Scouts in Britain. Baden-Powell replied that he was "sincerely grateful" for the book, adding that "It may interest you to know that I had been drawing up a scheme with a handbook to it, for the education of boys as scouts—which essentially runs much on the same lines as yours. . . ."

THE CHIEF SCOUT OF THE WORLD

The founder of Boy Scouting, Robert Stephenson Smyth Powell, was born in London on February 22, 1857. Stephe (pronounced "Steevie"), as his family always called him, would have few memories of his father, Baden Powell. A Church of England clergyman and a professor of geometry at Oxford University,

Baden Powell died when Stephe was barely three. A few years later, his widow changed the family surname to Baden-Powell to honor her late husband.

The task of raising Stephe and his five brothers and one sister (none of whom was older than thirteen or so when the Reverend Baden Powell passed away) fell to their mother, the former Henrietta Grace Smyth. By all accounts, Henrietta was a woman with a strong personality who urged her children to excel in everything that they did. Baden-Powell called her "that wonderful woman"; toward the end of his life he wrote, "The whole secret of my getting on lay with my mother."

As a young boy, Stephe showed a precocious talent for drawing, and, at school, for acting and singing. He also proved to be a good athlete, especially as a goalie on the football (soccer) team. While some boys were miserable in the often-harsh environment of an English boarding school in the Victorian era, Stephe enjoyed school life and was popular with his classmates. When his school, Charterhouse, moved from London to the countryside, Stephe developed a love of the outdoors. Soon he was slipping away, whenever he could, to take solitary hikes in the fields and forests that surrounded the school grounds. "It was here," he later wrote, "that I used to imagine myself a backwoodsman, trapper and Scout. I used to creep about warily

ABOVE (left) Boys, some aiming their bows and arrows at the camera, shown gathered at "Standing Rock Village," (right) Seton posing, dressed in the outdoor gear of the time, including tall boots and a wide-brimmed hat.

looking for 'signs' and getting 'close-up' observations of rabbits, squirrels, and birds."

Lackluster grades, however, kept Stephe from going on to university. Instead, he joined the army. The British Empire was at its height; for a young man like Baden-Powell, a military career could mean a life of adventure in exotic places, spiced with danger. After passing his officer's examination, Baden-Powell joined a cavalry regiment in India—the "jewel in the crown" of the British Empire—in 1876.

In India and in later postings around the empire, Baden-Powell showed himself to be a conscientious and competent officer, and he was steadily and rapidly promoted. At a time when one of the cavalry's main tasks was to go ahead of the infantry to locate enemy positions and determine their strength, he became an expert in scouting and reconnaissance. Such tasks also gave Baden-Powell an opportunity to use his ability as an artist. Baden-Powell may also have put his artistic and acting skills to use by working as a spy on occasion. (He famously claimed to have drawn a schematic of the enemies' fort within a sketch of a butterfly wing.)

Still, Baden-Powell saw little actual combat until 1896, when the Matabele people of Rhodesia in southern Africa (now the nation of Zimbabwe) rebelled against British rule. After leading a cavalry unit in action in this conflict (which even Baden-Powell, a staunch believer in the Empire, described as "a very one-sided fight"), Baden-Powell became a full colonel in command of his own regiment, at age forty.

THE SIEGE OF MAFEKING

As the 19th century drew toward its close, tensions were high in South Africa, which was then divided between British-governed territory and two republics ruled by the Boers—descendants of the region's original Dutch settlers. In 1899, the tensions flared into outright war.

At first the British expected to make short work of the Boers. Instead, the loosely organized but hard-hitting Boer "commandos" inflicted a series of defeats on the British forces in the early part of the conflict.

October 1899 found Colonel Baden-Powell in command of about 800 men—a mixed bag of regular troops and volunteers—in the dusty South African trading town of Mafeking. Surrounding the town were several thousand Boer fighters.

With his characteristic energy, Baden-Powell set up the town's defenses, organized food rationing—and even arranged cricket matches and other games and contests to keep up the morale of the defenders. By various methods, he also managed

ABOVE Baden-Powell family portraits. (left) Little Stephe posing on a chair. (middle) His father, Baden Powell, captured in a sketch. (right) Stephe's mother, Henrietta Grace Smyth.

to convince the besieging Boers that there were far more British troops in the town than there actually were. (For example, Baden-Powell's artillerymen would fire one of their small number of cannon, then move the gun to another emplacement, fire it again, move it again, and so on . . . making the Boers think that the defenders had considerable firepower at their disposal.) Despite the siege, messengers managed to keep Mafeking in contact with the outside world. Back in Britain, the public eagerly awaited Baden-Powell's calm and even lighthearted reports. A typical example: "All well. Four hours bombardment [by Boer artillery]. One dog killed."

Baden-Powell also organized Mafeking's boys into a "cadet corps." They carried messages (sometimes under fire), served as lookouts to spot Boer troop movements, and generally did all they could to support the town's defenders.

Finally, after a siege of 217 days, a British force broke through to Mafeking and the Boers retreated.

The siege of Mafeking was hardly a major victory. But when the news that the siege was over clattered over the telegraph lines on May 17, 1900, Britons—desperate for good news from the South African battlefronts—went wild with joy. On what would become known as "Mafeking Night," people poured into the streets, pounding on pots and pans and setting off fireworks. Baden-Powell instantly became a worldwide celebrity and a hero throughout the British Empire.

The British ultimately defeated the Boers in 1902—by which time they outnumbered the Boers by about 400,000 to 40,000. In the latter part of the conflict, Baden-Powell got the job of organizing defense and police forces in the territory won from the Boers. The uniform he designed for these troops—a khaki shirt and shorts, with a broad-brimmed hat and neckerchief to protect the wearer from the blazing African sun—would become the template for Boy Scout uniforms around the world for many years.

Baden-Powell returned to Britain in 1903 as the army's youngest major general. To his surprise, he found that he was now famous for something besides his defense of Mafeking.

One of Baden-Powell's last tasks before setting out for South Africa in 1899 was to put the finishing touches on his book *Aids to Scouting*. He never intended the book to be anything more than a military manual. Baden-Powell was inspired to write it by his observation that the men he'd commanded had little knowledge of how to move stealthily through rough country, to read the "signs" of nature, to take independent action when an

ABOVE Thousands of Britons crowd their home streets in celebration of "Mafeking Night," cheering British relief of the seige by Boers in South Africa.

ON THIS PAGE Baden-Powell's artistic skill was well suited for technical drawings and watercolors alike. (top foreground) Baden-Powell utilizes his cartography skills with a map showing coastline, terrain, and elevation. (bottom background) Watercolor sketch of a soldier in the hills overlooking a river valley. (bottom foreground) Two watercolor paintings of pastoral scenes of nature.

Mt Mavronoros

Bacchante Flats

Kalamus River

(Cock Covers   Marsh)

Map of **Levitatza** : approx^ly 2 miles to 1 inch.

BUTRINTO
Corfu in distance.

THE MAFEKING MAIL

Special Siege Slip.

ISSUED DAILY, SHELLS PERMITTING.   TERMS: ONE SHILLING PER WEEK, PAYABLE IN ADVANCE.

No. 112   Saturday, April 7th, 1900.   177th Day of Siege

of the whole public, and that it would be an inexcusably selfish action for anybody to remove a single paper from the room.

A shell from "Oud Greitje" smashed up the R.C.'s office-etcetras which he had just caused to be removed into the house formerly occupied by the late Capt. Girdwood.

We think that when medals are struck for this garrison, if one too many is made, it should be presented to the grey long haired Irish hound, called "Mafeking," belonging to Mr. Hamilton, the "special" war correspondent of the *London Times*. The poor animal has been three times wounded, twice with bullets, and once by a piece of shell.

MAFEKING GARRISON

GENERAL ORDERS

By Colonel R. S. S. Baden-Powell, Commanding Frontier Force.

MAFEKING, 7TH APRIL, 1900.

Court of Summary Jurisdiction — The Court of Summary Jurisdiction will meet on Monday, the 9th April, at the Court House, at 10·15 a.m., for the examination of such prisoners as may be brought before it. President : H. H. Maj. Goold-Adams, C.B., C.M.G. Member : Lieut.-Col. C. O Hore.

*Visiting Justice.—*The Visiting Justice to the Mafeking Gaol for the ensuing week will be Lieut.-Colonel C. O. Hore.

*Pay.—Appointment.—*Mr. Millar is appointed Commandant of the Refugee laager with pay at the rate of 10/- per diem from the 13th Oct., 1899, inclusive. Mr. Millar is not entitled to trench allowance in addition to pay.

*Establishment.—*With reference to General Order No. 3. of 31st March, 1900, the establishment of the Mafeking Cadet Corps is hereby increased to 24 privates from that date.

*Hospital Milk Supply.—*In consequence of the number of fever patients, convalescents, etc., for whom a sufficiency of milk is an absolute necessity, it has become necessary to prohibit entirely the sale of milk to private persons without the written authority of the D.A.A.G. (b). Any persons found selling or buying milk in future without such permit will be brought before the Court of Summary Jurisdiction, and will be liable for punishment for contravening this order.

By order,
E. H. CECIL, Major,
Chief Staff Officer.

NOTICE.

THE new issue of stamp bearing the Colonel's photograph, will be produced on Monday, the 9th instant. These stamps can only be issued on production of letter addressed locally (Mafeking or forts). No person can for the present be allowed to hand to the officer in charge of Siege Post Office more than one letter per diem.

J. V. HOWAT,
Postmaster.

Mafeking,
April 7th, 1900.

officer wasn't present to give commands, or to simply take care of themselves in the outdoors while on campaign.

Baden-Powell now learned that the book had become a popular success while he was in South Africa. Boys throughout Britain—also inspired by the deeds of the "cadet corps" at Mafeking—were buying the book and ganging together to apply its lessons in quests for outdoor adventure. In November 1900, the magazine *Boys of the Empire* began serializing *Aids to Scouting* under the title "The Boy Scout"—the first time the term appeared in print.

This new development tapped into a growing feeling of insecurity about Britain's youth and the future of its empire. In 1900, the British flag flew over approximately one-quarter of

challenge the mighty British fleet. Scary novels about German invasion plots made British best-seller lists in the early 1900s. If young British manhood had such a hard time subduing the Boers, people asked, how could they face the far greater threat from Germany?

When he returned to Britain after having spent most of the last three decades abroad, Baden-Powell could have looked forward to a few more years as a distinguished general, and then to a comfortable retirement. Instead, he threw himself into the task of making the small, informal, but growing British scouting movement into a coherent organization. He consulted with others of a similar mind-set—including the leaders of the YMCA and the military-oriented Boys' Brigade. He read deeply about

> Boys throughout Britain—also inspired by the deeds of the "cadet corps" at Mafeking—were buying [Baden Powell's *Aid to Scouting*] and ganging together to apply its lessons in quests for outdoor adventure.

the world's landmass, and one-quarter of the world's population lived under its folds. London was the world's undisputed financial capital, and despite challenges from America and Germany, Britain remained a formidable industrial power. And yet, even with its world power at its height, there were those in Britain who believed that the empire was rotting from within.

Britain's transition to an urban, industrialized society in the 19th century was even more rapid and wrenching than America's. The nation's upper classes lived in luxury, or at least in comfort, while its working class crammed into urban slums where disease, malnutrition, overwork (or unemployment), alcohol, and crime took an awful toll.

During the South African war, many Britons were shocked when an army general announced that more than half of the men who had volunteered to fight in the conflict weren't physically fit to serve. And while America didn't pose any military threat to the empire, the same couldn't be said for Germany, which was expanding its forces during the reign of the aggressive Kaiser Wilhelm II—including the building of a navy that could

the traditions of earlier cultures, from the Indians of North America to the legendary chivalry of King Arthur's court.

Baden-Powell then drafted a paper titled "Boy Scouts—A Suggestion." It set forth the goals he hoped to achieve with the new organization: "[T]o help in making the rising generation, of whatever class or creed, into good citizens at home or for the colonies."

But theory had to be put into practice. This would come in the summer of 1907, at a place called Brownsea Island—the world's first Scout camp.

BROWNSEA ISLAND AND SCOUTING FOR BOYS

A lot of thought went into Ernest Thompson Seton's "Indian camp," but it was still a local, relatively spontaneous affair. In contrast, the Brownsea camp was carefully planned to prove the potential of the Scouting idea to the British people.

Brownsea itself was a 500-acre island in the harbor of Poole in Dorset, on England's southeast coast. The island was owned by a wealthy businessman whom Baden-Powell had met

LEFT *The Mafeking Mail* article from the 177th day of the Boer siege. Notice the middle column, where Colonel R. S. S. Baden-Powell advertised "A Gymkhana Meeting," boasting of a list of games British soldiers could compete in to boost morale.

CURLEW

BULL

WOLF

RAVEN

on a fishing trip. Reachable only by ferry, Brownsea's relative isolation appealed to the general; while eager for publicity, he also worried that too much press attention might ruin what he dubbed "the experiment."

Twenty-two boys took part. The oldest was seventeen; the youngest—Baden-Powell's nephew, Dennis Baden-Powell—was nine. Despite the fact that British society was still deeply split along class lines at that time, B-P insisted that the boys be drawn from all classes. About half of the boys were students at elite "public" schools; the rest were "town boys" from nearby communities. They were organized into four patrols—Curlews, Ravens, Wolves, and Bulls—and each received a badge in the shape of a fleur-de-lis, which remains an emblem of Scouting. (Baden-Powell would later write, "It is the Patrol System that makes the Troop, and all Scouting for that matter, a real co-operative matter.")

Each of the eight days of the encampment began with B-P blowing on a trumpet made from the horn of a kudu—a species of African antelope—to assemble the boys. The day's activities revolved around a theme—woodcraft, chivalry, "saving a life," and so on. At Seton's Connecticut camp, the day ended with a campfire. The same was true at Brownsea. Years later, one of the Brownsea campers remembered B-P on these occasions: "I can still see him, as he stands in the flickering light of the fire—an alert figure, full of the joy of life, now grave, now gay,

answering all manner of questions, imitating the call of birds, showing how to stalk an animal, fleshing out a little story, dancing and singing round the fire . . ." Another Brownsea boy, Arthur Primmer, would recall, "You have to think back to what it was like in those days. . . . Nobody went camping. Not boys. The only camping that was done then was by the army."

After the campers went home on August 9, B-P pronounced the experiment a success. By then he'd already completed the manual of the Scouting movement in Britain, *Scouting for Boys*, at the urging of publisher Arthur Pearson, a close friend and staunch supporter of the Scouting idea. The work appeared in installments starting in January 1908 and in book form that May, with illustrations by B-P himself.

Scouting for Boys set forth the codes that became the basis of the Scouting movement worldwide:

- The Scout Motto: "Be Prepared." To B-P, this meant that the Scout must always "be in a state of readiness in mind and body to do [his] DUTY. . . ."
- The Scout Law: In its original form, a nine-point code beginning with "A Scout's Honour is to be trusted" and ending with "A Scout is thrifty." ("A Scout is pure in thought, word, and deed" was added later.)

ABOVE (left) Baden-Powell blows a trumpet made from the horn of a kudu to summon young Scouts at the Brownsea camp. (right) Emblems of the four animals representing the patrols among which the first Scouts were split.

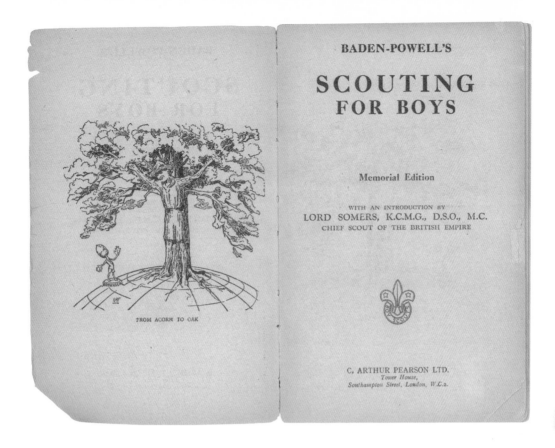

FROM ACORN TO OAK

BADEN-POWELL'S

SCOUTING FOR BOYS

Memorial Edition

WITH AN INTRODUCTION BY
LORD SOMERS, K.C.M.G., D.S.O., M.C.
CHIEF SCOUT OF THE BRITISH EMPIRE

C. ARTHUR PEARSON LTD.
Tower House,
Southampton Street, London, W.C.2.

- The Scout Oath:
  "On my honour I promise that I will do my best
  1. To do my duty to God and the King.
  2. To help other people at all times.
  3. To obey the Scout Law."
- The Scout Salute: Three fingers of the right hand touched to the forehead or hat brim.
- The Scout Handshake: Performed with the left hand. (B-P was inspired by the traditional handshake of the Zulu nation of South Africa.)
- The Scout Slogan: "Do a good turn daily."

The book was an instant best-seller and remained so for decades. Scout troops—each under the leadership of an adult Scoutmaster—sprang up across Britain. Baden-Powell described the movement's first couple of years as "rather a mushroom growth."

These first Scouts, though, encountered something that remains an issue for Scouts today: ridicule and hostility from their non-Scouting peers. To use a term coined much later, many boys looked at the Scouts' uniforms, their outdoor activities, and the movement's rules about clean living and good citizenship and decided Scouting wasn't "cool." An early British Scout later spoke of local boys teasing his troop with chants of "Here come the Brussels Sprouts, the stinking, blinking louts" as they set out on a hike.

Still, Scouting was on its way to becoming the biggest worldwide youth movement of the century.

COMING TO AMERICA

Just how and when the Scouting movement leaped across the Atlantic to America isn't known with any certainty. It's clear, though, that just as British boys used B-P's *Aids to Scouting* as a guidebook years before the movement became formally

ABOVE Title page of Baden-Powell's book *Scouting for Boys*. Baden-Powell laid the groundwork for Scouting in this manual. Illustrations drawn by him increased the appeal for children, such as the one shown of a young acorn growing into a tall, strong oak tree.

BOY SCOUTS OF AMERICA
National Council, New Brunswick, N. J.

FOR INTRA-ORGANIZATION COMMUNICATIONS

June 13, 1957

TO: MR. REBEL ROBERTSON

FROM: LEX R. LUCAS

Thank you for sending the leaflet about the Burnside Kentucky troop. This troop claims to be the first American Boy Scout troop. The Boy Scouts have had a long time policy of not recognizing or trying to determine the validity of claims to be "first". The situation is that in different sections of America there were troops organized through direct contact with Baden-Powell's office in London. It is almost certain that it would be impossible to determine which was the first even if it were important to do so. The fact is that the Boy Scouts of America started in 1910 and in that year a considerable number of troops were registered. No service before that time is counted.

As I said, this is the policy as I understand it and is one that should guide us when questions are asked.

Lex R. Lucas - mdh

American Indian community of Pawhuska, Oklahoma, in 1909.

Religious organizations certainly played a leading role in establishing Scouting in America. Leaders of the YMCA recognized that the movement could be a useful adjunct to their Boys' Work program. Individual churches also began sponsoring Scout troops, often as offshoots of Sunday school classes or Boys' Brigade companies. In Barre, Vermont, for example, a Scottish immigrant named William Milne used a copy of *Scouting for Boys* to start a troop at his adopted hometown's Baptist church in late 1909.

Elsewhere, groups of boys simply banded together and sought out an interested adult to serve as a Scoutmaster, and vice versa. In this, too, immigrants from Britain were influential. Albert W. Patzlaff would recall how Englishman O. W. Kneeves established a troop on the South Side of Chicago in the summer of 1909: "We made our own pup tents, and our uniforms were hand-me-down Army uniforms we got from surplus stores."

American Scouting was still an informal and decentralized activity as the first decade of the 20th century drew to a close. It would take the formidable energy and ability of one man—W. D. Boyce—and the hard work of a handful of his associates to turn Scouting into an organized national movement.

A GOOD TURN

Unlike the other "founding fathers" of Scouting, William Dickinson Boyce was not a writer, an artist, a naturalist, or a soldier. While he enjoyed hunting, fishing, and other outdoor activities, he felt no spiritual connection to nature. Boyce was a businessman first and foremost—and a phenomenally successful one.

Boyce's life story resembles one of the "rags to riches" novels so beloved by 19th-century Americans, in which a boy rises from modest circumstances to great wealth through hard work, intelligence, and a bit of luck. Born in Pennsylvania in 1858, he grew up on a farm, but the farming life was not for him. He taught for a bit, then traveled through the growing states and territories of the West, working variously as a fair manager, salesman, and census-taker before finding his true calling as a newspaper publisher.

organized, American boys were using his *Scouting for Boys* in much the same way not long after the book's publication.

There are several places that claim to be the "birthplace of Scouting" in the United States. It is known that in 1908 Mrs. Myra Greeno Bass organized an "Eagle troop" in Burnside, Kentucky. Bala Cynwyd, Pennsylvania, also claims a troop founded in that year. Some early U.S. troops were founded by British clergymen who brought their knowledge of the Scouting movement with them when they came to serve in American churches. Among them was a Church of England missionary, the Reverend John Mitchell, who founded a troop in the mostly

LEFT (background) Photograph of Burnside, Kentucky's, proud welcoming sign. (foreground) A response letter from the Boy Scouts of America regarding the leaflet, clarifying the official policy that no troop is the first troop. **ABOVE** An early leaflet for the Burnside troop.

While Boy Scouts Observe Anniversary—

Pawhuska Had First Troop

By MARTHA PLUMMER
Of The Tribune Staff

PAWHUSKA, Feb. 8—Today 4,100,000 Boy Scouts of America are honoring their founding and incorporation, which officially took place on this date in 1910.

But folks here in Pawhuska say 1910 was not actually the origin date of the Boy Scouts in this country. They maintain the first troop of Boy Scouts met in an Episcopal Mission church here in May, 1909, at the instigation of a young Episcopalian priest sent to Pawhuska as a missionary.

Two members of that first troop, Walter Johnson, of the Johnson Funeral Home, and Joe McGuire, real estate man here, are the only men out of the original 19 boy members that are still in Pawhuska. They have kept a scrapbook of pictures of that first group of boys in the United States ever to take the Scout oath.

The Rev. John Mitchell, founder of this first troop, had brought the idea of Scouting with him from England, when he was sent by the mother church to take charge of a Pawhuska mission church.

He had served as a chaplain for Sir Baden-Powell, founder of the Boy Scout movement in England, and saw an opportunity of organizing Pawhuska youths into a Scout group.

He discussed the project with the late W. E. McGuire, postmaster and father of Joe McGuire who agreed to aid him, and became the assistant Scoutmaster. McGuire was superintendent of the Methodist Sunday School, and he and Mr. Mitchell called together a group of Pawhuska boys one May evening in the Episcopal Church, and told them about the English Boy Scouts.

"He explained what fun they had, and then waved a picture of their uniform in front of us," Johnson said. "That uniform cinched it. We were fired with a desire to be Scouts."

That night, the United States' first Scout troop took the oath.

"After that, we mostly marched at our meeting," Johnson recalled. "We drilled, drilled and drilled."

MR. MITCHELL WROTE TO England for a charter for his troop and ordered them uniforms —probably the first uniforms in the United States. Insignia worn by the boys and their Scoutmaster was "A. B. S." or "American Boy Scouts."

The Episcopalian missionary was well-versed on the Scout movement, and he had ordered handbooks and other literature from his home. He especially emphasized, "Do a Good Deed Daily."

"We wore out all the old ladies in Pawhuska, pushing them from one side of the street to the other," Johnson recalls, for there weren't too many. Only about 1,200 to 1,400 persons here then."

Johnson said no one from this troop took any part in the incorporation of the Boy Scouts of America, which took place on Feb. 8, 1910, in Washington D. C. Instead, another troop of boys was the first to get a charter from the official organization. This explains why Pawhuskans have had to fight for national recognition as having the first uniformed, chartered Scout group in this country.

However, the Pawhuska troop did obtain a United States charter, and on March 2, 1910 shortly after the incorporation, set forth on what was to be their treasured memory—a trip to Bartlesville to organize a Scout troop there.

They had been designated a camping site in Bartlesville, and were to spend several nights there. The bigger boys rode out followed by the little ones on foot, and then the wagon of supplies. They were delayed at the outset, because some of the mothers felt the team which had been selected for the wagon was a little skittish, and it had to be switched.

The Pawhuska band preced-

See PAWHUSKA, page 45

REMAINING SCOUTS—Walter Johnson, left, and Joe McGuire are the only two members of the early Pawhuska Scout troop left at Pawhuska. Other members have scattered, and some have died. Johnson has the Johnson Funeral Home, and McGuire is in the real estate business. Both have taken an active part in Boy Scout work since 1909. Two members of the first troop live in Tulsa—D. F. Millard, of 2616 E. 34th St., and Robert McGuire, 3841 E. 39th St. Millard recalls that the first oath taken by the troop was to the King of England. (Tribune Staff Photo)

FIRST SCOUT TROOP—Pawhuskans point with pride to this picture of the first uniformed Boy Scout troop in the United States made in 1909. The uniforms were ordered from England through a Kansas City department store, and Pawhuskans defy any group to produce an earlier picture of Boy Scouts in uniform. The boys are pictured with their leader, the Rev. John Mitchell, who came to Pawhuska from England and founded the group in 1909. Boys pictured are Douglas Foote, Jack Hutchings, John I. Johnson, Robert McGuire, Lee Copeland, Cliff Ferguson, Thomas Leahy, Walter Johnson, Tim Leahy, Joe McGuire, Clyde Wilson, Dick Millard, Spider Hinkle, Clemmer Curtis, Roland Blanc, Alex Tinker, Jack Coffey, Roger Leahy and Roland McGuire. Tinker was the younger brother of the late Gen. Clarence Tinker, for whom Tinker Field is named. The general, then a young commissioned officer, once accompanied the scouts on a camping trip to Bartlesville.

THE TULSA TRIBUNE,

Pawhuska

From Page 35

ed them as they marched triumphantly from town.

After a glorious time in Bartlesville, including a flag-flying parade down the main street; street car rides to Dewey and saving a horse that fell into the Caney River, the Scouts started home.

"Halfway back, a dust storm hit, and we couldn't go any farther," McGuire remembers. "Johnson and I rode on into Pawhuska, and I got home at 4:30 a.m. We left the smaller ones to camp for the night."

John Long, team master for the trip, later wrote they were out of food, supplies and money—too many trolley trips to Dewey.

"We, boys and horses, pooled our sources. No one but Daubie (Roland) Blanc, complained of being hungry, and when he weighed in, he'd gained two pounds," Long said. (Blanc later was the editor of the Pawhuska paper.)

LATE IN 1910, MR. MITCHELL was called back to another post, and W. E. McGuire took over as Scoutmaster, a position he kept for 16 years, until the Pawhuska Boy Scouts had grown to 50 or 60 boys.

From time to time, Pawhuska citizens have tried to get the national organization to recognize the troop as the first in this country.

"So far, we haven't had any success, but I think they're coming around," Johnson said. "I heard that there was much talk of it at the last Jamboree."

Pawhuska has made several efforts to start a permanent memorial for the Boy Scouts. At present, a marker inscribed with the first troop's names and pictures, is in the middle of town. It was sponsored by the local Kiwanis Club. There has been talk of buying the original Episcopal Church, which later was moved and enlarged, and using it to house Boy Scout trophies and early souvenirs, but the fight has been hard.

Some Pawhuskans think the state legislature should pass a resolution designating the city and Oklahoma as being first in Scouting in the United States.

Thus, while some of the first 19 have drifted away and some have died, there has been no lapse of pride in Pawhuska for its first Scouts—and no doubting Thomases, either.

In the mid-1880s, Boyce hit on a scheme to provide a better class of newspaper for readers in rural areas. From his base in Chicago, Boyce sent ready-made printing plates to small-town newspaper editors. The plates had news and features from the big city. The editors just added local content. The first of Boyce's papers, the *Saturday Blade*, began publishing under this system in 1887. Several other papers and magazines followed over the next couple of decades. Local boys, working on commission, sold these periodicals in their communities. At one point as many as 30,000 boys distributed Boyce's publications—a fact that probably led to his later interest in boys' welfare. The success of the *Blade* and Boyce's other publications made Boyce a very rich man. He was eventually worth $20 million—an immense sum, particularly given the time.

Like other newspaper giants of the era, such as William Randolph Hearst, Boyce not only reported on the news—he made it himself, sponsoring expeditions to the Arctic. He also traveled to remote parts of the world with reporters and photographers in tow. Boyce was making arrangements for an African safari—in which he proposed to combine some big-game hunting with experimental photography using balloons—when he arrived in London in the summer of 1909 and had his fateful foggy meeting with the "Unknown Scout."

Boyce later stopped by Baden-Powell's office on Henrietta Street in London's Covent Garden district to pick up some literature on the movement, which he studied while in Africa. He decided that Scouting would be "a wonderful thing [for] our American boys." (Boyce was apparently unaware of the proto-Scout organizations in America like the Woodcraft Indians and the Sons of Daniel Boone, or the YMCA's scouting activities—although some historians believe he may have had some knowledge of them before his meeting with the "Unknown Scout.")

Back in London en route to America after the safari, Boyce again visited the Boy Scouts' Henrietta Street office to see if the organization would be interested in setting up in the United States. Baden-Powell wasn't there, but "whoever was in charge," in Boyce's words, told him that a better plan would be to "organize in the United States as the Boy Scouts of America."

Boyce returned to Chicago and set about doing just that, telling an Illinois newspaper, "We intend to take the British idea and Americanize it." On February 8, 1910, the Boy Scouts of America formally came into existence when Boyce filed incorporation papers in Washington, D.C. The papers stated that the organization was intended "to promote, through organization and cooperation with other agencies, the ability of

ABOVE (left) Photograph of W. D. Boyce, the wealthy businessman who officially launched Scouting in the United States. (right) Scouting ceremony at Gilwell Park, London.

boys to do things for themselves and for others, to train them in Scoutcraft, and to teach them patriotism, courage, self-reliance, and kindred virtues, using the methods which are in common use by Boy Scouts."

GETTING OFF THE GROUND

At the moment, though, the Boy Scouts of America was little more than a name. It was an organization with "no money [apart from the $1,000 per month Boyce soon pledged to support it], no members, and no standing."

The first order of business was to reach out to the "other agencies" referred to in the incorporation papers. The YMCA was at the top of the list. It was the nation's premiere youth organization; it had pioneered Scouting in America; and it already had an infrastructure in place, including around 400 summer camps.

In early May, Boyce met with three leaders of the Y's Boys' Work organization—Lawrence L. Dogget, Edgar M. Robinson, and J. A. Van Dis. The three YMCA men agreed to take the lead in turning the fledgling BSA into a viable organization. The forty-three-year-old Robinson, granted a year's leave from his YMCA duties, established an office for the BSA in the YMCA headquarters on East 28th Street in New York City the following month. Another Y man, John L. Alexander, came aboard as managing secretary.

Robinson quickly arranged a pair of "summit meetings" of leaders of various national youth groups—including Dan Beard

Scout movement, the creation of powerful newspaper publisher William Randolph Hearst. However, the ABS (later renamed the United States Boy Scouts) wasn't a good fit with the BSA anyway, as its focus was mostly on military training.

Boyce was happy with these rapid developments, noting that "[In] numbers there is strength, and the bringing together of the different boy organizations in the United States into the Boy Scouts of America would place the Boy Scouts on a firm foundation."

"I would rather be a Boy Scout than a dictator, king, or even President of the U.S.A."

DAN BEARD

and Ernest Thompson Seton—on June 15 and 21, 1910. Out of these meetings came a ten-member Committee on Organization, which would establish the BSA's basic framework. They also led to the merging of the Woodcraft Indians and the Sons of Daniel Boone with the BSA, along with several smaller scouting groups, such as the Boy Scouts of the United States and the National Scouts of America. The major holdout was the American Boy

The BSA was now more than a name. It had members, and the new organization's standing was boosted by the endorsement of prominent Americans, from President William Howard Taft (who agreed to serve as honorary president), former president Theodore Roosevelt (who was given the title "Chief Scout Citizen"), and a host of military men, politicians, writers, and social reformers.

ABOVE Edgar M. Robinson, the former YMCA leader who became an early leader of the Scouting organization. **RIGHT** W. D. Boyce filed papers for this, the bill for the incorporation of the Boy Scouts of America, in 1910.

61ST CONGRESS,
2D SESSION.

H. R. 24747.

IN THE HOUSE OF REPRESENTATIVES.

APRIL 20, 1910.

Mr. GRAFF introduced the following bill; which was referred to the Committee on Education and ordered to be printed.

A BILL

To incorporate the Boy Scouts of America, and for other purposes.

1 *Be it enacted by the Senate and House of Representa-*

2 *tives of the United States of America in Congress assembled,*

3 That W. D. Boyce, Frank W. Gunsaulus, Charles H. Stod-

4 dard, Roy O. West, of Chicago, Illinois; E. J. Spencer,

5 William H. Thompson, of Saint Louis, Missouri; William J.

6 Starr, of Madison, Wisconsin; James Gordon, of Okolona,

7 Mississippi; John A. Brashear, of Allegheny, Pennsylvania;

8 John J. Lentz, of Columbus, Ohio; and Colin H. Livingstone,

9 of Washington, District of Columbia, and their associates

10 and successors, are hereby created a body corporate and

11 politic in the District of Columbia.

12 SEC. 2. That the name of said corporation shall be

13 "Boy Scouts of America," and by that name it shall have

HOW SCOUTING WORKS

FROM THE TOP DOWN, here's an overview of the organizational structure of the BSA as it is today:

The governing body of the organization is the National Council, which since 1979 has been headquartered in Irving, Texas, a suburb of Dallas. The top official is the Chief Scout Executive—currently Robert J. Mazzuca, who took office in September 2007. Nationwide, the BSA is divided into four regions—Central, Northeast, Southern, and Western.

Regions, in turn, are subdivided into areas for administrative purposes. The basic "building block" of Scouting at the local level is the council—which, in populous parts of the country, is often contiguous with a county—administered by a professional council executive. Councils are governed by a volunteer board, and every professional position has a volunteer counterpart. Councils are in turn usually divided into districts, each with a professional district executive liaising with volunteer leaders.

There are three main programs within the overall BSA organization:

CUB SCOUTING: A family-oriented program for boys aged seven through ten, or the first through fifth grades: Tiger Cubs (first graders), Wolf Cub Scouts (second graders), Bear Cub Scouts (third graders), and Webelos Scouts (fourth and fifth graders). Cub Scouts are organized into dens of six to eight boys. Several dens form a pack, which is usually affiliated to a Boy Scout troop.

BOY SCOUTING: For boys who have earned the Cub Scout Arrow of Light Award and are at least ten years old, or who have completed the fifth grade and are at least ten, or who are at least eleven but not yet eighteen. Boy Scouts are organized into troops, each chartered to a local institution—which may be a church or other religious institution, a school, a business, or service clubs like Rotary International. Troops are composed of patrols, or units of up to a dozen or so boys.

VENTURING: For young men and women who are fourteen (and who have completed the eighth grade) through twenty. As the program's literature attests, Venturing's emphasis is on "high adventure, sports, arts and hobbies, religious life, or Sea Scouting," and the basic unit is the crew—or in the case of Sea Scouting, the ship.

The summer of 1910 also saw the first official Boy Scout camp when 120 boys—all YMCA members, although some appear to have also been members of groups like the Woodcraft Indians—gathered at Silver Bay, New York, in August. Ernest Thompson Seton—the BSA's first (and only) "Chief Scout"—was the star at the nightly campfires. William Edel, one of the campers, remembered how Seton "[T]alked about forest life and trees, finding your way from the way trees grow, and other things connected with woodcraft. He talked a lot about wild animals, and those of us who had read his books about animals were thrilled to hear some of the same stories." Edel also recalled how "The leaders of the camp were preaching Boy Scouts, and they convinced us, there's no doubt about that. I came to the camp a Woodcraft Indian and left as a Boy Scout." Among the leaders of the camp was another Y man, William D. Murray, who would go on to write the first history of the BSA.

Seton was also busy that summer writing and illustrating *Boy Scouts of America: A Handbook of Woodcraft, Scouting, and Life-Craft.* A full-scale manual along the lines of Baden-Powell's *Scouting for Boys* would have to wait, but in the meantime, the leaders needed some kind of handbook in print as soon as possible, so Seton largely adapted his *Birch-Bark Roll* with elements of B-P's book. From their New York office, Robinson and Alexander also produced two pamphlets, "Boy Scouts of America: Scouting for Boys" and "Hints for Local Councils or Committees."

The pamphlets were sorely needed, because the in-tray at the BSA's one-room office was overflowing with inquiries from boys wanting to become Scouts and men wanting to become Scoutmasters. According to one of Boyce's biographers, Janice A. Petterchak, the office received inquiries from some 150,000 boys in forty-four states, as well as the overseas territories of Puerto Rico and the Philippines, by the fall of 1910.

In October of that year, the Committee on Organization formally turned over management of the BSA to the Board of Managers (later renamed the Executive Council). Edgar Robinson was offered the position of permanent executive secretary of the BSA but decided to return to the YMCA. No one had done more than him to make the new organization a going proposition; Robinson is sometimes called the "unsung hero" of Scouting in America.

The board then turned to a thirty-four-year-old lawyer named James E. West, offering him a temporary appointment. West accepted the post, expecting to stay in it for no more than

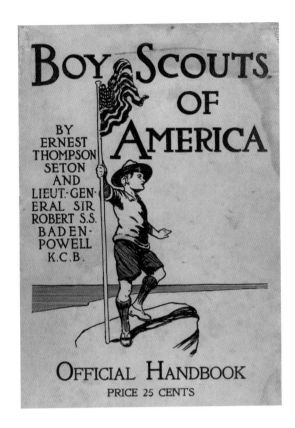

BY
ERNEST
THOMPSON
SETON
AND
LIEUT.-GEN-
ERAL SIR
ROBERT S.S.
BADEN-
POWELL
K.C.B.

OFFICIAL HANDBOOK
PRICE 25 CENTS

six months before returning to his law practice. Instead, as Chief Scout Executive, he would lead the BSA for more than three decades.

JAMES E. WEST AND THE GROWTH OF THE BSA

James E. West endured a wretched childhood. He was born in Washington, D.C., and both his parents died by the time he was six. Suffering from tuberculosis, which left one of his legs shorter than the other, he spent his childhood in dismal hospitals and orphanages. Over the opposition of the staff of Washington's City Orphan Home—who preferred that he remain on the grounds, cleaning its chicken coops—he insisted on going to high school, graduating at age nineteen and finally leaving the orphanage a year later. For the next few years he supported himself with odd jobs while working toward a law degree, finally winning admission to the Washington bar in 1901. After working in various government posts, he entered private practice a few years later.

West's early years filled him with a fierce desire to help others, especially young people. He worked for the YMCA while attending law school. He devoted his time, energy, and legal skills to causes like the National Playground Association and the National Child Rescue League, and worked to reform the juvenile court system. West's activities brought him to the attention of a Red Cross official, who recommended him when the BSA position opened up after Edgar Robinson's departure. In January 1911—with his salary paid by the Russell Sage Foundation—West opened the BSA's first real office at 200 Fifth Avenue in New York City, with a staff of seven.

West's personality could be prickly. Julian Salomon—whom we've already met as a Son of Daniel Boone, and who worked as an assistant in the BSA office's early years—later described his boss as "a real battler" who could be "ruthless." West was

"The American people recognize that Scouting today is one of the few organizations that has retained its basic values from its origin, and that is our best hope for future leadership of America. It is the only organization that completely endorses family value, which are being recognized belatedly by the American people as one of the real strengths and hopes for the future of our country."

**H. E. BOVAY JR., ADVISORY COUNCIL, BOY SCOUTS OF AMERICA,
AND PRESIDENT, MID-SOUTH TELECOMMUNICATIONS COMPANY, INC.**

ABOVE Ernest Thompson Seton's *Boy Scouts of America* handbook met the need of the surging nationwide interest in Scouting.

Boy Scouts

Buttons — The official buttons worn on the scout uniforms sel¹ for 10 cents per set for shirt and 15 cents per set for coat.

Merit Badges — Price 25 cents each.

Boy Scout Certificates — A handsome certificate in two colors, 6 x 8 inches, has been prepared for boy scouts who wish to have a record of their enrolment. The certificate has the Scout Oath and Law and the official Seal upon it, with place for the signature of the scout master. The price is 5 cents.

Directions For Ordering

Important ! When ordering supplies send exact remittance with order. If check is used add New York exchange. Make checks and money orders payable to Boy Scouts of America. All orders received without the proper remittance will be shipped C. O. D., or held until remittance arrives.

The Scout Oath

Before he becomes a scout a boy must promise:

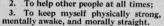

On my honor I will do my best:

1. To do my duty to God and my country, and to obey the scout law;

2. To help other people at all times;

3. To keep myself physically strong, mentally awake, and morally straight.

When taking this oath the scout will stand, holding up his right hand, palm to the front, thumb resting on the nail of the little finger and the other three fingers upright and together.

The Scout Sign

This is the scout sign. The three fingers held up remind him of his three promises in the scout oath.

The Scout Salute

When the three fingers thus held are raised to the forehead, it is the scout salute.

The scout always salutes an officer.

The Scout Law*

There have always been certain written and unwritten laws regulating the conduct and directing the activities of men.

*Result of work of Committee on Scout Oath, Scout Law, Tenderfoot, Second-class and First-class Scout Requirements:—
Prof. Jeremiah W. Jenks Chairman. Dr. Lee K. Frankel, George D. Porter, E. M. Robinson, G. W. Hinckley, B. E. Johnson, Clark W. Hetherington, Arthur A. Carey.

Scoutcraft

2. Dive properly from the surface of the water.

3. Demonstrate breast, crawl, and side stroke.

4. Swim on the back fifty feet.

Taxidermy

To obtain a merit badge for Taxidermy a scout must

1. Have a knowledge of the game laws of the state in which he lives.

2. Preserve and mount the skin of a game bird, or animal, killed in season.

3. Mount for a rug the pelt of some fur animal.

Life Scout

The life scout badge will be given to all first-class scouts who have qualified for the following five-merit badges: first aid, athletics, life-saving, personal health, and public health.

Star Scout

The star scout badge will be given to the first-class scout who has qualified for ten merit badges. The ten include the list of badges under life scout.

Eagle Scout

Any first-class scout qualifying for twenty-one merit badges will be entitled to wear the highest scout merit badge. This is an eagle's head in silver, and represents the all-round perfect scout.

BOY SCOUTS OF AMERICA

HANDBOOK FOR BOYS

in record time, in what Scouting historian Robert W. Peterson calls "a Herculean effort." It included sections on woodcraft by Seton, as well as contributions on natural history, animals, and the like from experts recruited from organizations ranging from the Audubon Society to the U.S. Geological Survey.

The *Handbook* also achieved Boyce's goal of "Americanizing" Scouting. The BSA retained Baden-Powell's Scout Oath, but replaced "the King" with "my country," and added a new line at the end: "to keep myself physically strong, mentally awake, and morally straight."

The BSA version of the Scout Law had twelve points, in contrast with the nine points of the British Scout Law in its original form. The first nine points were basically the same as B-P's, but expressed more simply:

1. A Scout is trustworthy.
2. A Scout is loyal.
3. A Scout is helpful.
4. A Scout is friendly.
5. A Scout is courteous.
6. A Scout is kind.
7. A Scout is obedient.
8. A Scout is cheerful.
9. A Scout is thrifty.

And the three additional points were:

10. A Scout is brave.
11. A Scout is clean.
12. A Scout is reverent.

The last point was especially important to the deeply religious West.

The *Handbook* also codified the BSA's fundamental structure—troops led by an adult Scoutmaster, patrols led by the boys themselves, groups of troops overseen by local councils—and its rules for membership and advancement.

Boys could join at twelve as Tenderfoot Scouts and rise through Second Class to First Class Scout rank by demonstrating proficiency in various skills. Once a boy was a First Class Scout, he could earn merit badges—each represented by a small round

particularly ruthless in going after anyone who infringed on the copyrighted Boy Scouts name for commercial purposes, or any organization that implied that it was somehow connected with the BSA when it was not. (William Randolph Hearst's American Boy Scout was apparently guilty of the latter, and it was a particular target of West's wrath.)

The new chief was also keenly aware that his impoverished urban childhood and the limp caused by his tuberculosis set him apart from outdoorsmen like Beard and Seton. (Beard, in fact, uncharitably said that West had "never seen the blue sky in his life.") The bespectacled West was also bothered by the fact that he didn't possess the kind of easygoing yet colorful personality that would allow him to easily "connect" with Scouts.

But West had the drive and organizational ability needed at a critical moment for the BSA. In Julian Salomon's words, "He *made* the organization, no question about that."

A major event of West's first year as chief was the publication of *Handbook for Boys*, the official full-length manual of the BSA, in August 1911. West and a small committee put the book together

ABOVE Photograph of James E. West in uniform, with his Scouting hat in hand.

cloth emblem—in different subject areas. (The first edition of the *Handbook* listed requirements for fifty-seven badges—from Agriculture to Taxidermy, and including surprisingly modern subjects like Aviation.)

Earning the First Aid, Athletics, Lifesaving, Personal Health, and Public Health merit badges won the boy advancement to Star Scout rank. Five more (in any subject) brought Life Scout rank. A total of twenty-one merit badges brought a boy to the pinnacle—Eagle Scout rank, which the *Handbook* described as representing "the all-round perfect scout."

The publication of the *Handbook* led even more boys and men to get involved in Scouting. There would be no national registration of Scouts and Scouters—adult leaders—until 1913, so—as with predecessors like the Woodcraft Indians and the Sons of Daniel Boone—it's impossible to say just how many

members the BSA had in its first two years, but the consensus seems to be roughly 60,000 around 1910–1912.

Thereafter the BSA began to grow by leaps and bounds. But, as with any organization, growth came with growing pains.

EARLY CONTROVERSIES

America in the early 20th century was a country in which there was still considerable tension between Catholics and Protestants, and not much in the way of ecumenical cooperation. The leadership of the Roman Catholic Church in America, for example, was wary of allowing its boys and young men to participate in Scouting because of the movement's close identification with the YMCA, then a staunchly Protestant organization—despite Edgar M. Robinson's assurance, in 1910, that "This national movement [the BSA] is not organically related in any way to the

ABOVE Early BSA troops were closely associated with the YMCA.

Young Men's Christian Association. . . ." In 1917, the Church finally allowed Catholic boys to join the Scouts, but only on the condition that "there shall be distinctly Catholic troops under a Catholic Scoutmaster, and that there shall be a Chaplain appointed by the proper ecclesiastical authority for each Catholic troop." Over time, and as Americans of all faiths embraced the idea of a more pluralistic society, this attitude changed; by the 21st century, almost 10,000 Catholic parishes across the country were involved in Scouting in some way, with no denominational restrictions on membership.

Other faiths immediately embraced the new organization. In 1913, for example, the Church of Jesus Christ of Latter-day Saints (popularly known as the Mormons) adopted the BSA as an official youth program after two years of study by the LDS's Young Men's Mutual Improvement Association. Today, more Scout units are chartered to the LDS than to any other organization.

The relationship between Scouting and the Mormon Church is one of the most fascinating and historically significant in the history of Scouting. The numbers themselves are illuminating: almost 10 percent of the Boy Scout Advisory Council are residents of Salt Lake City, well known as the home of the Mormon Church. Though Mormons make up less than 2 percent of the U.S. population, more than 21 percent of the boys in the Boy Scouts are members of the Mormon Church, followed closely by the United Methodist Church.

Though the relationship between the BSA and the Church of Jesus Christ of Latter-day Saints has lasted more than ninety years, it has not always been smooth sailing. The Mormons and the BSA began a formal relationship in 1913, when Scouting was recognized by the Church as an important character-building experience for its young boys. This sudden formal recognition, though, came as a shock to some members who remembered that just two years before, in 1911, the Church had firmly decided that Scouting was not going to be part of its members' lives.

The Mormon Church already had a program called the Young Men's Mutual Improvement Association, or MIA. This program was, in essence, a character-building organization like the Scouts, but had a decidedly Mormon agenda. The Church elders felt that Scouting was either superfluous or in conflict with their own "in-house" organization.

But Scouting took on a life of its own, and it came to the attention of the Church's governing body that Scout troops

A SCOUT IS REVERENT

JAMES WEST'S FINAL ADDED POINT in the Scout Law, a Scout is reverent, has rung true over the 100 years of Scouting. Its spiritual ideals and early affiliation with the YMCA led to some initial controversy among non-Christians over whether their children should be Scouts. However, Scouting has never been affiliated with any one faith, and does not favor one religion over another. The Boy Scouts of America has always encouraged Scouts to be faithful to their own individual religion. This ideal led to the religious emblem program, a way for Scouts of all religions to be recognized for their devotion and service to their faith. These programs vary, as they are designed and administered by the leaders of various religious groups. Differing religious groups have their own requirements for awarding medals, and each program also must be officially recognized by the BSA. With members of the Boy Scouts of America representing every major faith, there is a broad range of medals that are awarded for religious service. Dedication to one's faith continues to be one of the most important tenets that young Scouts embrace today.

The amazing variety of religious awards—which includes such faiths as Islam, Buddhism, and Baha'i—is proof of Scouting's adaptation to an increasingly diverse and multicultural America. At the same time, the BSA's religious awards connect the movement to one of its founding principles—that faith and spiritual development are necessary to doing one's best as a person and citizen, not just in youth but throughout life.

were organically popping up across the state of Utah without the sanction or even knowledge of the Church elders. This prompted the general board of the MIA to launch an inquiry into the Scouting movement among young Mormon boys. They determined that the existence of two character-building entities didn't make sense, and they again denounced the Boy Scouts. But even in light of the announced disapproval, Scout troops

> ## "The Boy Scouts of America has something for it that all the government welfare programs in America can't match: success. Besides family and religion, Scouting is probably this country's single best program for building character in boys, and has been for nearly a century."
>
> ### THE TIMES LEADER,
> ### WILKES-BARRE, PENNSYLVANIA

kept emerging all over Utah. The general board of the MIA had to reconsider its position on Scouting, as their own members were simply joining the Scouts regardless.

In a historic 1913 meeting, then-Scouting organizer Samuel Moffat made a trip to Salt Lake City by train to meet with Church officials. By the time he left Utah, it was clear that the relationship between the two organizations was inevitable. By 1913, 13,000 MIA boys had joined the Scouts and the relationship between the Church and Scouting was galvanized.

Mormon families lent their characteristic support for the Boy Scouts almost immediately. Land was donated and cleared for camps and meetings were attended with vehemence. The first Scout camp, Cache Valley, was originally created to accommodate 150 Scouts, but burst at the seams with the more than 1,000 Scouts who came that first summer. In the years following the Moffat visit, more than 500 Scout troops sprang up throughout the Western states.

By 1928, the BSA was growing steadily in popularity among Mormons. Many people are unaware that the BSA's creation of Exploring, a program for older Scouts, was in part due to the influence of the Mormon Church. The Church recognized the problem of keeping older boys interested in youth activities like the BSA. Like Scout troops in the rest of the country, Mormon boys after the age of fourteen would find sports or other after-school activities to be more enticing than the Boy Scouts. The Church formed a committee to find ways to keep these boys interested in Scouting, and formed a faction called the Vanguards as a result. The BSA was uncomfortable with the Utah council creating a new group without their permission, but later conceded and was inspired to form the Exploring program for much the same reason.

Today, the Mormon Church is an important and respected part of the Boy Scouts of America.

From the beginning, the BSA's official position on religion—largely formulated by James E. West—was that a belief in God was a prerequisite for good citizenship, and therefore a vital part of Scouting. This policy, however, was expressed in resolutely non-denominational terms, and was in place from the very first edition of the *Handbook for Boys*:

> The recognition of God as the ruling and leading power in the universe, and the grateful acknowledgment of his favors and blessings is necessary to the best type of citizenship and is a wholesome thing in the education of the growing boy. . . . The Boy Scouts of America therefore recognize the religious element in the training of a boy, but it is absolutely non-sectarian in its attitude toward this training. . . . If he be a Catholic boy scout, the Catholic Church of which he is a member is the best channel for his training. If he is a Hebrew boy, then the Synagogue will train him in the faith of his fathers. If he be a Protestant, no matter to what denomination of Protestantism he may belong, the church of which he is an adherent or a member should be the proper organization to give him an education in the things that pertain to his allegiance to God. The Boy Scouts of America, then, while recognizing the fact that the boy should be taught the things that pertain to religion, insists upon the boy's religious life being stimulated and fostered by the institution with which he is connected.

THEODORE ROOSEVELT
CHIEF SCOUT CITIZEN, PRESIDENT OF THE UNITED STATES

THEODORE ROOSEVELT LEFT THE WHITE HOUSE a year before the Boy Scouts of America's incorporation in 1910, but the popular former president's staunch support of the new movement gave a big boost to the organization in its early years. Roosevelt himself embodied many of Scouting's key values—service to the public, respect for the environment, physical fitness, and a devotion to doing one's best in all circumstances.

Born into a wealthy New York City family in 1858, Roosevelt was a weak and sickly boy. In response to his father's urging that he "must *make* his body," Roosevelt built up his strength through rigorous exercise. (As president, he sometimes exhausted visiting diplomats by inviting them to join him on his usual routine of hiking, horseback riding, swimming, and tennis.) He also became an enthusiastic naturalist as a boy, writing his first paper on the subject at the age of nine.

After graduating from Harvard in 1880, Roosevelt entered politics as a Republican member of the New York legislature. In 1884, he suffered a stunning double tragedy. His wife, the former Alice Lee, died just two days after giving birth; his mother died on the same day. Roosevelt spent the next couple of years as a rancher in the rugged badlands of the Dakota Territory, an experience that deepened his belief in the value of what he called "the strenuous life."

Returning to the East, Roosevelt remarried, to Edith Carow; they ultimately had five children. Roosevelt reentered politics, serving as commissioner of the federal civil service and, in 1895, head of the New York City Police Department. A scholar as well as a man of action, Roosevelt also published a steady stream of books on subjects ranging from his experiences in the badlands to biographies of notable Americans.

Appointed deputy secretary of the navy in 1897, Roosevelt readied the nation's fleet for a war with Spain that he believed was inevitable. When war did come in the spring of 1898, he resigned his post and raised a volunteer cavalry regiment, soon to be famous as the "Rough Riders," which included both Ivy League polo players and western cowboys. Serving as second-in-command of the regiment, Colonel Roosevelt led the men on a successful assault on Spanish positions on San Juan Hill, Cuba, on July 1, 1898.

Roosevelt's exploits in Cuba made him a national hero. He won election as governor of New York later that year, and in 1900 he became vice president of the United States as William McKinley's running mate in the presidential election. On September 6, 1901, an assassin shot McKinley, and Roosevelt succeeded to the presidency. At just forty-two years of age, he was the youngest president up to that time. Roosevelt was elected president in his own right in 1904.

In the White House, Roosevelt promoted the ideals of the Progressive movement in American politics, which called for greater government involvement in making life better for ordinary Americans. His administration saw the passage of the first federal laws regulating the purity of food and drugs, and he used executive powers to negotiate settlements in labor disputes. In foreign affairs, he flexed America's military muscles—for example, by supporting a revolution in Colombia that paved the way for the construction of the Panama Canal, which, when it opened in 1914, linked the Atlantic and Pacific oceans. But Roosevelt also oversaw the negotiations that ended a war between Russia and Japan, for which he received the Nobel Peace Prize in 1906.

Roosevelt was also the first president to make conservation of natural resources and preservation of wilderness areas a national priority. Starting in 1902, he established five national parks, four federal game preserves, and eighteen national monuments (including natural wonders such as the Grand Canyon and California's redwood forests), as well as setting up a National Forest Service.

This has remained the cornerstone of the BSA's policy ever since. Today, more than thirty different religious groups have created religious emblems programs to recognize their members' achievements in Scouting. Reflecting the growing diversity of American society, they now include faiths ranging from Hinduism and Islam to Baha'i and Zoroastrianism. (In fact, every major religious denomination in the United States is now represented in Scouting.)

At the time of the BSA's founding, America was a nation divided on racial as well as religious lines. Racial prejudice was widespread, and whether by law in the South or by custom elsewhere in the country, a system of segregation compelled African Americans to live separate and usually unequal lives outside the mainstream of white society.

Officially, the BSA was committed to inclusiveness in race as well as religion—W. D. Boyce, for example, agreed to provide funding for the organization with the understanding that it would not "discriminate according to race or creed." Some southern African American community leaders, inspired by Baden-Powell's *Scouting for Boys*, established troops even before the BSA officially came into being. In the North, some African American boys were accepted as members of mostly white troops in the movement's earliest days—and an African American troop formed in Elizabeth City, New Jersey, in 1911. A fully integrated troop was organized in a school for the deaf in the same state five years later.

But the BSA still had to deal with the prevailing social attitudes of the time. In 1911, for example, James E. West received a letter from the organizer of a New Orleans troop that wanted to affiliate with the BSA, but who feared he would be unable to keep white boys in the group if he also admitted African American boys. "There would be no necessity whatever of the New Orleans Boy Scouts admitting Negro Boys into their ranks," West wrote back. "The Negro interests of the Boy Scout Movement could be handled in the same way you handle the public school question in the South, that is, providing separate schools, separate teachers and administration."

In the 1920s, the BSA would begin to make a determined effort to bring African American boys into Scouting (see Part Two)—an effort that was especially commendable considering the opposition from white-supremacist groups like the Ku Klux Klan, which had a resurgence following World War I. Still,

Scouting—in the South at least—would largely be segregated until after World War II.

The BSA even had some initial opposition from America's organized-labor movement in its first years. In Baden-Powell's *Scouting for Boys*, the second point of the Scout Law called on boys to be loyal not only "to the King, and to his officers, and to his parents, [and] to his country," but to "his employers" as well, and this was repeated in some of the BSA's first publications. Some American labor leaders took this to mean that the BSA was opposed to the right to strike and the right to collective bargaining by workers.

In 1911, for example, members of a musician's union refused to participate in a parade in St. Louis, Missouri, in which Boy Scouts were marching; in 1912, labor activists protested at Baden-Powell's appearances during an American lecture tour. By that time, however, the newly published *Handbook for Boys*

had omitted the reference to loyalty to employers, and Samuel Gompers, head of the American Federation of Labor (AFL), was in talks with James E. West about cooperation with the BSA. Still, as with the Catholic Church, it took some labor organizations several years to fully accept Scouting as a worthy pursuit for the sons of their members.

Probably the biggest controversy facing the BSA was over accusations that it promoted "militarism." The Boy Scouts in Britain had faced similar accusations. In founding the movement, Baden-Powell had stressed the distinction between "peace scouts" and "war scouts." But Baden-Powell, of course, was first and foremost a military hero, and some people in Britain saw the Scouts as an organization aimed mainly at preparing boys for service in the country's armed forces.

The Chief Scout's own statements were sometimes ambiguous. In a 1910 paper, for example, he wrote, "We [the

LEFT Baden-Powell, a decorated war hero, wears his military uniform. **ABOVE** Young men wearing the first official BSA uniform.

THE EVOLUTION OF AN EAGLE

IT WASN'T THIS WAY AT THE BEGINNING. When the BSA was getting off the ground in 1910–1911, the top rank was called Wolf. But—apparently out of the desire to have a more uniquely American symbol—Wolf became Eagle. As the 1911 handbook put it, "Any first-class scout qualifying for twenty-one merit badges will be entitled to wear the highest scout merit badge. This is an eagle's head in silver, and represents the all-round perfect scout."

At first Eagle Scout wasn't so much a rank as a kind of "super" merit badge. Still, earning those twenty-one merit badges was a major achievement, and when the first Scout "qualified" in 1912, he was personally interviewed by James E. West and Dan Beard, and possibly by Ernest Thompson Seton, too.

That first Eagle Scout was seventeen-year-old Arthur Eldred of Troop 1, Oceanside, Long Island, New York, and he got his Eagle badge on Labor Day, September 2, 1912. Troop 1—founded in November 1910 by Arthur's older brother Hubert—had a reputation for being well uniformed and well disciplined, so it was chosen to serve as an honor guard when Baden-Powell arrived in New York City in January 1912 for a lecture tour. It's said that the Chief Scout was so impressed by Eldred's merit badge sash that he stopped and spoke to him personally before the welcoming ceremony began.

While Eldred waited for his Eagle Scout medal, he earned another distinction. While camping with his troop in August 1912, Eldred rescued a fellow Scout from drowning in a lake. For this he won the BSA's Honor Medal.

Eldred served in the U.S. Navy in World War I and went on to a distinguished career in the transportation business. He died in 1951 at his home in Clementon, New Jersey, aged fifty-five. His son and grandson also achieved Eagle Scout rank.

Twenty-one other Scouts reached Eagle Scout rank by the end of 1912. Throughout the 1920s and into the 1930s, attaining Eagle Scout status was still largely a matter of earning merit badges. (In 1927, the BSA authorized Eagle Palm awards—bronze, silver, and gold—for those who continued to earn merit badges after achieving Eagle Scout rank.) During this period, Eagle wasn't limited to youth members of the BSA—adults were eligible for the award, too, until 1952. The service-project concept was introduced that same year, but not refined into its present form until 1965. (The number of merit badges needed to advance to Eagle Scout—and which badges were required—has also varied since then.)

In 1972, the BSA established the National Eagle Scout Association (NESA) as a fraternal association of Eagle Scouts and a service organization with the goal of helping Scouts along the trail to the BSA's highest rank. NESA has its roots in the Knights of Dunamis, an unofficial "honor society" of Eagle Scouts dating back to the 1920s. NESA took over administration of the Distinguished Eagle Scout Award, bestowed by the BSA since 1969 to recognize Eagle Scouts who'd distinguished themselves "in business, professions, and service to others." Recipients of the award receive a gold Eagle medal. (Twenty-five years must have passed since attaining Eagle Scout rank for an individual to be eligible for the award.) As of 2007, about 2,000 Eagle Scouts have received the Distinguished Eagle Scout Award. A sample of the more famous recipients includes astronaut Neil Armstrong; top military commanders Admiral Elmo M. Zumwalt Jr. and General William C. Westmoreland; businessman and presidential candidate H. Ross Perot; entrepreneur-adventurer Steve Fossett; cartoonist Milton Caniff; scientist E. O. Wilson; and a long list of politicians— U.S. Senators Lamar Alexander, Bill Bradley, and Lloyd M. Bentsen Jr., and President Gerald Ford among them.

In 1982, Alexander Holsinger of Normal, Illinois, became the BSA's one-millionth Eagle Scout. As of this writing, about 1.7 million Scouts have attained Eagle Scout rank.

As Eagle Scout progressed from a tally of merit badges to Scouting's highest rank, so did its public profile. Nowadays, at Eagle courts of honor across the country, newly fledged Eagle Scouts are told by their Scoutmasters that they are "marked men"—while they've achieved much as boys, even more is expected of them in their lives and careers as men. As the saying goes, "Once an Eagle, always an Eagle."

Boy Scouts] do not take up soldiering as part of our main policy," noting that the Scouts' lack of official emphasis on outright military training helped bring in boys whose parents "object to military drill in any form." But Baden-Powell and other promoters of Scouting in Britain were also staunch believers that British youth needed to "be prepared" to meet what they saw as threats to Britain and its global empire. As Baden-Powell put it in a 1911 article, "… our policy is not to make the boys into soldiers, but as a first aim to make them good citizens, although the results show that a very large proportion of our boys who have left us have gone into the service."

The controversy carried over to the United States. In the 1910s, close to one in five Americans had been born overseas or to immigrant parents. Many of these immigrants had left Europe for America to avoid conscription—forced military service—in their homelands. There was also a strong pacifist trend among native-born Americans. And anti-militaristic feeling only intensified after World War I broke out in Europe in August 1914; while the U.S. remained neutral, Americans watched in horror as hundreds of thousands—ultimately millions—of young men were slaughtered in the trenches that soon stretched across the continent.

Thus, many Americans suspected that a youth organization that was organized into "troops" and "patrols," which stressed patriotism and citizenship, and which wore uniforms, must be just a sort of prep school for military service. A Missouri boy, Fielding Chandler, recalled much later that while his parents allowed him to take part in Scouting activities, they wouldn't let him join officially: "In those days there was some idea that the boys would graduate from Scouting to the Army."

The uniform didn't help this perception, either. The British Boy Scout uniform might have been based on a military pattern, but at least it looked rather sporty, with its shorts, neckerchief, and broad-brimmed hat. The first official BSA uniform (available from the Sigmund Eisner Company of Red Bank, New Jersey, at $4.05 for a "complete outfit") was pretty much a copy of the dowdy U.S. Army uniform of the time, complete with baggy trousers tucked into canvas leggings known as "puttees" and a four-pocketed tunic with a high "choker" collar. (Eisner's

ABOVE A young man wearing the first BSA uniform.

THE SUPPLY GROUP

Boy Scouts and Scout Masters

The Hill & Loper Co., Danbury, Conn., are making a special hat for you—a hat that's *built for scouting*—one that will *hold its shape and color* and all the snap and dash that are put into it, in spite of "wind and weather." It's made to supply the increasing demand for a *better* Boy Scout Hat. It's made from Fine Fur Felt — from the same stock and by the same skilled workmen that produce the Hill & Loper Co.'s famous "HI-LO" Felt Hats which are sold to the most particular trade all over the country. It's "*Scout*" style, through and through, and built on the thorough, thoroughly honest principles that your great organization stands for. It is approved by your National Council, and you'll approve it as soon as you see it and try it on. You can get one of these Boy Scout or Scout Master Hats from your local dealer or from National Headquarters, Boy Scouts of America. Be sure to look for the Boy Scout Seal, stamped on the Sweat Leather. None genuine without this seal. If there is no dealer in your locality send your size and the regular price—$2.00 for "Boy Scout" or $2.50 for "Scout Master" Hat, direct to

National Outfitter
SIGMUND EISNER
Red Bank   **New Jersey**

BOY SCOUT SHOES

OFFICIAL SEAL

Price
$2.50

Joseph M. Herman & Co., of Boston, the world famous manufacturers of Herman's **U. S. Army Shoes**, the kind the soldiers, sailors, marines and militia wear, have created the **most comfortable** and **best wearing shoe for boys that ever was known**. It is made on the **sensible orthopedic last** designed by army surgeons. The regular army stamp is on these shoes and so is the official Boy Scout seal. Look for these marks when buying. The genuine

U. S. Army — Boy Scout Shoe

is made of **Shrewsbury leather** with **double sole of solid oak leather reinforced** so that it **cannot break away**. The upper has a **cool lining** and is **soft and pliable**. This is not only the **best shoe for wear** that a boy can put on but is **handsome and snappy**—one that **any boy will be proud to show to his friends**. Be sure to **mention your size** when ordering. Send orders direct to

SIGMUND EISNER, National Outfitter, RED BANK, N. J.

THE BSA RECOGNIZED from the outset that its members would need a reliable, authorized, reasonably priced source for uniforms, instructional materials, and other gear. From 1910 to 1912, the BSA's National Council "[Made] arrangements with certain manufacturers to furnish such parts of the equipment as may be desired by the boys," as the BSA's Second Annual Report put it. In 1913, however, the BSA decided to centralize its supply operations, adopting a resolution "That the scope of the department shall be confined to such items and printed matter for which there might be . . . a real use in Scouting; . . .[and] that no attempt shall be made to develop a general sales department for the sake merely of profit, and it shall be the policy of the Supply Department, at all times, to sell goods of the best quality at the lowest possible prices consistent therewith."

To help manage this ambitious undertaking, the BSA hired an experienced executive from Montgomery Ward, one of the country's leading mail-order sales companies at the time. The Supply Service's first catalog (sent to Scoutmasters only) appeared in 1913, and the following year a catalog of fifty or so items was mailed to all registered Scouts and Scouters. While the Supply Service was faithful to its policy of not striving for profit for profit's sake, it proved so successful that, in 1918, an internal report noted "It is with considerable satisfaction . . . that through the Department of Scout Supplies a substantial portion of the expenses of the organization [the BSA as a whole] were met during the year 1917." In 1920, the Supply Service reported sales of $710,697—equivalent to about $7 million in 2006 dollars.

As Scouting grew in the 1920s, distribution branches were established in San Francisco and Chicago in addition to the main branch in New York City. Along with the BSA headquarters, the Supply Service would move to North Brunswick, New Jersey, in the early 1950s. Now known as the Supply Group, it operates a consolidated distribution center in Charlotte, North Carolina, and sells everything from uniforms to DVDs via a nationwide retail network of "Scout shops," distributors, and a Web site, www.scoutstuff.org.

LEFT Early advertisements for Scouting apparel, with the shoe ad boasting they have the same manufacturer as the U.S. Army. **RIGHT** A boy wearing a BSA-issued shirt and neckerchief. **ABOVE** A young man, Theo Gatz Jr., shows off his badges and the first BSA uniform, which closely resembled the U.S. Army uniform of the time.

advertisement in the first edition of the *Handbook for Boys* even boasted that the company was a "manufacturer of U.S. Army and National Guard Uniforms.")

In addition, some Scoutmasters of the era did indeed run their troops along quasi-military lines, with junior leaders designated as "sergeants" and "corporals" and emphasis on marching, close-order drill, and marksmanship. Albert Drompp, a Pennsylvania Scout, remembered that his Scoutmaster—a veteran of America's 1898 war with Spain—"[wasn't] too well-acquainted with Scouting, and his activities were marching and camping—things he knew something about."

The BSA's national leadership tried to steer a middle path through the controversy about "militarism" in the organization. James E. West was no fan of either military drill or firearms training. West was also struggling against the perception, in some quarters, that the BSA and William Randolph Hearst's avowedly militarist American Boy Scout movement were connected.

ABOVE (top) Young members of Hearst's militaristic group, the American Boy Scouts. (bottom) A member of the American Boy Scouts lowers his gun to reflect on the statue of Nathan Hale, the famed officer who gave his life for his country in the Revolutionary War, in New York City.

with the windows of his bedroom open both summer and winter.

It means also that he should take a cold bath often, rubbing dry with a rough towel. He should breathe through the nose and not through the mouth. He should at all times train himself to endure hardships.

In addition to these the scout should be a lover of his country. He should know his country. How many states there are in it, what are its natural resources, scope, and boundaries. He ought to know something of its history, its early settlers, and of the great deeds that won his land. How they settled along the banks of the James River. How Philadelphia, New York, and other great cities were founded. How the Pilgrim Fathers established New England and laid the foundation for our national life. How the scouts of the Middle West saved all that great section of the country for the Republic. He ought to know how Texas became part of the United States, and how our national heroes stretched out their hands, north and south, east and west, to make one great united country.

He ought to know the history of the important wars. He ought to know about our army and navy flags and the insignia of rank of our officers. He ought to know the kind of government he lives under, and what it means to live in a republic. He ought to know what is expected of him as a citizen of his state and nation, and what to do to help the people among whom he lives.

In short, to be a good scout is to be a well-developed, well-informed boy.

Scout Virtues

There are other things which a scout ought to know and which should be characteristic of him, if he is going to be the kind of scout for which the Boy Scouts of America stand. One of these is obedience. To be a good scout a boy must learn to obey the orders of his patrol leader, scout master, and scout commissioner. He must learn to obey, before he is able to command. He should so learn to discipline and control himself that he will have no thought but to obey the orders of his officers. He should keep such a strong grip on his own life that he will not allow himself to do anything which is ignoble, or which will harm his life or weaken his powers of endurance.

Another virtue of a scout is that of courtesy. A boy scout

ABOVE (foreground) Page from *Handbook for Boys* stating that a Scout should love his country and be a good citizen. (background) Scouts waving the American flag at an exhibition in Central Park.

The Setons . . .

Ernest Thompson Seton, side by side with Lord Baden-Powell and Daniel Carter Beard, hiked Scouting's first trails and built Scouting's first campfires. Together, these early pioneers mapped out a boy's program that would eventually become the largest youth organization in the free world -- the Boy Scouts of America.

Seton, already an author, artist and naturalist of world renown, was there in the very beginning -- and before. Some years before the Baden-Powell Scouting concept was born, Seton began promoting the development of young boys through outdoor skills with a youth organization he founded: the Woodcraft Indians.

Seton's contributions to Scouting during the formative years of the organization are impressive. He wrote the first Scout Handbook and was the first Chief Scout, a position he held for five years. Chief Seton received the Silver Buffalo Award for distinguished service to boyhood in 1926, the first year the award was given.

Chief Ernest Thompson Seton died October 23, 1946.

The generosity and forsight of his widow, Julia, have brought the Seton collections to Philmont.

A native of New York City, Mrs. Seton is a recognized lecturer and author. She received her Master's degree from Hunter College, where she taught before marrying Seton and moving to the Southwest.

ERNEST THOMPSON SETON
MEMORIAL LIBRARY AND MUSEUM

SETON MEMORIAL
LIBRARY AND MUSEUM

PHILMONT SCOUT RANCH
CIMARRON, NEW MEXICO

But there were other Americans who thought the BSA's program didn't emphasize the military-style training *enough*. After World War I started in Europe, some prominent Americans (including the "Chief Scout Citizen," ex-president Theodore Roosevelt) began arguing that the United States should enter the war in support of the Allies (Britain and France) in the struggle against the Central Powers (Germany, Austria-Hungary, and Turkey). A "Preparedness" movement sprang up, with young businessmen volunteering for military training under army officers in camps across the country. To some of these people, the BSA's position seemed, somehow, unpatriotic. Among them was the U.S. Army's chief of staff, Major General Leonard Wood. A charter member of the BSA's National Council, Wood resigned his position in 1914 over the organization's supposed anti-military stance. Theodore Roosevelt weighed in, saying that "certain [BSA] leaders . . . have used the Boy Scouts organization as a medium for the dissemination of pacifist literature and . . . as a propaganda [sic] for interfering with the training of our boys to a standard of military efficiency."

The BSA's Executive Board published a resolution denying the BSA was "anti-military," going on to say that "The Boy Scout Movement neither promotes nor discourages military training, its sole concern being the development of character and personal efficiency of adolescent boys."

The pacifism versus militarism controversy was a reflection of a wider rift between the men who had put together the BSA. When it came to deciding the goals and overall philosophy of the new organization, the founders had considerable differences of opinion.

Chief Scout Ernest Thompson Seton felt there was too much emphasis on patriotism and citizenship, and by 1915 he had left the BSA. He founded a new organization, the Woodcraft League of America, which was open to both boys and girls. He continued to publish his "animal stories," took U.S. citizenship, and died at eighty-six in New Mexico.

Much of Seton's contributions to the *Handbook for Boys* were cut out of later editions, and in the wake of his departure the role of "spiritual father" of the BSA passed on to Dan Beard. Still, Seton's influence on the Scouting movement in general and on the BSA in particular was profound. His legacy remains in the respect for American Indian folkways and the emphasis on closeness to nature that underpins so much of the BSA's program—and especially that of the Order of the Arrow (see pages 92 and 95).

LEFT (top) Announcement of Ernest T. Seton's death. (bottom) His collections were placed in a memorial museum at Philmont. **ABOVE** (left) Scouts mobilizing field hospital units at the Central Park exhibition, responding to their civic duty. (right) Boys from Hearst's American Boy Scouts stand at attention.

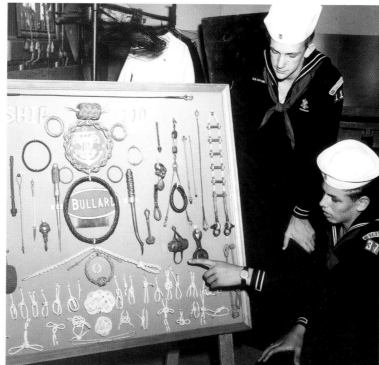

THE EARLY YEARS

Infighting among the BSA's leaders and the various controversies did little to stunt the organization's growth. Annual national registration of Scouts began in 1913 (cost: 25 cents), and the

be able to manage a boat, to bring it properly alongside a ship or pier," and he saw that many older boys were interested in all things nautical—not surprising, as Britain had the world's most powerful navy and its biggest merchant fleet at the time of

"It is obvious that the . . . seamanship and life on the water present quite as favorable opportunities for learning and practicing the Scout virtues as do the occupation of woodcraft . . . and there are, besides, a large number of boys to whose imagination the call of the sea appeals with greater charm than that of the woods."

FROM A BSA NATIONAL COMMITTEE REPORT ON SEA SCOUTING, 1913

membership rolls for the following year showed some 107,000 boys and 25,000 men taking part in the movement.

The year 1912 saw some important developments. In that year, Sea Scouting became an official program of the BSA. Like Scouting in general, Sea Scouting had its origins in Britain. In *Scouting for Boys*, Baden-Powell had written that "a Scout should

Scouting's founding. What's more, there was a nautical expert in the family—Baden-Powell's oldest brother, Warington, an experienced merchant seaman, yachtsman, canoeist, and later in life, an expert in maritime law. Baden-Powell wrote a preliminary pamphlet outlining the basics of Sea Scouting in 1911, but he turned to Warington to write a manual that would

ABOVE (left) Arthur Astor Carey, father of the Sea Scouts. (right) A Sea Scout points at a board of knots and tools for rope work.

ON THIS PAGE (right) Waving semaphore flags from a dock.

(middle) The requirements to earn the Seamanship merit

badge. (bottom) Sea Scouts say grace before a meal.

Seamanship

To obtain a merit badge for Seamanship a scout must
1. Be able to tie rapidly six different knots.
2. Splice ropes.
3. Use a palm and needle.
4. Fling a rope coil.
5. Be able to row, pole, scull, and steer a boat; also bring a boat properly alongside and make fast.
6. Know how to box the compass, read a chart, and show use of parallel rules and dividers.
7. Be able to state direction by the stars and sun.
8. Swim fifty yards with shoes and clothes on.

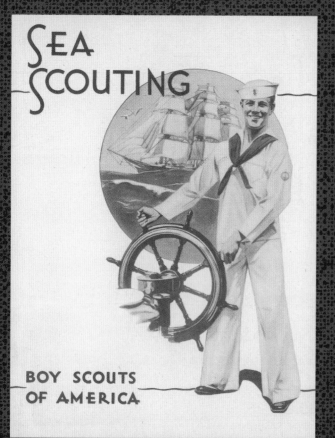

SEA SCOUTING

BOY SCOUTS OF AMERICA

Form 900-10M-2-34-D.

BOY SCOUTS OF AMERICA
SEA SCOUT APPLICATION

This blank should be sent to Local Council and retained by them—not sent to National Office of the Boy Scouts of America.

INCORPORATED FEBRUARY 8, 1910.   CHARTERED BY CONGRESS, JUNE 15, 1916

APPLICATION FOR MEMBERSHIP IN SEA SCOUT UNIT.

City_____ County_____ State_____

I hereby apply for membership in the Sea Scout Ship_____, Troop No._____
(Give Ship Name)

Boy Scouts of America, and agree to be guided by the rules of the Ship and the duly constituted Scout authorities.

If at any time I cease to be a Scout through fault of my own, I agree to return upon request of the Scout authorities my certificate, badge, and all other Scout insignia, which may have been purchased by me or loaned to me.

According to the requirements of the National Council I promise to make a part of my everyday life the Scout Oath, Scout Law, and the Sea Promise.

NOTE: The rules of the National Council positively forbid the enrollment of any boy under FIFTEEN YEARS OF AGE as a Sea Scout. NO EXCEPTION TO THIS RULE CAN BE MADE.

I enclose_____cents for my registration and membership dues.

Date_____ Name_____ Nationality_____
(Boy's Signature)

Residence_____ Phone_____

School or Employer_____ Highest Grade Reached_____

Employer's Address_____ Phone_____

Church Preference_____

Member of the following Boys' Organizations_____

Have been a Scout in the following Troops_____No. full years in Scouting_____Highest rank reached_____

If the candidate is not a member of the Institution with which the Sea Scout Ship is connected, it is suggested that the Skipper secure the approval of the Pastor, Priest, Rabbi, or other responsible head of same.

Application approved_____
(Head of Institution)   (Title)

PARENTS OR GUARDIAN'S APPROVAL

I HEREBY CERTIFY THAT_____

was born_____ I have read the Scout Oath and Law and am willing
(Month)   (Day)   (Year)

and desirous that he become a member of the Boy Scouts of America, Sea Scout Division, and will try to assist him in observing the rules of the organization. In consideration of the benefits derived from this membership if accepted, I hereby voluntarily waive any claim against the Boy Scouts of America for any and all causes which may arise in connection with the activities of the above organization.

Is his date of birth registered with the local health officer?_____

Business_____

Phone_____
(Signature of Parent or Guardian)

NOTE TO PARENTS OR GUARDIAN: The Sea Scout Program is at times one of strenuous outdoor activity which may include swimming, climbing, sailing, rowing and paddling. This calls for vigorous physical health and applicants for membership must be organically sound to be accepted. The following confidential information on the past health history and present physical condition of your son or ward, is required in order that his application may be considered. This, please understand, is for his protection. Please give all the information requested below and add anything desired under "Remarks" on opposite side.

Is there any one item of food which, if eaten, makes him ill?_____

Is he subject to: (Answer Yes or No)	Has he had: (Answer Yes or No)
Headaches?_____	Infantile Paralysis?_____ When?_____
Fainting Spells?_____	Typhoid Fever?_____ When?_____
Tonsilitis?_____	Pneumonia?_____ When?_____
Abdominal Pains?_____	
Cramps?_____ Where?_____	(Over)

One of the essential skills required of a Sea Scout is ability to signal by semaphore quickly. Above is a picture of some Sea Scouts in Manila, P. I., being instructed in semaphore signalling.

Above circle—After being taught how to row a boat a Sea Scout is taught how to sail one. This is easier and more exciting, that rowing and lots of fun.

Right—All Sailors sing at their work. The songs they sing are called Chanteys. These are work songs something like the spirituals. Here you see a group singing while they haul on a brace.

A Scout is clean. Cleanliness is essential on board ship. Cleanliness of person and uniform is insisted upon. Above you will see the Skipper of the Sea Scout Ship "Alert" inspecting his crew in the morning watch.

Even though the Sea Scouts like the water, sometimes they try to get as far away from it as possible, by climbing the masts. Sometimes they really have to go there to make some repairs. That is probably what these fellows are doing.

There is an art in getting into a boat. Most people do not know how, but Sea Scouts are carefully instructed on just how they should enter and leave a boat. The above group of Sea Scouts are getting this instruction.

The Sea Scouts in all of the towns around the coasts have been privileged by being asked to act as guards of honor on board the famous Frigate "Old Ironsides." Here is a picture of the Sea Scouts in Washington, D. C., sailing down the Potomac to welcome "Old Ironsides" as she came up to the Capitol City.

Above circle—Many Sea Scout Ships are fortunate in being presented with Navy Whaleboats. Above is a group being instructed in how to sail a 24 ft. Whaleboat with a sliding gunter rig.

Left—There is always a study period on every cruise held in the forenoon watch after the ship has been scrubbed down and all the bright work shined (that is, of course, if the weather is good.)

be the watery equivalent of *Scouting for Boys*. Warington's *Sea Scouting and Seamanship for Boys* appeared the following year. The Sea Scouts idea came to America a year later when Arthur Carey organized a troop aboard his schooner, the *Pioneer*, in Waltham, Massachusetts. The Sea Scouts set their membership age at fifteen and up, giving older boys with an interest in nautical subjects a program of their own.

Despite official recognition by the BSA, it took some years for the Sea Scouts to become firmly established, but the program was significant as an early attempt at dealing with what generations of Scouters would come to know as the "older-boy problem." From the beginning of the movement, adult leaders recognized that as boys entered their adolescent years, many dropped out of Scouting. Some became more interested in sports than Scouting, or decided that while camping and hiking and other activities may have been okay when they were just "boys," they were no longer worthy pursuits now that they were young men. Others left the movement in the face of peer pressure. In Britain, Baden-Powell responded to the "older-boy problem" by establishing Rovering in 1919. Rovering's twin goals were to retain young men in Scouting and to prepare them to serve as adult leaders. (The age for admission to Rovering in Britain was variable in its early years, but finally set at seventeen in 1921.) In his own words, Baden-Powell saw Rovering as "the third progressive step in the education of the Boy Scout," encompassed in a three-point program:

1. Service to self, career, health.
2. Service to the Scout Movement.
3. Service to the Community.

Like its "younger-boy problem" counterpart, Cub Scouting, Rovering came to the United States as an unofficial import. Copies of the Rovering handbook, *Rovering to Success* (first published in Britain in 1922), found their way into the hands of American Scouters, and in areas close to Canada—especially the Pacific Northwest and New England—American troops organized

LEFT (top left and bottom) Sea Scouting brochure cover and pages explaining the ropes of Sea Scouting and encouraging teens to stay involved with Scouting. (top right) Sea Scouting application form. Only boys fifteen or older were eligible to apply.

THE YOUNGER BOY PROBLEM AND THE OLDER BOY PROBLEM

THESE TWO TERMS CROP UP A LOT in the history of Scouting, and they describe two issues that have dogged the movement from its beginning. The "younger-boy problem" refers to the fact that boys not old enough to meet Boy Scouting's age requirements still want to take part in Scouting activities. Following British precedent, the BSA addressed this problem with the introduction of Cub Scouting (see page 89). Today, thanks to the Tiger Cubs program that began in 1982, boys who've reached the age of seven or who have entered the first grade can have a fun introduction to the world of Scouting.

The "older-boy problem" has been more challenging. Besides pressure from peers who think Scouting "isn't cool," Scouts hitting their teen years are subject to many competing interests and activities. In addition, many older Scouts—then and now—have had to take jobs to help their families or to save money for college, leaving less time for Scouting. And beyond these issues, older Scouts often want to take part in more challenging activities—backpacking, rock climbing, white-water rafting, etc.—that aren't safe for younger Scouts. Over the decades, the BSA has dealt with the "older-boy problem" with a variety of programs—from Rovering to Exploring to Varsity and Venturing—with a high degree of success.

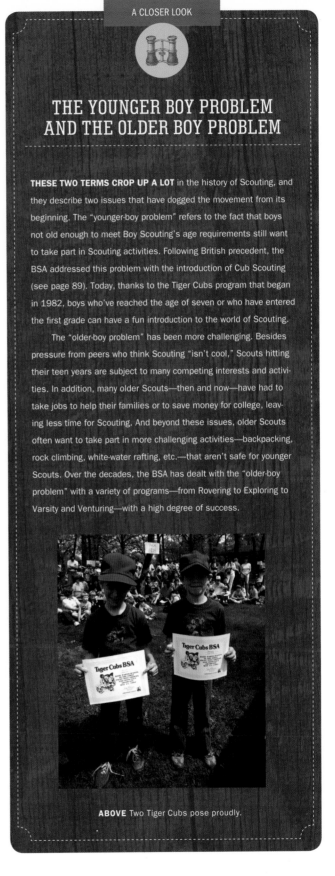

ABOVE Two Tiger Cubs pose proudly.

Rover "crews" in imitation of their brother Scouts north of the border. Other councils and individual troops adapted elements of Rovering into their own unique programs for older Scouts, some of which went by names like "Musketeers," "Foresters," and "Rangers." As with the Order of the Arrow (see pages 92 and 95), elaborate ceremonies often accompanied admission to the Rovers and similar groups; and also like the OA, Rovers performed outstanding service by maintaining local council camps.

While Rovering and its imitators made unofficial inroads in America, the BSA introduced Senior Scouting in the 1920s; by the mid-1930s, "Senior Scouting" had become an umbrella term that encompassed not only older boys and young men in individual troops, but all the BSA's "Senior Boy" programs (generally aimed at boys fifteen or older), including the Order of the Arrow, Sea Scouting, and (after 1942) Air Scouting.

Rovering became an official BSA program for boys and young men aged seventeen to twenty-five in 1933. Unlike the Cub Scouts, however, Rovering never really caught on in a big way in the United States. Estimates vary, but by the end of the 1930s there were probably fewer than 2,000 Scouts registered with the BSA's National Council as members of Rover crews. The Rovers faced competition from other "Senior Boy" programs, and, eight years after its inception, America's entry into World War II meant that the young men in the Rover age range would be wearing a different type of uniform. Although a few Rover crews continued to be active for decades after the war, the remaining Rovers were folded into the Explorer program after 1953.

Still, the basic principle of Rovering—"a preparation for life, and also a pursuit for life," as Baden-Powell put it—would ultimately underpin the Venturing program established by the BSA in 1998.

BOYS' LIFE

In 1912, an enduring element of Scouting in America appeared in print: the first "official" issue of *Boys' Life* magazine. The magazine had actually begun publishing in 1911 as the brainchild of George S. Barton, of Somerville, Massachusetts. The BSA then bought the magazine from its original publisher, the George S. Barton Company, for $6,000—or roughly $1 for

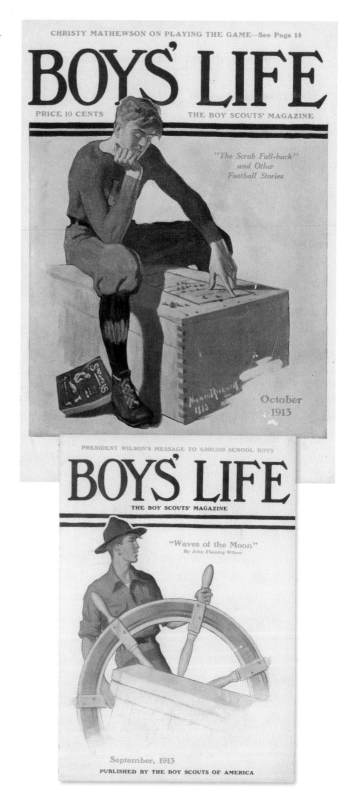

ABOVE Some of the very first covers of *Boys' Life* magazine illustrated by Norman Rockwell. By 1913, the price of the magazine had doubled to 10 cents.

PRESIDENT ROOSEVELT'S BSA SUPPORT

EVEN BEFORE HE BECAME the nation's chief executive, Roosevelt took a keen interest in the moral and physical health of America's boys and young men. In a 1900 essay on "The American Boy," published in *St. Nicholas*, one of the leading youth magazines of the era, Roosevelt wrote:

> Of course what we have a right to expect of the American boy is that he shall turn out to be a good American man. Now, the chances are strong that he won't be much of a man unless he is a good deal of a boy. He must not be a coward or a weakling, a bully, a shirk, or a prig. He must work hard and play hard. He must be clean-minded and clean-lived, and able to hold his own under all circumstances and against all comers. It is only on these conditions that he will grow into the kind of American man of whom America can be really proud.

When the newly formed BSA appealed for Roosevelt's support, the former president responded with all of his celebrated energy and enthusiasm. He accepted the post of honorary vice president of the BSA (the honorary presidency went to William Howard Taft, the current occupant of the White House—beginning a tradition that continues to this day). The BSA also conferred the unique designation of "Chief Scout Citizen" on Roosevelt.

Roosevelt contributed a section on "Practical Citizenship" to the 1911 edition of the *Handbook for Boys*, raising points he echoed in an article in an early issue of *Boys' Life*:

> Through *Boys' Life* I want to send this message, not only to the Boy Scouts, but to all the boys of America. The prime lesson of the Boy Scout movement is teaching that manliness in its most vigorous form can be and ought to be accompanied by unselfish consideration for the rights and interests of others. Indeed I can go a little further. I wish that I could make the especial appeal to the American boy to remember that unless he thinks of others he cannot fit himself to the best work in any great emergency.

In 1912, Roosevelt made another run for the presidency as candidate of the Progressive Party, which became known popularly as the "Bull Moose Party" when Roosevelt proclaimed that he was "fit as a bull moose." He certainly showed his fitness on October 14, 1912, when he insisted on making a campaign speech in Milwaukee—with a would-be assassin's bullet lodged in his chest.

Roosevelt came in second in the popular vote in the presidential election of 1912, but his third-party candidacy split the Republican vote and helped Democrat Woodrow Wilson win the White House. After the election, Roosevelt (accompanied by his son Kermit) led an expedition to map the unexplored Rio Negro (now the Rio Roosevelt) in the Brazilian rain forest. Racked by tropical diseases, the former president barely survived the harrowing journey through the jungle.

When World War I broke out in Europe, Roosevelt argued for American intervention on behalf of the Allies in the fight against Germany. When the U.S. finally entered the war in April 1917, Roosevelt appealed to President Wilson for a combat command. He was turned down.

Suffering from poor health and grieving over the death in action of his son Quentin, a fighter pilot, Roosevelt died at his Long Island, New York, home, Sagamore Hill, on January 16, 1919. He was sixty years old. For decades afterward, Boy Scouts—often led by Dan Beard—made an annual pilgrimage to his grave.

Sixty-fourth Congress of the United States of America;

At the First Session,

Begun and held at the City of Washington on Monday, the sixth day of December, one thousand nine hundred and fifteen.

AN ACT

To incorporate the Boy Scouts of America, and for other purposes.

Be it enacted by the Senate and House of Representatives of the United States of America in Congress assembled, That Colin H. Livingstone and Ernest P. Bicknell, of Washington, District of Columbia; Benjamin L. Dulaney, of Bristol, Tennessee; Milton A. McRae, of Detroit, Michigan; David Starr Jordan, of Berkeley, California; F. L. Seely, of Asheville, North Carolina; A. Stamford White, of Chicago, Illinois; Daniel Carter Beard, of Flushing, New York; George D. Pratt, of Brooklyn, New York;* Franklin C. Hoyt, Jeremiah W. Jenks, Charles P. Neill, Frank Presbrey, Edgar M. Robinson, Mortimer L. Schiff, and James E. West, of New York, New York; G. Barrett Rich, junior, of Buffalo, New York; Robert Garrett, of Baltimore, Maryland; John Sherman Hoyt, of Norwalk, Connecticut; Charles C. Jackson, of Boston, Massachusetts; John H. Nicholson, of Pittsburgh, Pennsylvania; William D. Murray, of Plainfield, New Jersey; and George D. Porter, of Philadelphia, Pennsylvania, their associates and successors, are hereby created a body corporate and politic of the District of C[...] shall be.

SEC. 2. That the name of this corporation s[...] and by that name it shall have perpetual suc[...] sued in courts of law and equity within the [...] to hold such real and personal estate as shall h[...] and to receive real and personal property by g[...] seal, and the same to alter and destroy at ple[...] its business and affairs within and without th[...] several States and Territories of the United S[...]

* Dr. Charles D. Hart, Philadelphia, Pa. [...]

Form 512—3M—10-22—B.P.S.

PROTECTION OF UNIFORM, BADGES,
INSIGNIA AND WORDS DESCRIPTIVE

OF THE

BOY SCOUTS OF AMERICA

GRANTED BY
TWO ACTS

OF U. S. CONGRESS

1. ACT OF CONGRESS, GRANTING FEDERAL CHARTER
   TO BOY SCOUTS OF AMERICA AND EDITORIAL
   COMMENTS.

2. SECTION 125 OF ARMY REORGANIZATION LAW,
   EXCEPTING BOY SCOUTS OF AMERICA FROM
   PROHIBITION AGAINST WEARING UNIFORMS SIMILAR
   TO THOSE WORN BY U. S. ARMY, NAVY OR
   MARINE CORPS.

NATIONAL HEADQUARTERS

BOY SCOUTS OF AMERICA
200 FIFTH AVENUE, N. Y. CITY

each current subscriber. In 1913, the magazine hired a young illustrator named Norman Rockwell—beginning an association between Rockwell and Scouting that would last more than sixty years (see page 142). A magazine for Scoutmasters, *Scouting*, began publication around the same time.

The BSA's first years also expanded public-service efforts. Scouts assisted at reunions of Civil War veterans and at state fairs. A contingent performed crowd-control duty at President Woodrow Wilson's inauguration in 1913—and Scouts have served at presidential inaugurations ever since.

When major floods hit the Midwest later that year, Scouts helped local authorities.

National recognition of the BSA took a big step forward on June 15, 1916, when Congress granted the organization a national charter. The charter read, in part: "That the purpose of this corporation shall be to promote, through organization and cooperation with other agencies, the ability of boys to do things for themselves and others, to train them in Scoutcraft, and to teach them patriotism, courage, self-reliance, and kindred virtues, using the methods which are now in common use by

LEFT (background) Congress grants the Boy Scouts of America a charter as a national organization, signed by Wilson on June 15, 1916. (foreground) A telegram to James E. West announcing that the bill was passed. **ABOVE** (left) Twenty-eighth President of the United States Woodrow Wilson, a great friend to the Scouts. (right) The two acts of Congress that granted the BSA a national charter and protected its right to wear uniforms.

Boy Scouts." Thanks to the legal protections afforded by the charter, the BSA now had sole claim to the name "Boy Scouts." Another law, passed by Congress around the same time, barred competing youth organizations from wearing the BSA's official military-style uniform.

THE BSA IN WORLD WAR I

The event that firmly established the Boy Scouts as America's foremost youth organization was the nation's entry into World War I in April 1917. Before the guns fell silent on November 11,

Troops hiked through their local forests to locate groves of black walnut trees, whose wood was needed for rifle stocks and airplane propellers. They collected tons of peach pits, a component used in filters for gas masks. Under the auspices of the War Garden Project, and with the slogan "Every Scout to feed a soldier," Scouts established more than 12,000 "Scout Farms" to raise much-needed food. In addition, Scouts designated as "dispatch bearers" distributed some 30 million pieces of government literature, while others patrolled bays and harbors on the East Coast to give warning if any enemy ships should

During the was and its aftermath, the Boy Scouts became a symbol of patriotic resolve and volunteer service to the nation.

1918, Scouts participated in a wide variety of activities aimed at aiding the country's war effort on what soon came to be called the "home front." (When America entered the war in 1917, the BSA, with 268,000 members, actually outnumbered the 200,000-man U.S. Army.)

appear, or guarded defense plants and depots against sabotage.

The BSA's biggest contribution to the war effort, though, was helping to raise the money needed to fight the war. In cooperation with the U.S. Treasury Department, Scouts helped sell Liberty Loan bonds and War Savings Stamps. Over the

ABOVE (left) The BSA ID card, with letter from Wilson entrusting Scouts as dispatch bearers on the back. (right) Scout effort to raise funds for World War I in 1917. **RIGHT** Letter addressed to Colin H. Livingstone, the first president of the BSA, from President Wilson, asking for help from Scouts to distribute Liberty Loan applications.

19 May, 1917

My dear Mr. Livingstone:

It will be most gratifying to me as Honorary President of the Boy Scouts of America to have the Boy Scouts, their scoutmasters and leaders throughout the United States lend their aid to the Secretary of the Treasury in distributing applications and securing popular subscriptions to the Liberty Loan. This will give every Scout a wonderful opportunity to do his share for his country under the slogan "Every Scout to Save a Soldier."

I feel sure this request will find a unanimous and enthusiastic response from Boy Scouts everywhere.

Sincerely yours,

Woodrow Wilson

Mr. Colin H. Livingstone, President,
National Council, Boy Scouts of America,
Washington, D. C.

BOY SCOUTS OF AMERICA

ORIGINALLY INCORPORATED, FEBRUARY 8, 1910
GRANTED FEDERAL CHARTER, BY CONGRESS, JUNE 16, 1916

HEADQUARTERS NATIONAL COUNCIL
THE FIFTH AVENUE BUILDING
NEW YORK CITY
TELEPHONE: GRAMERCY 4680

GEORGE D. PRATT
Treasurer

JAMES E. WEST
Chief Scout Executive

May 21st, 1917.

EMERGENCY CIRCULAR #7

Every Scout to SAVE a Soldier

The President calls for service: Act Today.
Prove Boy Scouts of America an Asset to our Country.

Dear Fellow Workers:

For the first time in the history of the Boy Scout movement the President of the United States has personally joined in a specific request to the Boy Scouts of America for cooperation with the National Government. An exceptional opportunity is forcibly presented by the enclosed letter from President Wilson addressed to Mr. Livingstone, President of the Boy Scouts of America, and the reply of President Livingstone with reference to the Boy Scouts of America serving our country in connection with the Liberty Bond issue.

THE EXECUTIVE BOARD APPROVES PLAN.

The Executive Board of the National Council at meeting held today definitely approved plans to invite every Scout official and registered scout to cooperate as requested by the President. This furnishes the Boy Scouts of America a real opportunity for service in a very vital matter at a time when our country needs the unqualified support of each and every one.

FOR OUR COUNTRY, HUMANITY AND DEMOCRACY.

Aside from the actual need of our Government for cash, there will be a real vital psychological benefit if the Liberty Bond issue is completely taken by June 15th - the closing day for applications. If the response of our people is such as to produce applications for two or three times the amount of the issue, the psychological value will be increased tremendously. Indeed it may materially shorten the duration of the war and thus save hundreds of thousands, yes, even possibly a million lives. It is for this reason that the Boy Scouts of America feel especially appropriate that they should engage in this work under the slogan, "EVERY SCOUT TO SAVE A SOLDIER." Furthermore, everyone who takes part in this campaign will perform a real patriotic service and materially help the world war for liberty, humanity, justice and democracy.

SHORT TERM BOY SCOUT CAMPAIGN FOR LIBERTY BOND SUBSCRIPTIONS.

A National Boy Scout short term campaign will be conducted June 11th, 12th, 13th, and 14th simultaneously throughout the country under the slogan "Every Scout to Save a Soldier." The plan involves the distribution of 10,000,000 pieces of printed matter furnished by the U. S. Treasury Department explaining the Bond issue, containing an application blank addressed to a local bank requesting the allotment of one or more of these bonds, and providing a window card for those who agree to subscribe.

In cities where there are councils of the First Class the organization of the city into districts and definite assignments of such districts to troops of scouts and sub-assignments to individual scouts or teams of scouts for a systematic house-to house canvass will be under the leadership of the Council. In other communities the scoutmasters are asked to organize themselves into a committee for the purpose of preventing duplication. In cases where there is but one troop of scouts, the scoutmaster will be charged with the responsibility of making sure that the most effective plan is developed for covering the entire community.   (over)

"BE PREPARED"   "DO A GOOD TURN DAILY"

ABOVE J. C. Leyendecker's 1918 Lady Liberty poster.

EARNING AN EAGLE SCOUT RANK

THE DESIGNATION OF EAGLE SCOUT RANK is American Scouting's highest achievement: Only about five percent of boys who enter Scouting have the medal pinned on their uniform by a proud parent at a troop court of honor. As of 2007, requirements for Eagle Scout include reaching Life Scout rank and earning twenty-one merit badges, twelve of which—ranging from Camping to Family Life—are mandatory. In addition, a contemporary candidate for Eagle Scout needs to earn either the Emergency Preparedness or Lifesaving merit badge, and at least one from a selection of Cycling, Hiking, and Swimming merit badges.

Earning the required merit badges is just part of the Eagle Scout equation. The candidate also has to plan and carry out a service project to benefit his community—some examples include organizing a blood drive, collecting food and clothing for a homeless shelter, helping to train guide dogs for the blind, or planting grass to halt beach erosion. Finally, the Eagle Scout candidate attends both a Scoutmaster conference and a board of review in which his adult leaders evaluate his "attitude and practice of the ideals of Scouting." These conferences now occur at every level of advancement, but in the case of Eagle Scout candidates, the results have to be approved not only by the troop but also by the local district and council and, ultimately, the BSA's National Council. And all this has to be accomplished before a boy's eighteenth birthday (although age requirements can be waived for Scouts with disabilities).

ABOVE The medal awarded to the first Eagle Scout.

course of five Liberty Loan "drives," Scouts marched in parades to promote sales, helped adult volunteers collect from buyers, and put up posters. (Illustrator J. C. Leyendecker's 1918 poster depicting a Scout handing a sword inscribed "Be Prepared" to a figure of Lady Liberty remains an enduring emblem of Scouting's wartime service.)

The Treasury Department awarded badges for bond sales; among the top sellers was Joseph D. Wooding of Troop 1, Garretsford, Pennsylvania, who racked up sales of more than $150,000. Wooding recalled that "I had one customer who was a very wealthy man and he gave me a check for $50,000. Here I am, a fourteen-year-old kid with a check for $50,000 in my pocket. I thought I was John D. Rockefeller." All told, Scouts sold 2,350,977 bonds worth $147,876,902 and $53,043,698 worth of stamps.

"The war is over," the BSA proclaimed in late 1918, "but our work is not." The end of the conflict coincided with a worldwide epidemic of a deadly form of influenza, a respiratory disease that ultimately killed more than 600,000 people in the U.S. alone. Once

"Boy Scouts and beans—they came together tumultuously at the [New York] Hippodrome yesterday morning, and if the boys have their way with the beans, back yards, flower beds, vacant lots, and window boxes from the Battery to Yonkers will bear beans by the bushel, which will feed soldiers at the front and women and children at home. For the Boy Scouts have been called to the ranks of the agricultural army and have volunteered to do their bit with the hoe."

THE NEW YORK TIMES, APRIL 22, 1917

again Scouts across the country pitched in, this time to help local governments and health authorities deal with the epidemic—for example, by distributing literature about how to avoid the disease. As the *Minneapolis-St. Paul Star Tribune* reported on October 13, 1918, "Boy Scouts are being mobilized and will be put into action tomorrow distributing placards and literature to all stores, offices and factories in the downtown district."

During the war and its aftermath, the Boy Scouts became a symbol of patriotic resolve and volunteer service to the nation. They appeared at Memorial Day and Fourth of July parades and other patriotic gatherings in countless communities; as one Scout of the time recalled, "Hardly a week went by that we weren't called out to march in a parade or help with traffic control for one." It's likely that many Americans got their first glimpse of uniformed Scouts on these occasions, and they liked what they saw. The BSA's home-front activities gave men and boys who were too young, too old, or otherwise unable to serve in the military a way to "do their bit" for the war effort. As a result of all this, membership more than doubled during the war years, rising to about 420,000 by the end of 1918.

LEFT (bottom) New York Scouts using the poster of a Scout handing Lady Liberty a sword to sell bonds. (top) A stream of uniformed Scouts working together to sell Liberty Loan war bonds. **ABOVE** Dozens of Scouts turn out with Lady Liberty posters to promote war bonds during World War I.

PART TWO

SCOUTING GROWS UP

1920 – 1945

LEFT Ephemera from 100 years of Scouting.

On July 30, 1920, 8,000 Boy Scouts from thirty-four countries gathered in London for the opening of Scouting's first worldwide jamboree. Among them were 301 American Scouts and Scouters, including James E. West. At the end of the weeklong event, presided over by Baden-Powell (now Sir Robert Baden-Powell—he'd been knighted in 1909) he was proclaimed "Chief Scout of the World."

The BSA's participation in the jamboree was a fitting kickoff to its second decade. There were now nearly a half-million boys enrolled. At the top level, the organization was adding professionals to support the growing volunteer structure, with 274 employees in the national office in New York and a field force of Scout executives helping to administer twelve regions. Among the new professionals was Danish-born William Hillcourt, who joined the BSA's Service of Supply in 1926—the start of a forty-year career in Scouting (see page 52).

The 1920s also saw the adoption of the Order of the Arrow as an official program. Scouts of the 1920s had a spiffy new uniform, introduced in 1919, and several Scouts wore them on well-publicized adventures around the world. In 1927, three Sea Scouts boarded the sailing ship *Northern Light* for an exploring cruise in the Arctic under the auspices of Chicago's Borden-Field Museum. The following year another Sea Scout, Paul Siple, went to the opposite end of the earth as a member of naval officer Richard Byrd's first Antarctic expedition, while three Boy Scouts accompanied the husband-and-wife exploring team of Martin and Osa Johnson on an expedition to Africa.

Scouting was now a household word. Still, membership growth in the 1920s dropped off from its World War I highs. In response, the BSA stepped up its efforts to bring as many boys as possible into the movement—including those with physical disabilities (the BSA introduced the first achievement awards for disabled Scouts in 1924), those who lived in rural areas without access to organized troops, and African Americans.

THE INTER-RACIAL SERVICE REACHES OUT

While Scouting had been open to African American boys since the beginning, there were probably only about 5,000 African

ABOVE (top) Scouts in the 1920s sported new uniforms, as illustrated in this January 1920 *Scouting* article. (bottom) The three lucky Scouts who accompanied Martin and Osa Johnson to Africa: David R. Martin Jr. (left), Robert L. Douglas Jr., and Douglas L. Oliver. **RIGHT** (top) The African contigent with their guide get up close with the lions in Africa in 1928. (bottom) With local hunters in Africa.

PAUL SIPLE AT THE SOUTH POLE

IN 1928, U.S. NAVY OFFICER RICHARD E. BYRD—who had won worldwide fame two years earlier for making the first airplane flight to the North Pole—announced his intention to do the same at the South Pole. And he decided to take a Boy Scout along. (Byrd's decision may have been inspired by the British explorer Sir Ernest Shackleton, who brought along a Scout, John Marr, on his final Antarctic expedition of 1921–1922.) The selection process was rigorous. Applicants had to be between seventeen and twenty years of age, in peak physical condition, and with proven leadership ability. Chief Scout Executive James E. West wrote that the BSA's national office received "literally thousands of applications." The office winnowed these down to six finalists, who were invited to New York to interview with Byrd and to undergo a battery of physical and mental tests. In the end, however, the final selection was up to the finalists themselves; each was asked to vote for the two candidates they thought best qualified. The majority voted for nineteen-year-old Paul Siple.

Born in 1908 in Montpelier, Ohio, Siple moved with his family to Erie, Pennsylvania, ten years later. A Sea Scout as well as Boy Scout, Siple earned the Eagle Scout rank, amassing no fewer than sixty merit badges. When he heard about the Byrd expedition, Siple had just completed his freshman year at Allegheny College, where he majored in biology.

On August 25, 1928, Siple and thirty-two other men sailed for Antarctica aboard the ship *City of New York*. After rendezvousing with a supply ship carrying Byrd and his aircraft, the expedition established a base camp—dubbed "Little America"—at McMurdo Sound on the Antarctic coast. Over the next few months, Siple learned to drive sled dogs as the explorers established emergency supply depots on the ice.

Then the brutal polar winter set in, with months of complete darkness and temperatures plunging as low as 70 degrees below zero. Thanks to his training in biology, Siple's tasks during the winter included helping the expedition's scientists in dissecting and cataloging penguins, seals, and other Antarctic wildlife. Siple soon earned the respect of the expedition members for his physical strength, good humor, and devotion to his duties. One later wrote, "Perhaps no Boy Scout ever so belied his name. He was six feet tall, weighed in midwinter more than two hundred pounds. . . . He worked hard. . . . He had the poise of a much older and experienced man."

The expedition achieved its main goal on November 29, 1929, when Byrd and three companions flew a Ford Trimotor plane to the pole and back in nineteen hours. After the expedition returned to America in 1930, Siple wrote a book about his Antarctic experiences, *A Boy Scout With Byrd*.

This expedition was just the start of Siple's Antarctic adventures. Over the next quarter century he accompanied Byrd on several other trips south and led expeditions of his own. Siple became an accomplished scientist in several fields, eventually becoming "special scientific adviser" to the U.S. Army's Office of Research and Development. Among his achievements was the development (with Charles F. Passel) of the wind-chill scale, now a staple of meteorology.

Siple capped his polar career in 1956–1957 by spending the winter at the South Pole as a member of a party charged with establishing a permanent research station. By then, he'd spent more of his life in Antarctica than any other person up to that time. Four decades after his death in 1968, Siple remains an inspirational figure to adventure-loving Scouts.

Public Banquet

Honoring

Eagle Scout Paul A. Siple

on his return from

The Antarctica

Masonic Temple
Saturday, June 28, 1930
at
Erie, Pennsylvania

Souvenir Program

BYRD ANTARCTIC EXPEDITION

RADIOGRAM

RECEIVED BY
The New York Times

88 WFBT Little America Feb 8th   0547gmt

Finley

Times NY

You certainly can. You are familiar with my attitude
towards the Scouts. I consider it a great movement for the best
kind of progress. Paul Siple is living up to the high standards
and I am proud of him. He sends his greetings. You have my permission
to quote me any way you like about this or any other subject
as you have my perfect confidence. Kindest regards.

Byrd

1253am/8th

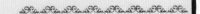

LEFT Paul Siple on the cover of the book he wrote about his year and a half spent on the Byrd expedition in Antarctica. **ABOVE** (top) Richard E. Byrd flanked by the six Boy Scout finalists, including Siple on the far left. (bottom left) Page from a souvenir program for a banquet to honor Paul Siple. (bottom right) Radiogram from Byrd sent from Antarctica.

REPORT OF
COMMITTEE ON INTER-RACIAL ACTIVITIES
BOY SCOUTS OF AMERICA
1929

(Submitted for the Committee by BOLTON SMITH, Chairman)

NATIONAL COMMITTEE ON INTER-RACIAL ACTIVITIES

BOLTON SMITH, *Chairman*, Memphis, Tenn.
LEO M. FAVROT, *Vice-Chairman*, Baton Rouge, La.
PERCY JACKSON, *Vice-Chairman*, New York
STANLEY A. HARRIS, Amantha, N. C.

DIVISION OF NEGRO WORK

LEO M. FAVROT, *Chairman*	DR. E. P. ROBERTS, New York
DR. GEORGE J. FISHER, New York	DR. J. H. DILLARD, Charlottesville, Va.
B. E. LOVEMAN, Chattanooga, Tenn.	DR. J. D. TRAWICK, Louisville, Ky.
RT. REV. THOS. F. GAILOR, Memphis, Tenn.	MELL R. WILKINSON, Atlanta, Ga.
DR. THOS. JESSE JONES, New York	A. L. JACKSON, Chicago, Ill.
DR. W. T. B. WILLIAMS, Tuskegee Inst., Ala.	FATHER JOS. GLENN, Richmond, Va.

DIVISION OF INDIAN WORK

PERCY JACKSON, *Chairman*	DAVID OWL, Iroquois, New York
LEWIS MERIAM, Washington, D. C.	JOHN COLLIER, Washington, D. C.
DR. THOS. JESSE JONES, New York	DR. CLARK WISSLER, New York
REV. HENRY ROE CLOUD, Wichita, Kan.	DR. FRED W. HODGE, New York

EXECUTIVE OFFICERS

STANLEY A. HARRIS, *National Director of Inter-Racial Activities*
J. A. BEAUCHAMP, *Assistant to National Director*
A. J. TAYLOR, *Assistant to National Director*
Work of the Committee is under supervision of
DR. GEORGE J. FISHER, *Deputy Chief Scout Executive*
Office, 2 Park Avenue, New York City.

---

moral training. Scouting does reduce cr... improve the boys' surroundings. We ca... reduction of this crime bill. Our orga... to do its full part in this great and pa... National Charter and our monopoly of ... on an implied promise to do this.

It Works

That the Scouting Spirit really functions in the life of Negro Boy Scouts is literally illustrated by hundreds of examples. I mention only two. At New Bern, North Carolina in November a Troop was organized and in less than a month after organization the Troop had so caught the spirit of Scouting that every boy in the Troop participated with his own money and labor to provide twelve Thanksgiving dinners which they personally delivered to poor old men and women —one a sick widow with several little children. At Fort Worth, Texas a thirteen year old Negro Boy Scout found a lady's pocket-book with more than $300.00 currency in it and returned the pocketbook. The liberal reward offered, the little boy simply declined by saying, "No madam, I am a Boy Scout and cannot take a tip for doing my duty." In the name of justice and for the good of America we urge that this spirit of Scouting be made available to every boy in America.

Below are listed some of the Southern cities where Scout Troops are in operation among Negro boys under the direction of the local Council.

Baltimore, Md.	3	McKenzie, Tenn.	1	Tulsa, Okla.	5
Cumberland, Md.	2	Smithfield, N. C.	1	Oklahoma City, Okla.	3
Washington, D. C.	12	Lexington, N. C.	1	Muskogee, Okla.	3
Richmond, Va.	6	Thomasville, N. C.	1	Okmulgee, Okla.	1
Petersburg, Va.	3	Columbia, S. C.	2	Shawnee, Okla.	4
Lawrenceville, Va.	1	Augusta, Ga.	3	Bartlesville, Okla.	1
Newport News, Va.	2	West Point, Ga.	1	Chickasha, Okla.	1
Norfolk, Va.	9	Jacksonville, Fla.	3	Enid, Okla.	1
Hampton, Va.	2	St. Augustine, Fla.	1	Ada, Okla.	1
Roanoke, Va.	3	Lakeland, Fla.	2	Boley, Okla.	1
Charlotte, N. C.	2	W. Palm Beach, Fla.	2	Langston, Okla.	1
Gastonia, N. C.	3	Ft. Lauderdale, Fla.	1	Sapulpa, Okla.	2
High Point, N. C.	3	Miami, Fla.	3	Wewoka, Okla.	2
Greensboro, N. C.	4	Tuskegee, Ala.	2	Dallas, Tex.	5
Reidsville, N. C.	1	Opelika, Ala.	1	Corsicana, Tex.	1
Leaksville, N. C.	1	Eufaula, Ala.	1	Ft. Worth, Tex.	3
Henderson, N. C.	1	Enterprise, Ala.	1	Wichita Falls, Tex.	2
Wise, N. C.	1	Sipsey, Ala.	1	Beaumont, Tex.	3
Raleigh, N. C.	3	Corona, Ala.	1	Orange, Tex.	3
Washington, N. C.	1	El Dorado, Ark.	5	Port Arthur, Tex.	1
Goldsboro, N. C.	2	Little Rock, Ark.	5	Texarkana, Tex.	4
Monroe, La.	1	Hot Springs, Ark.	2	Corpus Christi, Tex.	1
Lake Charles, La.	2	Ft. Smith, Ark.	15	El Paso, Tex.	1
Meridian, Miss.	4	Van Buren, Ark.	1	Huntsville, Tex.	1
Piney Woods (Jackson)		Louisville, Ky.	31	Prairie View, Tex.	1
Chattanooga, Tenn.	10	Bowling Green, Ky.	2	Galveston, Tex.	3
Rockwood, Tenn.	1	Earlington, Ky.	1	Kansas City, Mo.	14
Knoxville, Tenn.	3	Russellville, Ky.	1	St. Louis, Mo.	22
Bristol, Tenn.	3	Paducah, Ky.	2		
Memphis, Tenn.	10				

...Program

...al Councils training program were con-...following cities:

Gastonia, N. C.	...Okla.	Ft. Smith, Ark.
Greensboro, N. C.	Chickasha, Okla.	Augusta, Ga.
Norfolk, Va.	Oklahoma City, Okla.	Danville, Ill.
Portsmouth, Va.	Tulsa, Okla.	Portsmouth, Ohio
Richmond, Va.	Shawnee, Okla.	Wheeling, W. Va.
Cumberland, Md.	Little Rock, Ark.	W. Palm Beach, Fla.
Chattanooga, Tenn.	Ada, Okla.	Jacksonville, Fla.
Knoxville, Tenn.	Wewoka, Okla.	Memphis, Tenn.
Dallas, Tex.	Okmulgee, Okla.	Monroe, La.
Ft. Worth, Tex.	Boley, Okla.	Lake Charles, La.
Beaumont, Tex.	Muskogee, Okla.	Goldsboro, N. C.
Miami, Fla.	Sapulpa, Okla.	New Bern, N. C.
Huntsville, Tex.	El Dorado, Ark.	Raleigh, N. C.
	Hot Springs, Ark.	

Indian Work

The following qualified group of men have been designated as a Committee on Indian work with the approval of the National Council:

Percy Jackson, Chairman, New York
Lewis Meriam, Washington, D. C.
Dr. Thos. Jesse Jones, New York.
Rev. Henry Roe Cloud, Wichita, Kan.
David Owl, Iroquois, N. Y.
John Collier, Washington, D. C.
Dr. Clark Wissler, New York.
Dr. Fred W. Hodge, New York.

Early in his administration of the Department of the Interior, Secretary Wilbur requested the cooperation of the Boy Scouts of the Indian reservations and in the Indian schools. After Commissioner Rhoads' appointment conference was held, attended by Secretary Wilbur, Commissioner Rhoads, and Superintendent of Indian schools and the following working agreement was made.

"Indian boys to be in mixed Troops where possible and, if not mixed Troops, then to have three or more occasions annually where Troops of Indian boys are brought into contact with other Boy Scouts. Jamborees, camps, and Courts of Honor to be emphasized for this purpose.

"Scouts at Indian Schools to be allowed to attend meetings of Troops nearby and when it is practical to mix them with the boys of the town in which the school is located.

"Schools to work out system by which Scouts may earn a uniform where his parents are not able to provide it for him. If money should be provided from any source to purchase uniforms, the Scout is not to have the uniform until he has done enough so that he will feel he has earned it.

"The Boy Scouts have a Regional Executive in charge and a local Scout Executive immediately supervising all the territory where Indian schools and reservations are located.

"Local Scout Executives to be requested to call upon superintendents of Indian schools and reservations, and the Commissioner to request his superintendents to cooperate with the local Scout Executive in finding capable leadership for Troops and Home Patrols. The sug-

American Scouts by the mid-1920s. In the South, where the majority of African Americans lived at this time, Scouting was almost completely segregated. An African American Scouter in South Carolina later recalled that "We operated parallel to the [local] council, with our own president, commissioners, and so forth. We had a separate camp for the Negro Boys; it wasn't second-class—it was about sixth class." In some Southern communities, Scouts weren't even permitted to wear the uniform.

Bigotry wasn't limited to the South. The 1920s saw a revival of the Ku Klux Klan across the country. Founded by ex-Confederates after the Civil War, the KKK terrorized freed slaves before being driven underground in the 1870s. The "new" Klan—proclaiming itself the defender of "100 percent Americanism"—targeted Jews, Roman Catholics, and immigrants, too. An African American troop camping in Pennsylvania in 1924, for example, found itself confronted by gun-toting Klansmen and a fiery cross. In other areas, the Klan attempted to keep Catholics and Jews out of Scouting.

In 1927, the BSA set up an Inter-Racial Service under the leadership of Stanley Harris to promote African American Scouting, especially in the South. Thanks to its efforts, all but one Southern council accepted African American troops

LEFT The BSA's 1929 Report of Committee on Inter-Racial Activities. **ABOVE** A large African American troop poses proudly.

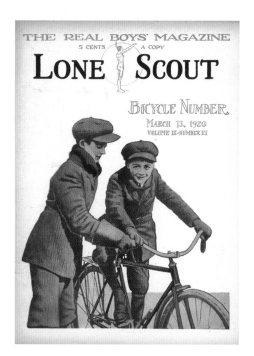

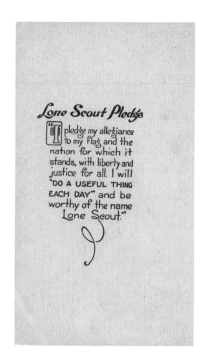

(again, still segregated) by the late 1930s. Still, African American participation in Scouting continued to lag far behind that of whites.

THE LONE SCOUTS JOIN THE BOY SCOUTS

As the BSA's second decade approached, the organization's leadership was keenly aware that about half of all American communities lacked an organized Scout troop. And so W. D. Boyce reenters our story.

Busy with his publishing empire and his travels, Boyce had little direct involvement with the BSA in its earliest years. But a few years after the BSA's incorporation, Boyce became concerned that boys who lived in communities without Scout troops were missing out on the program—especially boys in the rural communities that were the main customers for his newspapers and magazines. As he put it, boys in these communities still "needed some opportunity and guidance along the lines of Scouting." Boyce was also concerned that some boys stayed away from Scouting because they or their parents couldn't afford the cost of uniforms, equipment, and troop dues.

The British Boy Scout movement had already recognized

this problem, and in response, a young English Scout leader named John Hargrave established a "Lone Scout" program, outlined in *Lonecraft—The Hand-book for Lone Scouts* (1913). Boyce initially tried to convince the BSA's leadership to establish the Lone Scouts in the U.S. as an official program. Boyce ran into opposition from James E. West, however, who felt that membership in a troop was a key element of Scouting. West and other BSA leaders may also have been concerned that the program Boyce proposed would be too closely tied to his publishing empire.

So Boyce set up a separate movement, the Lone Scouts of America (LSA), which was incorporated on January 9, 1915. The organization's stated goals were to encourage "patriotism, discipline, obedience, courage, self-reliance, gallantry, courtesy, thrift, usefulness, helpfulness, and cheerfulness."

Although the Lone Scouts weren't affiliated with the BSA, the two organizations shared common roots in looking to American Indian culture for inspiration. Boyce styled himself as the organization's "Chief Totem," for example, and to become a Lone Scout, a boy needed only to "choose a starlit night, face the north, the land of the totem, slowly raise your arms in the peace

ABOVE (left) Cover of Boyce's *Lone Scout* magazine. (middle and right) Cover and pledge from the *Official Handbook of the Lone Scouts of America*, from 1913. To join, a boy had only to earnestly recite the pledge by himself at night.

How to Become a Lone Scout

THE boy who joins the Lone Scouts of America has taken an important step, one which will count greatly for his future. For he has not only allied himself with an organization whose program will add to the joys properly a part of boyhood; he is building for the time to come. Benefits will come to him thru three channels: He will

Tribe in Camp

be enriched mentally, built up physically, and strengthened in his moral structure.

The Lone Scouts of America is an organization for boys everywhere. It was originated by W. D. Boyce (who started the Boy Scout movement in the United States) because he was interested in all boys, and wanted to offer them, whether living in cities, small towns, villages or on the farm, the advantage of belonging to an organization without the necessity of joining a group of boys in the same neighborhood. Hence the name Lone Scout.

The Organization was incorporated in Washington, District of Columbia, in 1915. At the first meeting of the incorporators by-laws were adopted and W. D. Boyce was elected Chief Totem, or head of the Organization.

sign of the Indian, and with uncovered head repeat solemnly 'I pledge allegiance to the flag and the Nation for which it stands, with liberty and justice for all. I will do a useful thing every day, so as to be worthy of the name Lone Scout.'"

To lead the new organization, Boyce recruited a prominent Chicago Scoutmaster, Frank Allen Morgan, whose son Warren (one of the first Eagle Scouts) became "Lone Scout Number One." Many of the first Lone Scouts were drawn from the 20,000-plus boys who distributed Boyce's publications across the Midwest. In fact, Boyce "appointed" each of his newsboys as a Lone Scout and urged them to bring their friends into the movement.

The element that united the group was its weekly magazine, the *Lone Scout*, which began publication in October 1915 with Frank Morgan as editor. Boyce's acumen as a publisher came to the fore here. *Lone Scout* was filled with exciting stories and interesting articles, and it featured colorful covers and illustrations from a talented artist, Perry Emerson Thompson. Advertising kept costs down—the initial subscription price was 1 cent, raised a few years later to 5 cents. And that penny or nickel was the only cost for membership in the Lone Scouts—

there were no uniforms to buy or dues to pay. (The LSA would introduce a uniform—cost, $6.00—in 1917.)

When *Lone Scout* started up, Boyce told one of his associates that "my guess is that the boys will do it themselves if you give them the chance." He was right. Before long, the Lone Scouts themselves were eagerly contributing most of the magazine's content. The LSA even established a special award—the Golden Quill—for excellence in writing. One young contributor later recalled: "Budding authors sent their short stories, feature articles, poems, cartoons, 'How To Do It' plans and constantly sought to make their bits different. . . . Many were the future editors, writers, newspapermen, printers, etc. who served their apprenticeship in the pages of *Lone Scout*."

The LSA gave its members a path of advancement similar to the BSA's, although advancement was expressed in "degrees" (there were seven in all) instead of ranks—a system that was likely inspired by Boyce's membership in the Freemasons. To reach the highest degree, a Lone Scout had to demonstrate his proficiency in a variety of areas, from traditional woodcraft (using an ax, administering first aid) to more modern skills (mastering Morse code, repairing a pump valve).

ABOVE (left) Opening page from the *Official Handbook of the Lone Scouts of America*, showing a tribe of boys camping in tents outdoors. (right) Official logo of the Lone Scouts of America.

Official Magazine

OF THE

LONE SCOUTS OF AMERICA

Incorporated 1915, Under the Laws of the District of Columbia

LONE SCOUT MOTTO:

"<u>Do</u> a <u>U</u>seful <u>T</u>hing Each <u>D</u>ay"

LONE SCOUT

Successor to Every Boy's Magazine

PUBLISHED EVERY SATURDAY BY

W. D. BOYCE COMPANY, CHICAGO, ILL.

500 North Dearborn Street

Copyright, 1916, by W. D. Boyce Company. Entered as second-class matter at the postoffice at Chicago, Ill., under act of March 3, 1879.

Subscription Rate

50 cents a year   25 cents 6 months
15 cents 3 months

A boy can become a member of the LONE SCOUTS OF AMERICA by sending in 15 cents for 3 months' subscription to the Lone Scout magazine and complying with requirements of the organization, signing pledge, etc., as explained on Page 15 of this magazine.

In applying for membership, address W. D. BOYCE, Chief Totem, 500 North Dearborn St., Chicago, Ill

This interesting story began in "Lone Scout" No. 8, issue of December 18, and it is continuing from week to week. Back copies of "Lone Scout" can be obtained from our office.

CHAPTER X.—(Continued.)

THE TRAVELING MAN'S STORY.

IT WAS evident that the traveling man was much pleased by the attention the men and boys were giving him, and he quickly resumed his account of the rain-making experiment.

"The professor explained that there was no danger to any of the persons engaged in the experiment," he said. "The bombs that would be taken up in the balloon would be fitted with internal percussion caps and fuses, and the fuses could be cut to any length, so that they would explode the bombs in any number of seconds decided upon. The impact of exploded dynamite is principally downward, so that the balloon and its occupants would be safe.

"'You've got the scheme, professor! It's just the thing!' exclaimed Mr. Burns with enthusiasm. 'If others will not chip in money sufficient, I'm going to sell the south forty acres of the farm and make the experiment myself. We've got more land than we need, anyway; besides, if we don't find some way to get more rain no one's land in this section is going to be worth much.'

"Professor Dinks smiled. 'The air-waves created by the detonations at separate points would create very great atmospheric agitation, somewhat like the turmoil of water created by ocean billows rushing together. No doubt such agitation would materially aid in the production of fluid precipitation.'

"Mr. Burns arose and grasped the professor's hand and wrung it fervently. 'All right,' he exclaimed, 'you look after the ordering of the balloon an' the touchin' off of the stuff and I'll see that the bills are paid.'

"It was on the third day of July, I remember, that preparations to apply the Dinks-Burns stimulus to Heaven's natural laws were pronounced complete. Probably, as far as the production of moisture was concerned, the sky was in need of a tonic, for no rain had fallen during the month of June, and the fields lay wilted. The parching fever of July and August would surely lick up the soil's last drop of sap.

"On the soft slope of the hillside near the village, and just inside of the 'ice inclosing one of Hayden Burns' eat fields, a wrinkled mass of silk—ed canvas hung in a wooden frame. Beneath it stood a big tank of gas, ready for inflating the giant sack. Along the spine of the ridge above, arranged in a double line, stood one hundred sheet-iron cylinders filled with gas and prepared for explosion by means of connecting fuse, the cans to be exploded in duplicate with ten seconds elapsing between detonations. By the balloon stood a box of dynamite bombs, each bomb being fitted with a little tail fuse and a percussion cap.

"This was the status of preparation when night fell on July third. On the morrow the Kymoose country should be treated to a 'racket' befitting the glorious Fourth, such noise as had not been heard in that quarter since primeval earthquakes reared the mountains. At least, so Professor Dinks said.

"Of course, the thing was a dangerous and crazy experiment, but rain making in the arid belt was attempted at many times and in many ways during those years. Davie and I had numerous confabs about it. We were anxious to go up in the balloon and fire

The Boy Inventors

By Alvah Milton Kerr

(Editor of the Chicago Ledger)

"Davie Saved the Town From the Indians," Said the Traveling Man.

off the dynamite, a perfectly silly idea. Mr. Burns and Mrs. Burns and Professor Dinks strenuously opposed this desire. 'Something might happen,' they said, and—something did happen.

"Two questions of importance finally reached decision. Professor Dinks would supervise the firing of the gas cylinders, while Hayden Burns ascended in the basket of the balloon and exploded the dynamite.

"During those years—back in the seventies—there was on the far frontier a whisper in the air of impending Indian attacks much of the time. Happily, actual disaster from the red men rarely materialized. Thruout the Kymoose region rumors of restlessness among the tribes of the mountain valleys to the westward had been persistent for months, indeed, so long that apprehension had fallen dormant. But security was fancied rather than real, for near midnight on July third a

wounded man rode into Kymoose City from the west with a report that whitened the faces of women and children and caused the scalp of many a male head to creep and prickle with fear and horror. Several families had been massacred up near the mountains, and the Cheyennes and Sioux tribes had joined forces to the number of two thousand and were moving down the Kymoose. They were armed and in war paint and would probably strike the settlement about daybreak. That was the terrifying news the injured courier brought.

"Jonas, the hired man, had gone into solitary bivouac for the night, down by the balloon. Rolled in a blanket, one might sleep anywhere out of doors in that high, arid region, but Jonas, being set to watch over a great and precious interest, was instructed not to sleep. However, keeping awake all night in a silent field, under the stars, requires

fortitude, and Jonas, by midnight, felt the need of a tonic. He therefore left the balloon and went down into the town in quest of a stimulant. That which he found was far more exciting than anything spirituous,—wild news of a mad peril pressing upon the very threshold of the community.

"At once, and as wildly as his legs would carry him, he carried the news of the Indian uprising to Hayden Burns' house. His words brought the family out of slumber. Soon Jonas and his employer were striding toward town, each with a rifle on his shoulder, while Mrs. Burns and Davie followed. Davie had not slept that night, but had lain in bed staring at the darkness, seeing great pictures of the morrow painted on the gloom.

"In the streets of the little town they found a giddy fever of action. Lamps were aglow in all the houses, people were running to and fro and organization for defense was shaping thru the united effort of Tiger Jones, gambler and 'bad man,' and Rev. Talcott Hunt, pastor of the First Church, all differences forgotten in the general peril.

"Thruout the latter half of the night and during the early morning settlers came hurrying into the town from all quarters, those from up the Kymoose River barely escaping the foe, and, in a few cases, leaving behind members of families to such fate as no one cared to fancy.

"Still, while the general influx was to the town, some went hastily out of it eastward by the road that followed the Kymoose. Among the latter were—fessor Dinks and his family. a threatening disaster, naturally from rain and the making of it ceased to influence the professor. Hayden Burns, also, forgot both the experiment and the Fourth of July. But Davie did not. A vision blossomed in his young imagination, so large and vivid it made his eyes shine with excitement. He found me among the fear-inflamed people of the street and detached me from the crowd with a whistle and jerk of the head. When we were apart from the others, Davie seized me by the wrist and hurried me thru an alley.

"'I'm going up in the balloon to see where the Indians are,' he whispered. 'I want you to help me. Keep mum; the folks would stop me if they knew!'

"I gasped, but was at once full of enthusiasm. 'All right,' I cried, and we hurried away to the field. When we paused beside the balloon, Davie at once turned the stop-cock of the gas tank and the gas began to whistle thru the inflating pipe and stir like a thing of life in the mighty sack. He had been Professor Dinks' chief aid at every step of preparation, and now his procedure was sure and direct.

"By four o'clock in the morning the balloon stretched upward, a gigantic bubble, swaying softly in a slow eastern wind. The early summer dawn broke in muffled glory. Davie carefully placed a lot of the dynamite bombs in the basket of the balloon and climbed in.

"'Untie the stay-ropes, Tuck,' he said to me. 'In five minutes I'll know where the Indians are, I think. I'll shout down to you and you trot down and tell Tiger Jones and the preacher.'

"'All right,' I replied, and three minutes later the huge bag of gas leaped upward like a bubble blown by a quick breath. Davie saw the earth fall away from under him like a swiftly expanding ring, then suddenly the balloon tugged and quivered and the world and its vast map of fields and mountains

(Continued on Page 15.)

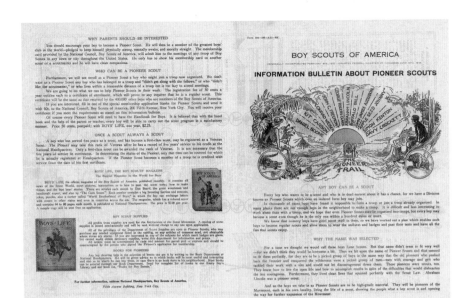
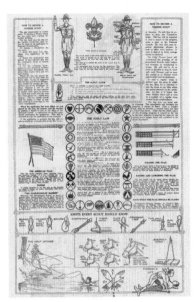

The Lone Scout was on his honor when it came to reporting his progress through the degrees. But as former Lone Scout Walter MacPeek put it, "No one worried very much about a Lone Scout failing to do what exactly was expected of him in meeting the requirements for advancement. Somehow, boyhood had its code and here the responsibility for honest performance rested on the boy's own shoulders."

While (in Lone Scout Number One Warren Morgan's words) "every attempt was made to keep the degrees simple enough so that they could be explained in the Lone Scout and performed by even a single boy working on his own in some remote part of the United States," the LSA encouraged boys to form "tribes" of five or so members. In addition, Lone Scouts formed "mail tribes" of "pen pals."

The Lone Scouts was a great success; within two years it boasted about 225,000 members. Not all of them were in rural areas, either; the movement gained a surprising following in towns and cities. Some of these Lone Scouts were boys who were interested in Scouting but not entirely comfortable with joining a troop. As one such urban Lone Scout recalled:

Re-reading the small print [in the Lone Scout] that told about the organization, we noted that Mr.

Boyce had established the organization largely for country boys who could not join the troops of the Boy Scouts of America. Some of us, who lived in big cities where there were plenty of Boy Scout troops, wondered if Mr. Boyce had us in mind too. Many of us were shy boys. The thought of walking around to a troop meeting and saying: "I'd like to join," scared us stiff.

In addition, an unknown number of boys were enrolled in *both* the Lone Scouts and the BSA.

Inevitably, though, the rise of the LSA led to friction with the BSA. James E. West certainly recognized Boyce's contribution to Scouting in America, writing in 1916 that "We have every desire to maintain a friendly relationship with Mr. Boyce because we believe that at heart he is genuinely interested in boys and because a great deal of credit is due to him." But West qualified this statement by writing that "Many of [Boyce's] friends are greatly disappointed because he has seen fit to develop his Lone Scout plan along the lines he has, but we believe that he will in time discover wherein his plan is wrong and make such changes as should be made." In that same year the BSA introduced a Pioneer Division, with the same goal as

LEFT Page showing an illustrated story from a February 1916 issue. **ABOVE** (left) Bulletin on the Pioneer Scouts division, the BSA's counterpoint to the Lone Scouts. (right) Information inside the bulletin on how to become a Pioneer Scout, with the familiar twelve points of the Scout Law in the center.

A REAL BOYS' MAGAZINE

2 CENTS A COPY

LONE SCOUT

VOL. V   CHICAGO, ILL., SEPTEMBER 16, 1916   NO. 47

Racing Number

How to make a Pushmobile

ON THIS PAGE Two covers of *Lone Scout* magazine, illustrated by Perry Emerson Thompson: how to build a pushmobile (left); learning to canoe (right).

A REAL BOYS' MAGAZINE

2 CENTS A COPY

LONE SCOUT

VOL. V   CHICAGO, ILL., JULY 15, 1916   NO. 38

OUR
Movie

1

LEARNING
THE
PADDLE
STROKE

2

PERRY
EMERSON
THOMPSON

3

TOP VIEW
SHOWING FINISH
OF STROKE

DECREE III
TEST
9

See
page
4

CANOEING

the Lone Scouts—to bring Scouting to rural boys. Unlike the LSA, however, the Pioneer Scouts could only advance under the guidance of a local adult leader, such as a teacher or clergyman. The program proved unpopular, never numbering more than a couple of thousand boys—a fraction of the LSA's membership.

Despite its undoubted success in its first half decade, the LSA ran into problems as the 1920s began. For one thing, the *Lone Scout*, the keystone of the organization, was losing money. Even with the Lone Scouts themselves contributing most of the content, a change to monthly rather than weekly publication, and a price rise to 10 cents per issue, the cost of putting out a full-color magazine proved too much even for W. D. Boyce's deep pockets. By some accounts the magazine was in the red $100,000 per year in the early 1920s. Also, LSA membership declined after World War I—probably because the U.S. was rapidly urbanizing, putting more and more boys within the reach of the BSA's troop-based program.

In early 1924, Boyce agreed—with some sadness—to a merger between the LSA and the BSA. "Mr. Boyce has felt so much pleased with the management and success of the Boy Scouts of America that he has sought to have its benefits made available to the Lone Scouts of America. . . ." wrote James E. West in a "welcome message" in the April issue of the *Lone Scout*. "During the last nine years, over 500,000 boys have been enrolled as members of the Lone Scouts of America. All of those still interested and active are to be given the benefits of the facilities and leadership of the Boy Scouts of America."

The 500,000 figure included all the Lone Scouts who had ever joined the group, regardless of whether or not they were still members. When the merger officially took place, in June 1924, the number of active Lone Scouts integrated into the BSA was probably more like 45,000 boys.

Despite the merger, Lone Scouting endured within the wider context of the BSA. Scouts without local troop affiliations could continue to advance through the LSA degrees until the mid-1930s, when BSA ranks were adopted. Today, the BSA still maintains a Lone Scout plan to accommodate boys "who cannot take part in a nearby Cub Scout pack or Boy Scout troop on a regular basis because of such factors as distance, weather, time, or disability."

The Lone Scouts of America lasted fewer than ten years as an independent organization, but the half-million boys who had participated remained proud of their involvement with the movement. Many LSA "mail tribes" kept up their correspondence for decades, and the LSA's literary tradition continued through two magazines, the *Lone Indian* and the *Elbeetee*. The LSA's alumni included such notable Americans as Hubert Humphrey (senator from Minnesota and vice president in President Lyndon Johnson's administration), folksinger Burl Ives, and actors Fred MacMurray and Broderick Crawford. (MacMurray went on to play a Scoutmaster in the beloved 1966 Walt Disney movie *Follow Me, Boys!*)

Besides the merger with the LSA, the BSA formed a Committee on Rural Scouting, which worked with 4-H clubs to develop merit badges that would appeal to farm boys. In the

ABOVE Advertisement calling for boys to join the Lone Scouts, with *Boys' Life* named as its official magazine. **RIGHT** Lone Scouts pamphlet announcing its merger with the Boy Scouts of America and offering a subscription form for *Boys' Life* magazine along with an application form to join the Lone Scouts of America.

BOY SCOUTS of AMERICA

200 FIFTH AVENUE
NEW YORK CITY

My dear Friend:

Of course you are interested in becoming a Lone Scout of the Boy Scouts of America; every manly boy wants to become one just as soon as he hears about it. Nearly 600,000 Lone Scouts since the organization was started ten years ago by W. D. Boyce of Chicago.

It is one of America's best boys' work programs, as it is truly a boys' program. It offers plans for both individual and group training without a loss to the boy as a unit citizen or as a member of a community group.

Lone Scouting has character building, fun, adventure and challenge to manly boys to become real men. A Lone Scout is a Boy Scout and a brother to all other scouts. As a Lone Scout you will take the same oath, obey the same scout laws and achieve distinction in service, obtain rank as Life, Star and Eagle Scout, the same as all other scouts do.

As a Lone Scout, you will win the three great Lodge ranks and many fine titles, honors, merit badges and awards.

The President of the United States is our Honorary President and scores of America's greatest men are officers and Board members of our organization. O course, you will be proud to be a Lone Scout and w the name.

If you live in a Boy Scout council territory, of course, can join through your local office. Ju as soon as you have joined, you can then get four boys to join so you can organize a real Lone Scout tribe, with Tribe Guide, Chief, Sachem, Scribe and pum Bearer as officers.

Read carefully the other side of this letter; if you really want to be a Lone Scout send us your application blank or, better still, send it to you local scout executive and we'll all be glad to bid "Welcome" into Scout brotherhood.

Scoutingly yours,

James E. West

Chief Totem,
Lone Scouts—Boy Scouts of Ame

BOYS' LIFE,
The Official Monthly Magazine of the Lone Scouts of America

WHEN you become a Lone Scout you may be sure you will be interested in the official Magazine. As one boy put it: "While the stories are interesting and full of pep, BOYS' LIFE is a wonderful educational value, too. It awakens the ambitions of the boy." And another: "I figure that for the $2.00 price of BOYS' LIFE, I get at least $7.00 worth of reading."

BOYS' LIFE is published monthly. It contains 64 or more big pages, and has serial stories, regular short stories, feature articles, cartoons, directions for making things, and special departments for just about every interest of boy life. Best of all, it prints stories written by your brother Lone Scouts, and you can write for it, too.

You will want BOYS' LIFE, and the best way to subscribe for it when you join. If you can't do that, then at least you should send for a sample copy—it will cost you only 20c and that will be the best investment you ever made.

TO SUBSCRIBE TO BOYS' LIFE

Date ....

Inclosed please find .... (in stamps, coin or money order)
(Give Amount)

for which you are to send me BOYS' LIFE for ....
(How Long?)

Name ....

Address ....

BOYS' LIFE will be sent you one year for $2.00; six months for $1.00. Send 20c for a sample copy.

If you want to join
The LONE SCOUTS of AMERICA

Here's your application blank

Date ....

I have, with the consent of my parents or guardian, taken the following pledge of the Lone Scouts of America, which I have read and understand:

I pledge my allegiance to my flag and the nation for which it stands, with liberty and justice for all. I will "DO A USEFUL THING EACH DAY" and be worthy of the name Lone Scout.

Enclosed find .... cents to cover the cost of enrolling me as a member. (For membership and Handbook only the fee is 15 cents. If you wish the Membership Badge also, send 30 cents.)

Name ....

Nationality and Color ....

St. No., P. O. Box or R. F. D. No. ....

Town .... State ....

The Lone Scouts of America
500 North Dearborn Street
Chicago, Illinois.

L 2883 S

mid-1920s, the BSA also introduced "Railroad Scouting": With the cooperation of several railroad lines, professional Scouters traveled to small towns along their routes to distribute Scouting literature and organize troops.

The BSA honored Boyce's great contributions to the Scouting movement in 1926, when the publisher became one of the first three recipients of the Silver Buffalo Award, established by the BSA that year for "distinguished service to boyhood." (The other initial awards went to Baden-Powell and to the "Unknown Scout" that Boyce had encountered on that foggy day in London in 1909.) After the ceremony Boyce wrote:

> As the future of our country depends on the character and health of those who come after us, I know of no movement for the betterment of our civilization than that of training of youth. "As the twig is bent the tree is inclined," and I hope to live long enough to see that day when it can be truthfully said that one out of every two boys in the United States . . . has at some time been an active Boy Scout or Lone Scout.

W. D. Boyce didn't live long enough to see his hope fulfilled;

he died at his Ottawa, Illinois, home in June 1929, a few days short of his seventy-first birthday. Thirty-two Scouts served as honorary pallbearers at his funeral.

CUB SCOUTING

The most significant development in American Scouting in the years between World War I and World War II was the establishment of Cub Scouting as an official program in 1930. It was a process that stretched back to the beginnings of the BSA.

As discussed in Part One, from the start, Scouting faced not only an "older-boy problem"—keeping boys interested in Scouting once they hit their teen years—but also a "younger-boy problem." Younger boys saw their older brothers and neighbors hiking, camping, and learning to do interesting and exciting things; naturally, they wanted in. Determining just how to accommodate the needs of boys younger than twelve within the framework of the BSA, though, took the better part of two decades.

In the BSA's preliminary 1910 handbook, Ernest Thompson Seton stated that "in special cases" boys as young as nine could become members of Scout troops. A couple of years later, Seton proposed a program called Cubs of America for younger boys, with a bear cub as its "totem." This was the first, but by no

LEFT July 1959 issue of the *Elbeetee*, with the Lone Scout symbol saluting the title. **ABOVE** Members of a Lone Scouts of America tribe. The LSA more firmly embraced American Indian elements.

LONE SCOUTS of AMERICA First Degree

Tepee Lodge

BADGE (BRONZE)
S 1898 O   **BOOK ONE**

LONE SCOUTS of AMERICA Second Degree

Tepee Lodge

SECOND DEGREE
BADGE (BRONZE)
S 2001 O   **BOOK TWO**

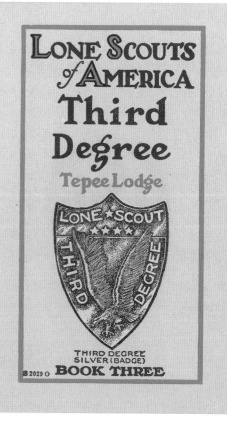

LONE SCOUTS of AMERICA Third Degree

Tepee Lodge

THIRD DEGREE
SILVER (BADGE)
S 2029 O   **BOOK THREE**

ON THIS PAGE The seven degrees boys could attain in the Lone Scouts of America. Each degree required mastery of a number of different outdoor skills. The first three degrees earned a boy a place in the Tepee Lodge, and three different badges. The next three degrees merited a boy the Totem Pole Lodge. The seventh, and final, degree made a boy worthy of the Sagamore Lodge.

LONE SCOUTS
of AMERICA

Fourth Degree

Totem Pole Lodge

BOOK FOUR

TOTEM POLE LODGE BADGE
(ROMAN GOLD)

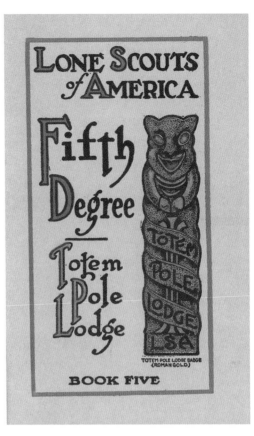

LONE SCOUTS
of AMERICA

Fifth Degree

Totem Pole Lodge

BOOK FIVE

TOTEM POLE LODGE BADGE
(ROMAN GOLD)

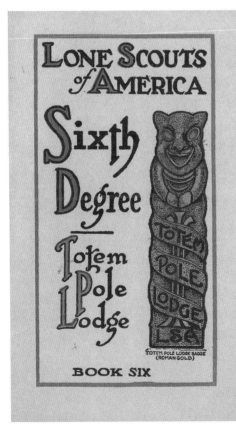

LONE SCOUTS
of AMERICA

Sixth Degree

Totem Pole Lodge

BOOK SIX

TOTEM POLE LODGE BADGE
(ROMAN GOLD)

LONE SCOUTS
of AMERICA

Seventh Degree
(Sagamore Lodge)

Woodcraft, Pioneering
and Camping

SAGAMORE LODGE BADGE
(BLUE AND GREEN-GOLD)
BOOK SEVEN

ORDER OF THE ARROW

THE ORDER OF THE ARROW, the BSA's national honor society, traces its roots back to the Philadelphia, Pennsylvania, council's summer camp on Treasure Island in the Delaware River. There, in the summer of 1915, camp director E. Urner Goodman and his assistant, Caroll A. Edson, decided to found an honor society, the Order of the Arrow, among Treasure Island's campers, aimed at keeping boys coming back to the camp in following years and promoting Scout camping in general. Goodman and Edson devised a solemn induction ritual based on the lore of the local American Indians—the Delaware, or Lenni Lenape nation—mixing in elements from novelist James Fenimore Cooper's *The Last of the Mohicans*.

(While Goodman was the OA's founder, it should be noted that this accomplishment was just part of his long and distinguished Scouting career—a career that began in 1911, when he became Scoutmaster of Philadelphia's Troop 1. Goodman served as the BSA's program director from 1931 to 1951, and he continued his involvement with the OA until his death in 1980 at the age of eighty-eight.)

The first twenty-five Arrowmen underwent induction on July 16, 1915. Each of them had been selected by their fellow Scouts. This remains a hallmark of the OA to this day. Boys (and adult leaders) can't just apply for membership; they must be elected as candidates by their fellow Scouts.

Over the next few years the OA spread to other councils on the East Coast and the Midwest. In 1922, the BSA approved the OA as an experimental program. While there was concern that an "honor society" like the OA would be "elitist" and might distract members from normal Scouting activities, OA members stressed that the society's purpose was to strengthen regular Scouting, not to substitute for it. In 1948, the BSA officially adopted the Order of the Arrow as its "national brotherhood of honor campers," recognizing Scouts and Scouters who "best exemplify the Scout Oath and Law in their daily lives."

The OA is organized into lodges, each of which is chartered to the local BSA council; larger councils may also be divided into chapters—one for each of the council's districts. Lodges in the same general geographic area form a section. Nationally, the OA is divided into four regions coordinated by a national committee. Each section holds an annual gathering known as a conclave; a national meeting takes place every other year.

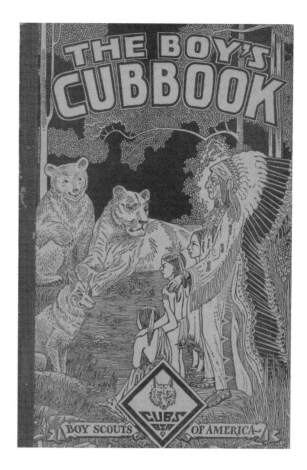

means the last, official mention of what came to be known as the "younger-boy problem."

Across the Atlantic, the British Boy Scouts Association was also grappling with the younger-boy problem. Baden-Powell established a "Junior Section" in 1914, which evolved into Wolf Cubbing, introduced in 1916 for boys between ages nine and twelve and outlined in *The Wolf Cub's Handbook*. The handbook drew heavily on the writings of Rudyard Kipling, particularly *The Jungle Book*. (Kipling, a commissioner in the British Scouting Program, was both a friend of Baden-Powell and an enthusiastic supporter of Scouting.) Wolf Cubs were organized into packs, with a Cubmaster (who could be either a man or a woman) in the Scoutmaster role. While the Wolf Cubs learned simplified versions of Scouting skills such as knot tying and first aid, "the overall emphasis was on self-discovery rather than discipline" (in the words of Tim Jeal, one of Baden-Powell's

ABOVE Cover of *The Boy's Cubbook*, the BSA guide for Cub Scouts.

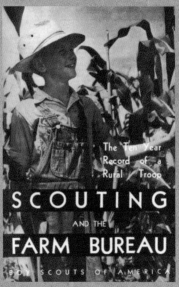

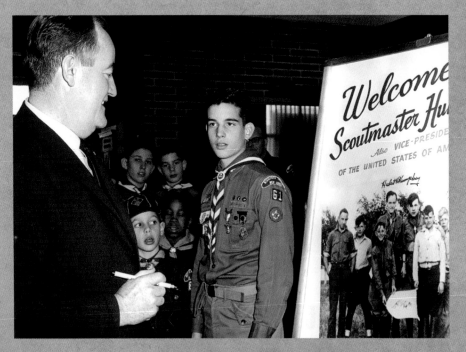

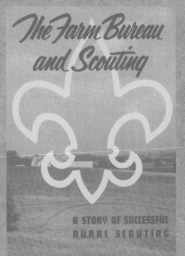

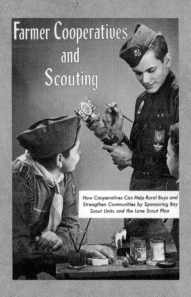

biographers), "with acting, drawing, and modeling receiving plenty of attention."

Just as interested Americans and British immigrants had used Baden-Powell's *Scouting for Boys* to establish troops before the rise of the BSA, copies of *The Wolf's Cub Handbook* found their way into the hands of American Scouters—often by way

including the American Eagles, the Tribesmen, and the largest and most successful, the Boy Rangers of America.

The BSA watched the growth of these separate groups with interest, as well as the proliferation of the Wolf packs associated—however unofficially—with local BSA troops and councils. As early as 1918, for example, the BSA acquired the

"The call of the pack all over the world is 'We'll do our best. . . .'"
LORD BADEN-POWELL

of Canada. And in the somewhat freewheeling days of Scouting in the United States, many troops simply ignored the twelve-year-old age minimum and permitted younger boys to join; often they were organized into auxiliary units called "Cadets," "Mascots," or "Junior Scouts." In addition, some non-BSA-affiliated but clearly Scout-influenced groups for younger boys sprang up in communities across the country in the 1910s,

U.S. publishing rights to *The Wolf Cub's Handbook* and sold it through the organization's Supply Service—even though Wolf Cubbing didn't have the BSA's official blessing. In a way, this was bowing to necessity; Wolf Cubbing was so popular that by the early 1920s some BSA councils (particularly those in the Pacific Northwest and Rocky Mountain states bordering Canada) were giving wholehearted support to the movement.

ABOVE An early Cub Scout pack from New York in the 1930s.

BECOMING AN ARROWMAN

"It's an honor . . . the whole premise of the Order of the Arrow is that non-members lift up the members of the society."
—Eagle Scout and OA member Cameron Barber, 2007

THE PROCESS OF BECOMING AN ARROWMAN begins when a Scout is elected as a candidate by a majority vote of his troop or Varsity Scout team—an election that takes place just once a year. To be eligible as a candidate, the Scout must be of First Class rank and have at least fifteen days and nights of camping, including an "extended" camping period of at least six days and five nights. (Adult candidates are nominated by unit, district, or council representatives, subject to approval by the lodge audit selection committee and council Scout executive.)

Next, candidates are "called out" by an Arrowman in Indian regalia. The calling-out can take place at a troop meeting, during weekend or summer camp, or at some other Scouting-related event.

Then comes the Ordeal. At this annual event, which typically takes place at the local council's camp, candidates endure a weekend in which they are expected to keep a pledge of silence, sleep a night alone from their fellow candidates, and eat little food while spending a day in arduous labor—usually making improvements to the camp—without complaint. A stirring ceremony follows the completion of the Ordeal, and the new Arrowman receives a white sash embroidered with a red arrow. He is now an Ordeal member of the Order of the Arrow.

After ten months, an Ordeal member who can show knowledge of the OA's purposes and traditions can take part in the Brotherhood ceremony, which signifies full membership in the Order. He then receives a new sash with bars on either end of the arrow.

After two years as a Brotherhood member, an Arrowman who has demonstrated "exceptional service, personal effort, and unselfish interest, [and] made distinguished contributions beyond the immediate responsibilities of their position or office to one or more of the following: their lodge, the Order of the Arrow, Scouting, or their Scout camp" may be selected by the Vigil Honor nominating committee of his lodge for the Vigil Honor. (Vigil is a high distinction indeed—in any given year, lodges are limited to one Vigil candidate for every fifty members.) Vigil Honor members wear a sash with a triangle on the arrow, and receive an Indian name, which usually reflects the Arrowman's personality: A Vigil honoree with a reputation for individualism, for example, might get the name Mawat Gentgeen Tschetshepi Pohonasin—which translates to "One who dances to a different drum."

As Scouting's national honor society, the Order of the Arrow is an integral part of the council's program. The OA's service, activities, adventures, and training for youth and adults are models of quality leadership development and programming. It helps extend Scouting to America's youth.

By mid-2005, the OA had a membership of about 180,000, representing 12 to 13 percent of overall BSA membership. Above all, the OA remains committed to "cheerful service" to Scouting in general and camping in particular. Much of this effort takes place within local districts and councils, but today the OA also provides "trail crews" to maintain trails at Philmont Scout Ranch and runs a mentoring program within the BSA's Scoutreach Division (see page 239). In 2008, the OA launched "ArrowCorps[5]," a major environmental program in partnership with the U.S. Forest Service.

ABOVE Arrowmen can earn a number of badges and distinctions, including the white sash with a red arrow awarded after completing the Ordeal.

CUB SCOUTING'S IDEALS

THE CUB SCOUT PROMISE

The Promise is written in boy language, short and simple, so every boy of Cub Scout age can grasp its meaning.

"Be square" is one of the key points in the Promise. Help your boys to see that it is not always easy to be fair to the other fellow. Sometimes fairness requires unselfishness and placing himself second to someone else. To "be square" the Cub Scout must treat other people as he would like them to treat him.

THE LAW OF THE PACK

The Cub Scout follows Akela.—In Cub Scouting the word Akela (*pronounced Ah-kay'-lah*) means "good leader." To a Cub Scout, Akela is his mother or father, his teacher, his Cubmaster, his Den Mother, or his den chief. Akela is anyone who has shown that he or she is able and willing to be a good leader for the Cub Scouts to follow. (See "Story of Akela," *Wolf Cub Scout Book*.)

Another point to stress here is the fact that in order to be a good leader one must first learn to be a good follower. So the key in the first part of the Law of the Pack is "follows."

The Cub Scout helps the pack go.—When a boy becomes 8 years old, he is beginning to realize that his wishes and desires are not the only things for him to consider. Cub Scouting may give him his first experience as a member of an organized group. That means he is taking on a new obligation. He is no longer just a boy, but a member of a den and a pack. He can "help the pack go" by being a loyal Cub Scout, by attending all meetings, by following his leader, and by making his pack better because he is a member. The key word in this portion of the Law is helps.

The pack helps the Cub Scout grow.—This part of the Law of the Pack helps the Cub Scout to see that, in meeting his obligations to other people, he brings more fun and satisfaction to himself. He helps the pack go, and in return the pack helps the Cub Scout grow—grow in fun and in spirit. Here the key word is helps.

124

CUB SCOUT PROMISE

I,_____. promise

To do my best

To do my duty

To God and my country,

To be square, and

To obey the Law of the Pack.

THE LAW OF THE PACK

The Cub Scout follows Akela.

The Cub Scout helps the pack go.

The pack helps the Cub Scout grow.

The Cub Scout gives goodwill.

So the basic principle of extending Scouting to younger boys was, in effect, already semi-tolerated by 1924, when the BSA's National Executive Board decided that the "adoption of a younger boy program at the earliest date, [which] should be kept entirely distinct from Scouting, [and] should prepare for graduation into the Scout movement" was a priority.

The BSA's leadership, however, moved cautiously in implementing such a program, insisting on a thorough and objective study first. In 1925, three members of the National Council—John N. Finley, Jeremiah W. Jenks, and William D. Murray—formed an exploratory committee. The committee expanded two years later under the leadership of psychologist Huber W. Hurl. Its efforts were partly financed by a grant from the Rockefeller family and included input from Scoutmasters, educators, and leaders of other youth organizations—including Ernest Thompson Seton. In 1929, "demonstration" Cubbing units were established in more than 106 communities.

Cubbing finally became an official program of the BSA on April 1, 1930, when the National Council authorized registration of Cub packs, although Cubbing (the program would not officially be known as Cub Scouting until 1945) would be considered "experimental" until May 1933. William C. Wessel became Cubbing's first national director.

Boys aged nine entered the program as Bobcats and advanced through the Wolf, Bear, and Lion ranks until they were old enough, at twelve, to join the Boy Scouts proper. In 1941, Cubbing added the Webelos rank (from an abbreviation of "We'll be loyal Scouts") for boys who had turned eleven-and-a-half, earned the Lion badge, and fulfilled certain requirements for the Boy Scouts' Tenderfoot rank.

Cub packs were divided into two or more dens of six to ten boys, which at first were under the leadership of a Boy Scout from a local troop—the den chief—and dens usually met each week or a couple of times a month in members' homes. While the BSA encouraged the mothers of Cubs to form neighborhood groups to "encourage" Cubbing in their communities, women, at first, had only a semi-official role in the new movement. As you can imagine, though, the task of dealing with a bunch of rambunctious nine, ten, and eleven-year-olds often proved too

much for teenaged den chiefs, and the leadership role often fell to the "den mother"—a term first introduced in 1932.

It wasn't until 1936, though, that den mothers could officially register with the BSA, and a year later the BSA published the first *Den Mother's Denbook*. By mid-1938, there were about 1,100 registered den mothers. (The actual number was likely much

ABOVE (top) John N. Finley, member of the National Council on the committee exploring the benefits of Cubbing. (bottom) William C. Wessel, the first national director of Cubbing.

higher for this and years following, as registration remained optional until 1948.)

The original *Den Mother's Denbook* set forth the qualities that the BSA believed necessary for the job:

1. An even temper;
2. A kindly and not too distant friendliness;
3. A quick, buoyant smile;
4. A sense of humor . . .
5. Much patience and hope;
6. A recognition that normal boys are increasingly different from normal girls and less quiet and more active;
7. Tact in dealing with people . . .
8. Ability to put one's self in other people's shoes.

For millions of boys, for more than seven decades, the den mother was the person who introduced them to Scouting; their first stop on the trail to Eagle and beyond was the den mother's basement or living room, where they and their friends acquired

> "We should all realize that every right implies a responsibility, every position a duty, and that the most effective sermon is expressed in deeds instead of words."
>
> **WAITE PHILLIPS**

some basic Scouting skills, had fun playing games and doing crafts, and learned to recite the Law of the Pack.

Cubbing kept some elements of its British predecessor, Wolf Cubbing, including the use of Akela—the wise wolf from Kipling's *The Jungle Book*—as a symbol of leadership, and the Cub Scout salute is two-fingered (rather than the three-fingered Boy Scout salute) to emulate the ears of an alert wolf. In keeping with the traditions of American Scouting, though, Cubbing also

ABOVE (top) A group of Cub Scouts give the salute. (bottom) Uniformed Cub Scout demonstrating the two-finger wolf ears salute. **RIGHT** Early advertisement for Cubbing outfits, 1930.

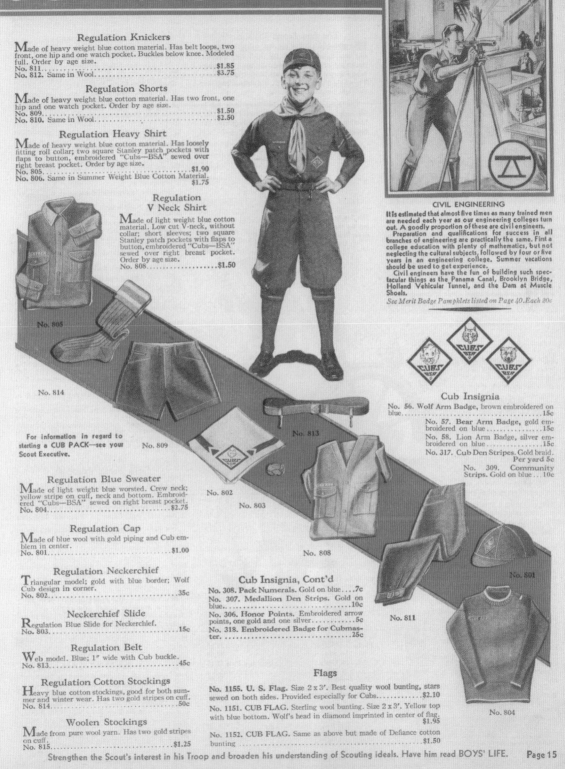

CUB OUTFITS

Regulation Knickers

Made of heavy weight blue cotton material. Has belt loops, two front, one hip and one watch pocket. Buckles below knee. Modeled full. Order by age size.
No. 811...$1.85
No. 812. Same in Wool...............................$3.75

Regulation Shorts

Made of heavy weight blue cotton material. Has two front, one hip and one watch pocket. Order by age size.
No. 809..$1.50
No. 810. Same in Wool...............................$2.50

Regulation Heavy Shirt

Made of heavy weight blue cotton material. Has loosely fitting roll collar; two square Stanley patch pockets with flaps to button, embroidered "Cubs—BSA" sewed over right breast pocket. Order by age size.
No. 805..$1.90
No. 806. Same in Summer Weight Blue Cotton Material.
....$1.75

Regulation V Neck Shirt

Made of light weight blue cotton material. Low cut V-neck, without collar; short sleeves; two square Stanley patch pockets with flaps to button, embroidered "Cubs—BSA" sewed over right breast pocket. Order by age size.
No. 808..$1.50

No. 805

No. 814

No. 809

For information in regard to starting a CUB PACK—see your Scout Executive.

Regulation Blue Sweater

Made of light weight blue worsted. Crew neck; yellow stripe on cuff, neck and bottom. Embroidered "Cubs—BSA" sewed on right breast pocket.
No. 804...$2.75

Regulation Cap

Made of blue wool with gold piping and Cub emblem in center.
No. 801...$1.00

Regulation Neckerchief

Triangular model; gold with blue border; Wolf Cub design in corner.
No. 802..35c

Neckerchief Slide

Regulation Blue Slide for Neckerchief.
No. 803..15c

Regulation Belt

Web model. Blue; 1″ wide with Cub buckle.
No. 813..45c

Regulation Cotton Stockings

Heavy blue cotton stockings, good for both summer and winter wear. Has two gold stripes on cuff.
No. 814..50c

Woolen Stockings

Made from pure wool yarn. Has two gold stripes on cuff.
No. 815..$1.25

No. 813

No. 802

No. 803

No. 808

No. 811

No. 801

No. 804

CIVIL ENGINEERING

It is estimated that almost five times as many trained men are needed each year as our engineering colleges turn out. A goodly proportion of these are civil engineers. Preparation and qualifications for success in all branches of engineering are practically the same. First a college education with plenty of mathematics, but not neglecting the cultural subjects, followed by four or five years in an engineering college. Summer vacations should be used to get experience.

Civil engineers have the fun of building such spectacular things as the Panama Canal, Brooklyn Bridge, Holland Vehicular Tunnel, and the Dam at Muscle Shoals.

See Merit Badge Pamphlets listed on Page 40. Each 20c

Cub Insignia

No. 56. Wolf Arm Badge, brown embroidered on blue..15c
No. 57. Bear Arm Badge, gold embroidered on blue..15c
No. 58. Lion Arm Badge, silver embroidered on blue...15c
No. 317. Cub Den Stripes. Gold braid. Per yard 5c
No. 309. Community Strips. Gold on blue...10c

Cub Insignia, Cont'd

No. 308. Pack Numerals. Gold on blue....7c
No. 307. Medallion Den Strips. Gold on blue...10c
No. 306. Honor Points. Embroidered arrow points, one gold and one silver...........5c
No. 318. Embroidered Badge for Cubmaster..25c

Flags

No. 1155. U. S. Flag. Size 2 x 3′. Best quality wool bunting, stars sewed on both sides. Provided especially for Cubs.............$2.10
No. 1151. CUB FLAG. Sterling wool bunting. Size 2 x 3′. Yellow top with blue bottom. Wolf's head in diamond imprinted in center of flag.
....$1.95
No. 1152. CUB FLAG. Same as above but made of Defiance cotton bunting $1.50

Strengthen the Scout's interest in his Troop and broaden his understanding of Scouting ideals. Have him read BOYS' LIFE.

SCOUT SONGS

WHETHER IT'S A CASUAL CAMPFIRE during a troop's weekend campout, the campwide gathering that traditionally marks the end of a week at summer camp, or the closing-night ceremony at a national jamboree, whenever Scouts get together, there'll be cheers, skits, and stories (silly, spooky, or serious). And songs. Scouts love to vocalize—a tradition that perhaps began with Baden-Powell, a fine singer.

American Scouts certainly enjoy belting out their country's folk songs, from "She'll be Comin' Round the Mountain" to "Oh! Susannah" to "On Top of Old Smokey," but there are plenty of tunes specific to Scouting. Some are known to practically all Scouts; others are particular to a local camp or even to a single troop, passed down from generation to generation of new Scouts.

ABOVE Scouts singing around the campfire, an important ritual on overnights.

Any Scout who's been to summer camp will probably remember singing the following ditty while waiting for a meal to be ready:

Here we sit like birds in the wilderness
Birds in the wilderness
Birds in the wilderness
Here we sit like birds in the wilderness
Waiting for the food to come . . .

And if it's a rainy day, this might be followed with:

It ain't gonna rain no more, no more
It ain't gonna rain no more
How the heck can I wash my neck
If it ain't gonna rain no more . . .

. . . followed by any number of similarly cheeky verses.

Boys being boys, they love "gross-out" songs, too. For example:

At camp with the Boy Scouts
They gave us a drink
We thought it was Kool-Aid
Because it was pink
But the drink that they gave us
Would have grossed out a moose
'Cause the good-tasting pink drink
Was really bug juice . . .

"Bug juice" being the Scouts' nickname for the punch that often appears on camp menus.

In a more serious but no less enthusiastic vein, campers at an interfaith service might sing "This Little Light of Mine," "Kumbaya," or this favorite, sung to the tune of the spiritual "Joy in My Heart":

I've got that Scouting [or Cub Scouting] spirit
Up in my head
Up in my head
Up in my head
I've got that Scouting spirit
Up in my head
Up in my head to stay . . .

. . . with the verses continuing through "down in my feet," "deep in my heart," and so on.

Campfires often conclude with the "Scoutmaster's Minute," in which an adult leader tells a brief story illustrating an important moral lesson. This might be followed by one of Scouting's most beloved and solemn songs, "Scout Vespers":

Softly falls the light of day
As our campfire fades away
Silently each Scout should ask
Have I done my daily task?
Have I kept my honor bright?
Can I guiltless sleep tonight?
Have I done and have I dared
Everything to be prepared?

Which the leader might follow with the Scout Benediction:

"And now, may the great Master of all Scouts be with us till we meet again."

MARCH, 1934
Vol. XXII, No. 3

Scouting

A Magazine of Information for All Scouters

The President's Address

From the White House 12 Noon February 10, 1934

FELLOW Scouts: I am happy to participate in the twenty-fourth anniversary celebration of our organization, the Boy Scouts of America. Nearly a million of us are mobilized at this time in all parts of the country as a part of the program for this week of celebration. Home Patrols and Farm Patrols and Troops of farm boys are joining with their brother Scouts in the big cities.

In front of the City Hall in San Francisco, and I think it's 9 o'clock in the morning there now, thousands of Scouts join with other thousands in the Hippodrome in New York in carrying on the cause of world-wide brotherhood in Scouting.

As most of you know, Scouting has been one of my active interests for a great many years. I have visited hundreds of Troops in their home towns and in their camps. I know, therefore, from personal experience the things that we do and stand for as Scouts. We have ideals. We're a growing organization. We believe that we're accomplishing fine American results not only for our own membership, but also for our families, our communities and our nation.

Summed up in one sentence, the aim of Scouting is to build up better citizenship. I believe that we are contributing greatly to that objective.

Jamboree in Capital

And today I am especially happy to extend personal greetings and congratulations to the Scouts and the leaders who have earned the President's Award for progress in the year 1933, as a part of the Ten Year Program. And it is appropriate also that we are planning for the celebration of our Silver Jubilee, the twenty-fifth anniversary of the Boy Scouts of America, which will culminate in a great national Jamboree here in the nation's capital in the summer of 1935. Of course it would be physically impossible for us to have the whole membership of the Boy Scouts of America, a million strong, come to Washington at one time, but I much hope that it will be possible to have every nook and cranny, every section of our nation represented.

Request For National Service

As a preliminary to this Silver Jubilee next year, and in line with the emphasis of service for others which we have always stressed, I suggest to you that it is time once more for us to do a National Good Turn.

As many of you know, we are doing everything possible in this emergency to help suffering humanity. I called on the Federal Emergency Relief Administrator, Harry Hopkins, to tell me what kind of a National Good Turn would be of the greatest service, and he has recommended that during the balance of the month of February every Troop and every Scout shall do everything possible in their separate localities to collect such household furniture, such furnishings, bedding and such clothes as people may be able and willing to share as gifts to those who greatly need them.

Therefore, I ask you, under the direction of your own local officers and in conference with the representatives of the Federal Relief Administration and other local social agencies, to gather up such of this material as may be available for distribution.

Public to Cooperate

I am confident that the American people will generously cooperate and respond, and indeed, I am hoping that in many cases they will telephone or send letters to the local Scout offices to offer their help to carry through this National Good Turn.

Already I have received offers of co-operation from Governors of States, from mayors of cities and other community leaders. May you carry out this new service and rededicate yourselves to the Scout Oath.

And now I ask you to join with me and with the Eagle Scouts and our President and the Chief Scout Executive who are with me in the White House at this moment, I ask you to join with me again in giving the Scout Oath.

All stand!

Give the Scout Sign!

Repeat with me the Scout Oath!

On my honor I will do my best:

To do my duty to God and to my country and to obey the Scout Law;

To help other people at all times;

To keep myself physically strong, mentally awake and morally straight,

Los Angeles Boy Scouts stand at attention as the President's voice comes over the air

included American Indian symbolism, like the Arrow of Light, the badge worn by Webelos Scouts preparing for graduation to the Boy Scouts. The official uniform, topped with a "beanie" cap, was blue trimmed with gold—a combination that remains the Cub Scout color scheme today. (While short pants were optional for Boy Scouts, shorts were official wear for Cubs until the late 1940s.)

The new program certainly seemed like an ideal solution to the younger-boy problem. In Cubbing's first years, though, the BSA's National Council still stressed that Cubbing should remain separate from Boy Scouting: An official memo of 1932 urged Cubmasters not to "unconsciously imitate or parallel Scouting" and "keep it home-centered."

But there was no arguing with success. By the end of 1931, there were 25,662 registered Cubs; in 1933, when the program's "experimental" status ended and the BSA accepted that Cubbing be "aggressively promoted as a part of the Boy Scout program,"

that number had doubled; by 1940, there were 286,402 boys and 49,161 pack leaders enrolled in Cubbing. By then it was clear that Cubbing not only did a fine job of bringing the benefits of Scouting to younger boys—a 1935 study pronounced the program "excellent in every field of operation"—Cubbing was also feeding a steady stream of boys into the BSA itself.

SCOUTING IN THE DEPRESSION

By the time Cubbing took off, America was mired in its worst national crisis since the Civil War—the Great Depression. The crash of the New York Stock Exchange in October 1929 sent shock waves through the economy; by 1933, perhaps one-quarter of all Americans were jobless, and the unemployment rate was considerably higher in many communities. Hunger and homelessness stalked the country.

Unless they were very rich or very lucky, few American families had any spare cash, and many found that even the modest

LEFT *Scouting* magazine publishes FDR's address to the Boy Scouts of America. **ABOVE** Scouts collecting items for the poor, 1933.

> ## "The record of Good Turns, small and large, that have been done by Scouts since the day Scouting was founded is truly impressive."
>
> ### *THE BOY SCOUT HANDBOOK*

costs of Scout registration, troop dues (usually 5 cents a week at this point in time), uniforms, and camping fees were now beyond their means. Hardship wasn't limited to the boys. Employees at the BSA's headquarters accepted a pay cut of 15 percent. And many professional Scouters in local councils couldn't get paid at all as banks failed across the nation. According to some accounts, professional Scouters in urban areas took to selling apples, pencils, or matches on the street to survive, like so many other unemployed or underemployed Americans.

But Scouts and Scouters found ways to adapt to the miserable economic situation. Some troops dropped all uniform requirements so boys who couldn't afford uniforms wouldn't be embarrassed. When camping, Scouts also proved adept at making meals from bones and scraps of meat begged from their local butcher, along with potatoes and whatever else they could scrounge from their parents' kitchens. Most boys responded to the situation with good humor—after all, most everybody was in the same boat—and resourcefulness. A Wisconsin Scout of the time said later, "I can recall that for the Second Class cooking test you had to cook a quarter-pound of steak. A lot of the boys said, 'I'd better make it this time because I'm not going to get another piece if this one is spoiled.'"

In February 1934, the BSA responded to a call for help from none other than the president of the United States—Franklin Delano Roosevelt, who'd been elected two years before promising a "New Deal" for the Depression-ravaged American people.

In anticipation of the twenty-fifth anniversary of the BSA's incorporation the following year, FDR made a radio broadcast in which he addressed the nation's Scouts directly:

> As many of you know, we are doing everything possible in this emergency to help suffering humanity. I called upon the Federal Emergency Relief Administrator, Mr. Harry L. Hopkins, to tell me what kind of National Good Turn would be of the greatest service. He has recommended that during the balance of the month of February every troop and every Scout do everything possible in their separate localities to collect such household furnishings, bedding and clothes as people may be able to share as gifts to those who greatly need them.
>
> Therefore, I ask you, under the direction of your own local officers, and in conference with the representatives of the Federal Relief Administration and other local social agencies, to gather up such of this material as may be available for distribution.

ABOVE Scouts in service, 1933.

FIFTEEN CENTS   July 12, 1937

TIME

The Weekly Newsmagazine

Volume XXX

Circulation Office, 330 East 22nd

BELOW Marching at the 1937 jamboree in Washington, D.C. **LEFT** James E. West on the cover of *Time* magazine; the issue covered the 1937 jamboree.

JAMBOREE!

SO HOW DID THE TERM *jamboree* enter the language? According to one of his biographers, Baden-Powell adopted a 19th-century American slang term for "a noisy, revel, carousal or spree" as the name for a worldwide Scout gathering when he first proposed the idea in 1916. The word also crops up in Rudyard Kipling's 1889 novel *Stalky & Co.* Given Kipling's many years in India, and his friendship with Baden-Powell and involvement in the early Scouting movement, it may be that *jamboree* actually has its origins in Hindustani or another Indian language. Whatever its etymology, *jamboree* quickly became synonymous with national and international Scout gatherings, and the term has been modified to describe smaller events—like the "camporees" regularly held by local Scout districts.

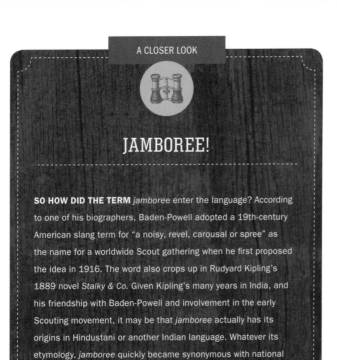

I am confident that the American people will generously cooperate and respond. Indeed, I am hoping that in many cases they will telephone or send letters to the local Scout offices to offer their help to carry through this National Good Turn.

The broadcast ended with the president joining James E. West and a delegation of Eagle Scouts in reciting the Scout Oath.

In the following weeks troops across the nation raided their own attics and basements and went door-to-door in their communities to collect the "furnishings, bedding, and clothes" that the president requested, which were then turned over to local authorities for distribution to the poorest of the poor. Some 2 million articles were collected.

ABOVE (top) FDR waves his hat to the crowd of cheering Scouts as he is driven down Constitution Avenue. (bottom) The motorcade continues past an orderly line of men in uniform.

"Philmont means more than just a series of scenic mountain camps or a collection of exciting programs. It is more than just a physical challenge. It is an experience in living together and cooperating with others under sometimes difficult circumstances. . . . Set your goals high and resolve to achieve them. You can do it. You will be better for it and your Philmont experience will become even more meaningful. It will never really end."

THE BOY SCOUT HANDBOOK

Even before this National Good Turn, however, and for years afterward, many individual councils and troops did everything they could for the poor in their communities—by collecting deposit bottles, for example, and parlaying the proceeds into food. In the darkest days of the Depression, impoverished families were cheered by the sight of Boy Scouts bringing baskets of food or coal to their doors, especially on holidays such as Thanksgiving and Christmas.

The BSA endured a disappointment in 1935, when the first national jamboree—organized to celebrate the movement's Silver Jubilee—had to be canceled just a couple of weeks before the event was scheduled to begin in Washington, D.C. The cause was a local outbreak of polio, a disease that killed or crippled many young Americans until Dr. Jonas Salk developed an effective vaccine in the 1950s. The BSA decided that gathering thousands of boys in one place was just too risky. President Roosevelt—a victim of the disease himself—announced the cancellation.

The following year, in another radio address to "my fellow Scouts," FDR announced that the postponed jamboree would take place in 1937: "We are going ahead [and] planning to have a city of tents rise here in the Capital, actually within the shadow of the Washington Monument."

More than 27,000 Scouts and Scouters attended the 1937

ABOVE (left) A Scout leads a mule on a ranch in the midst of the hilly scenery. (right) Waite Phillips, the donor who gave Philmont to the BSA.

ON THIS PAGE (top) Hiking through the Philmont wilderness.
(bottom) A long view of the majestic landscape.

"Leave this world a little better than you found it."

BADEN-POWELL'S LAST MESSAGE (PUBLISHED 1945)

jamboree. Many were able to come because James E. West persuaded railroad executives to offer a special jamboree fare of 1 cent per mile. (A ticket to the event cost each Scout $25.00.) They included about 400 Scouts from overseas, including two Canadian Scouts who bicycled all the way from British Columbia.

Time magazine reported on some of the logistical challenges of the event: "250 chefs in 25 big kitchen tents had the job of frying 100,000 flapjacks for breakfast, of coping with 30,000 quarts of milk, 70,000 eggs, two tons of sugar, 13,000 lb. of meat delivered every morning and serving it more or less hot to over 800 mess tents. Telephone connections and mail deliveries to the camp sites had to be organized on a similar scale." The jamboree ended with the assembled Scouts cheering President Roosevelt and First Lady Eleanor Roosevelt as they were driven down Washington's Constitution Avenue.

Nineteen thirty-eight saw the founding of one of the BSA's most cherished institutions: Philmont. In that year, Oklahoma businessman Waite Phillips gave 36,000 acres of land along the Cimarron River and the Sangre de Cristo Mountains in New Mexico to the BSA for the establishment of a wilderness camping area. Three years later, he added another 90,000 or so acres and set up an endowment from his business holdings. As Phillips said to a Tulsa newspaper: "That [land] represents an ideal of

ABOVE Scouts reflecting on the sign at the Philmont Scout Ranch.

my youth . . . and has meant a lot to my son and his pals. Now I want to make it available to other boys." The land was originally named the Philturn Rockymountain Scoutcamp—"Philturn" came from Phillips's name and the Scout slogan of doing a Good Turn daily. In 1942, it was renamed the Philmont Scout Ranch. Only a few hundred Scouts, though, were able to enjoy Philmont's stunning beauty and opportunities for backwoods adventure during its early years, because of gasoline rationing and other wartime travel restrictions. Philmont really took off in the early 1950s, with about 5,200 Scouts arriving in 1951—a number that rose to about 7,000 a few years later. The BSA also designated Philmont a National Training Center in 1950.

Around the same time that Philmont was established, the BSA received another generous gift. The philanthropist in

this case was Irving Berlin, one of the nation's most popular songwriters. Born Israel Baline in Russia in 1893, Berlin came to America with his family five years later. After working as a "singing waiter" in New York City's cafes, he went on to write more than 900 songs, including classics such as "There's No Business Like Show Business" and "White Christmas."

In 1938, to mark the twentieth anniversary of the end of World War I, Berlin wrote a patriotic song, "God Bless America," for singer Kate Smith. "God Bless America" quickly became something of an unofficial national anthem. Two years later, Berlin set up the God Bless America Fund and assigned one-half of the song's royalties to the BSA's Greater New York Council. In the words of the fund's charter, "The completely nonsectarian work of the Boy Scouts and Girl Scouts is calculated

LEFT Scouts survey a craggy hillside. **ABOVE** Irving Berlin with boys from the BSA, his favorite youth organization.

WORLD SCOUTING

"They all camped together, all races and all colors linked not by any discipline imposed by older men but by the secret code of youth itself and by an enthusiasm for playing the game of life according to the ideals of loyalty and efficiency and comradeship . . . and the spirit of adventure."

—British journalist Sir Philip Gibbs, reporting on the 1929 World Jamboree

IT DIDN'T TAKE LONG for Scouting to spread around the world after the publication of Baden-Powell's *Scouting for Boys* in 1908. Given the movement's British origins, it's no surprise that Scouting first took hold within the British Empire—which, at the time, included roughly 25 percent of the world's population. By the end of 1908, there were Scout troops in the British colonies of Malta and Gibraltar; over the next couple of years Scouting spread to Canada, India, Malaya (now Malaysia), and South Africa. Besides the U.S., Chile was the first nation outside of the British Empire to establish a national Scout association. By the end of 1910, eleven other nations in Europe and Latin America had followed suit.

When World War I broke out in 1914, some feared the conflict would mean the end of international cooperation in Scouting. Even before the war ended, however, Baden-Powell expressed the hope that when the war was over, world Scouting would play a role in maintaining peace: "The roots of Scouting have grown among young people of all civilised countries and are developing more each day," he wrote in 1917. "It might be thought that if in years to come, a considerable proportion of the future citizens of each nation forms part of this brotherhood, they will be joined by a bond of personal friendship and mutual understanding such as has never existed before, which will help to find a solution to terrible international conflicts."

By 1922, when Scouting's First International Committee met in Paris, there were thirty-one national Scouting organizations around the world. In each of these countries, Scouting adapted to local conditions, but each organization also held fast to the principles laid down by Baden-Powell: the Scout Oath and Law and the "Scout Method" of instruction, which emphasized hands-on learning through practical (but fun) activities.

Unfortunately, the 1920s and 1930s saw the rise of totalitarian governments in many nations. As a result, Scouting was banned in some countries and replaced by state-controlled organizations like the Hitler Youth in Nazi Germany and the Young Pioneers in the Soviet Union. In some places, Scouts and Scout leaders were imprisoned or even killed. World Scouting recovered after World War II; by 1950, the number of countries with national Scout organizations reached fifty. But Scouting remained suppressed in countries under Communist rule—a situation that eased after the end of the Cold War in the late 1980s. The BSA played an important part in supporting the revival of Scouting both in the aftermath of World War II and after the fall of the "iron curtain" (see page 219).

Today, the World Organization of Scout Movements (WOSM), headquartered in Geneva, Switzerland, is the "umbrella organization" for worldwide Scouting. Besides organizing world Scout jamborees every four years, the WOSM's three component bodies—the World Scout Conference, the World Scout Committee, and the World Scout Bureau—promote international Scouting in a variety of ways, including training volunteer and professional Scout leaders and raising funds to help foster Scouting in developing nations. The WOSM also represents Scouting in the United Nations. As of 2007, the WOSM recognized 155 national Scouting organizations. That figure doesn't include various territories and a number of countries in which Scouting exists but lacks a national organization. When all these figures are combined, as of 2007, there are only six countries around the world (Andorra, Burma, the People's Republic of China, Cuba, North Korea, and Laos) without any form of Scouting—a testament to the enduring cross-border appeal of Baden-Powell's vision.

ABOVE (top) Photo from an international Scouting conference, 1929. (bottom) Photo from international Scouting conference in Sweden, 1935.

**BOYS'
LIFE**

JULY 1942 20 CENTS A COPY
2.00 PER YEAR

BUY UNITED STATES WAR SAVINGS BONDS AND STAMPS

to best promote unity of mind and patriotism, two sentiments that are inherent in the song itself." Over the decades the song has earned millions of dollars for the organization.

The early 1940s saw the passing of two of Scouting's founding fathers. Baden-Powell—who had been in poor health for some years—died in Kenya in January 1941, aged eighty-three. Scouting's founder was buried in a churchyard near his African retreat, Paxtu Cottage. His gravestone bears a circle with a dot in the center—a trail symbol that means "I have gone home."

Daniel Carter Beard passed away at his home in Rockland County, New York, later that year, just days short of his ninety-first birthday. The memory of buckskin-clad "Uncle Dan" has been honored in many ways, including a campsite at Philmont and a mountain—Mt. Beard—near Mt. McKinley (Denali) in Alaska.

THE BSA IN WORLD WAR II

By the time Baden-Powell and Beard passed away, much

of the world was at war—and the U.S. would soon join the global conflict.

International tensions that had simmered for years boiled over in September 1939 when Germany invaded Poland, beginning World War II. As in World War I, the United States declared neutrality at first, but the nation began to ramp up its defenses in response to events overseas. As early as 1940, the BSA began working with the newly established Office of Civilian Defense. Scouts began collecting pots, pans, scrap rubber, and old newspapers, for example, for use in defense industries.

War finally came to America when the forces of imperial Japan bombed Pearl Harbor, Hawaii, on December 7, 1941. During the attack and its aftermath, Boy Scouts in Honolulu fought fires, served as messengers, administered first aid, and kept watch against what some expected would be a full-scale invasion of the island territory. Within hours of the attack, James E. West offered "the full and whole-hearted co-operation of our organization"—which by now numbered about 1.5 million boys—to President Roosevelt. Within a week, Scouts across the country had already distributed more than 1 million civil-defense posters.

All in all, the BSA responded to more than sixty-nine different requests for help from the federal government over the next four years. Scouting's contributions to the war effort included:

- Continuing to collect metal, paper, rubber (30 million pounds in a single two-week period in 1942), fats (for use in making explosives), and the pods of the milkweed plant (for use in life jackets).
- Collecting books, musical instruments, and sporting goods to send to servicemen and -women overseas, as well as clothing for refugees in Europe and Asia.
- Planting "Victory Gardens" (some 184,000 in all) as part of the nationwide effort to conserve food. (In addition, more than 100,000 Scouts volunteered to work on farms and ranches to replace men who were serving in the military.)

ABOVE (top) The American flag flies on a wartime cover of *Boys' Life*, 1942.

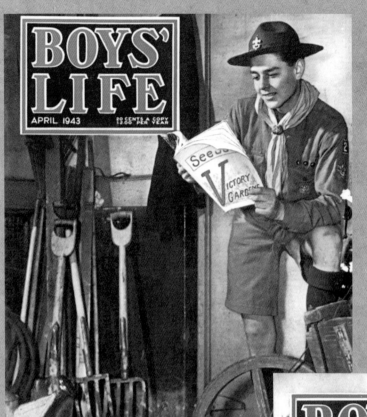

BOYS' LIFE

APRIL 1943 20 CENTS A COPY $2.00 PER YEAR

1743 – THOMAS JEFFERSON
BY HENDRIK WILLEM van LOON

PRODUCE and CONSERVE
FOOD

SCOUTING'S VICTORY PROGRAM FOR 1943
100,000,000 HOURS OF PRODUCTIVE SERVICE

ON THIS PAGE Calls for action from the Scouts to assist in the war effort (clockwise, from top left): Victory Garden promotion on the cover of *Boys' Life*, 1943; Victory program cover, 1943; a Scout in his Victory Garden on the cover of *Boys' Life*, 1942.

BOYS' LIFE

SEPTEMBER 1942 20 CENTS A COPY $2.00 PER YEAR

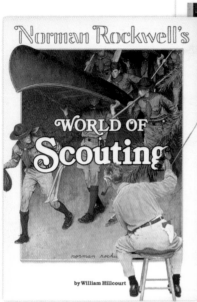

- In February 1943, President Roosevelt formally asked Scouts "to take an important commission as Government Dispatch Bearers for the Office of War Information." In this role, they distributed posters, pamphlets, and other materials—including Norman Rockwell's classic "Four Freedoms" poster—for the Office of War Information. This was a particularly important part of the BSA's wartime service.

- Distributing "pledge cards" in an effort to sell war bonds and savings stamps. While the BSA didn't take a direct role in helping the U.S. Treasury finance the war, as it had done in World War I, Scouts managed to raise close to $2 billion anyway.

- Setting up an Emergency Service Corps of older Scouts that assisted local police, fire, and civil-defense departments in many communities.

- Helping civil-defense authorities keep watch on the skies and coastlines for enemy planes and ships. Fortunately, these never came, but one Scout—Harvard Hodkins of Maine—spotted a pair of German spies who'd landed from a submarine and reported them to the FBI in 1944.

All branches of Scouting "did their part," including a new branch, the Air Scouts, established in 1942. Members of Air Scout squadrons learned navigation, aircraft mechanics, and aerodynamics, but they were forbidden from actually flying; as a result "air-minded" boys tended to join the Civil Air Patrol, which did allow flying, so Air Scout membership numbers rose to only about 11,000.

In one of the darker episodes of the World War II home front, more than 100,000 Japanese Americans—most of them American citizens—were deemed "security risks" and relocated from the Pacific Coast to grim internment camps inland. Even behind barbed wire, though, many Japanese American boys and men continued in Scouting. Junichi Asakura, a junior assistant Scoutmaster at the Heart Mountain camp in Wyoming, later recalled, "Every day we raised and lowered the American flag at the camp headquarters. We were very loyal to the United States." And in December 1942, Scouts at

ABOVE (left) Cover of Norman Rockwell's World of Scouting program. (right) Inside the program are Rockwell's posters for the Four Freedoms that were used to sell war bonds: freedom of speech, freedom from fear, freedom of worship, and freedom from want.

ON THIS PAGE (top) A group of Scouts on bicycles collects books during World War II. (bottom) Scouts help out.

AIR SCOUTS
BOY SCOUTS OF AMERICA
2 Park Avenue • New York, N. Y.

most of the internees American citizens, but that Scouting was strong among the boys at Heart Mountain.

When the two groups met, "We got to talking and got easier with each other, as kids do," in Simpson's words. "We talked about homes and merit badges and stories that you tell when you are twelve years old. We had contests between the two Scout troops, things like knot-tying. . . ."

Mineta and Simpson hit it off especially and became lifelong friends. Both boys went on to distinguished political careers—Mineta as a Democratic representative from California and secretary of transportation in George W. Bush's cabinet, and Simpson as a Republican senator from Wyoming. In the 1980s, both men worked together to secure compensation for former internees.

The war ended with Japan's surrender in September 1945. More than 16 million men and women had served in the armed forces during the war; some 400,000 gave their lives for their

> Within hours of the [Pearl Harbor] attack, James E. West offered "the full and whole-hearted co-operation of our organization"—which by now numbered about 1.5 million boys—to President Roosevelt.

the Manzanar camp in California put their physical safety on the line to demonstrate that loyalty by keeping a handful of pro-Japanese internees from storming the flagpole and tearing down the American flag.

A touching example of how Scouting could still bring boys of different backgrounds together, even under difficult wartime circumstances, is the story of two twelve-year-old Scouts who met at the Heart Mountain camp in 1943. Japanese American Norman Mineta's family had been "evacuated" from San Jose, California; Alan Simpson belonged to a troop in nearby Cody, Wyoming.

One day Simpson's Scoutmaster announced that the troop was going to meet with Scouts at the camp. More than forty years later, Simpson recalled the "befuddlement" with which he and his fellow Scouts greeted the news: Weren't all Japanese "the enemy"? The Scoutmaster explained that not only were

country. While the number of former Boy Scouts who served can't be determined, it was certainly a significant percentage. Many former Scouts who fought would record that the outdoor skills they'd learned as boys helped keep them alive in the jungles of the South Pacific or the fields and forests of Europe.

Coordinating the BSA's World War II service capped the career of James E. West. He stepped down as Chief Scout Executive in 1943 after three decades of service, and died five years later. Thanks in large part to West's longtime leadership, American Scouting was poised to enter a "golden era" when the GIs came home.

LEFT (top) Scouts collect scrap metal for the war effort. (bottom) Scouts load a truck with baskets of food. **ABOVE** Cover of Air Scouts pamphlet.

PART THREE

BOOM YEARS FOR THE BSA

1945 — 1965

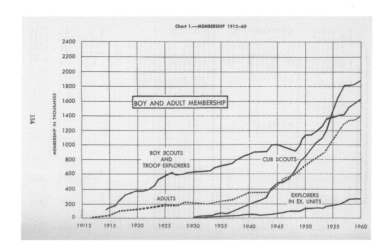

Between 1945 and 1964, about 76 million children were born in the United States—a "baby boom" that would have a reverberating effect on American society as well as on the Boy Scouts of America. Membership growth was phenomenal once the boys of the new generation reached the age of admission to Scouting—which was lowered to eight for Cub Scouts and eleven for Boy Scouts in 1949. After 1954—when the first baby boom boys were eligible to don the blue and gold of the Cub Scouts—overall new membership in the

Understandably, America in this era became a youth-centered society. Having survived the Great Depression and fought World War II—whether in uniform or on the home front—the parents of the baby boomers wanted only the best for their children, and they eagerly enrolled them in youth movements from the Boys & Girls Clubs of America to Little League and Pop Warner Football to the 4-H. Despite the competition, the Boy Scouts proved most successful in winning the allegiance of American boys and their parents.

> "I was holding a close friend in my arms as he died in battle, and I said to myself: 'I'm going to go back home and be a Scoutmaster, and I'm going to teach kids how to survive life—not the jungle, not a war—but life.' That's what I did. It's the greatest program any man ever designed."
>
> **THOMAS PARKER EMERY, WORLD WAR II VETERAN**

BSA averaged about 200,000 a year into the early 1960s. In 1955, overall active membership exceeded 4 million—more than twice the 1940 figure—and the BSA's national headquarters (which had just moved from New York City to North Brunswick, New Jersey) proudly reported that there were now more than 100,000 chartered units in the U.S. and its territories. A decade later, active membership stood at about 5.7 million.

Scouting's growth in its "golden age" wasn't just the result of a high birthrate. There were other trends at work. For one thing, despite the tensions of the Cold War with the Communist powers (which would flair into a hot war in Korea in 1950), the twenty years that followed the end of World War II marked a time of peace and prosperity for many Americans. The economy entered a period of unprecedented expansion,

ABOVE Chart of the rising BSA membership, 1912–1960. **RIGHT** (top) Cover of *The Scout Administrator*, with artwork by Norman Rockwell. (bottom) Inside *The Scout Administrator*, showing uniform specs and prices.

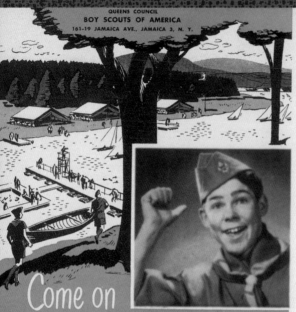

with low unemployment and rising living standards. With more money in their pockets, American families no longer found the modest costs of Scouting—membership fees, troop dues, the purchase of uniforms and equipment—to be a burden, as many had during the pinched years of the Depression.

Even more important, adult Americans had more leisure time than ever before. The eight-hour day and the five-day work week became the standard during these years, and plenty of Americans used their free evenings and weekends to serve as Scoutmasters, Cubmasters, and den mothers, or to serve on troop committees and other "auxiliary" organizations. The rise in youth enrollment in the BSA was more than matched by the rise in adult membership, which went from a pre-World War II figure of about 34,000 to 1.3 million by 1960.

Many of these adult leaders (women as well as men) were veterans, and for some, the experiences they'd had in World War II were an inspiration to devote their time and energy to Scouting. As Thomas Parker Emery, a paratrooper who saw combat in New Guinea and the Philippines, recalled: "I was holding a close friend in my arms as he died in battle, and I said to myself: 'I'm going to go back home and be a Scoutmaster, and I'm going to teach kids how to survive life—not the jungle, not

a war—but life.' That's what I did. It's the greatest program any man ever designed."

Many of these veterans took advantage of the inexpensive mortgages provided by the GI Bill to move their young families to the new suburbs springing up around major cities. Most Americans could afford cars now, too, and in the 1950s a network of interstate highways connected the country. These developments led to a big increase in weekend camping by troops; state and national parks and other prime camping areas were now within easy range. In the words of one Scoutmaster of the time, "When I was a Boy Scout in 1926, if you went camping 100 miles from home, that was a heck of a long trip so most of your camping was close by. Beginning in the fifties, 100 miles was a jaunt."

Campers also enjoyed newer and better gear, much of it courtesy of the U.S. military. The end of World War II and the defensive buildup of the Cold War meant an abundance of military surplus equipment; as early as 1946, an article in the *New York Times* reported that the U.S. Army had sold more than $1 million worth of sleeping bags and tents to the BSA under regulations classifying Boy Scout councils "as non-profit institutions entitled to buy surplus [government] property

ABOVE (left) Scouts securing their pitched tent. (right) Stringing the tent framework for their campsite. **LEFT** Camp brochure showing off different uniforms, 1950.

at wholesale prices with special priority." New "convenience" foods like canned Spam and powdered beverages (which Scouts usually dubbed "bug juice") made campfire cooking easier, too. Of course, adult leaders grumbled that today's boys had it so much easier than *they* did when they were Scouts.

Summer camping flourished as well. The postwar era saw the culmination of a trend that began in the 1930s—troop-based summer camping. Going to camp for a week or two was a feature of Scouting from the BSA's earliest days. But for the BSA's first couple of decades, it was rare for troops to go to summer camp as a unit; most boys went to their local council's camp as individuals. This caused various problems, not the least of which was that some Scouts got lonely and homesick away from their friends. Keith Monroe, who attended camp under the old system, recalled:

The camp I attended as a Scout would seem strange today, though it was typical of its time. It was a "mass camp" with rows of big tents, all alike. I was the only Scout from my troop, but if the whole troop had happened to come I might have felt almost as alone, because we would have been scattered at random among the ten-boy tents in the visitors' sector.

A sixteen-year-old staffer, called a "patrol leader," was in charge of each tent. There were no troops, just makeshift patrols which lined up thrice daily on the parade ground, ate together in the dining hall, but otherwise saw little of one another.

Each day I checked in at merit badge classes if I chose, joined in the afternoon camp swim, and whiled away hours on handicrafts or stood in line at the archery range or just sat and dreamed. Other Scouts did much the same.

After studying the matter, the BSA recommended a switch to whole troops going to camp together and staying in their own campsites. It took many years for the new system to take hold, but by the 1960s, 65 percent of all troops went to summer

ABOVE Putting the finishing touches on their tents.

camp as a unit. Because troops brought their own adult and junior leaders with them, troop-based camping freed up camp staff to focus on teaching merit-badge skills and running "program areas" like aquatics, crafts, rifle and archery ranges, and so on.

By now the jewel in Scout camping's crown was New Mexico's Philmont Scout Ranch. There, boys could live out true "Wild West" adventures—hikes into the hills with mules carrying supplies, horseback riding, and mountain climbing. Some 17,000 Scouts a year enjoyed the incomparable experience of Philmont by the mid-1960s. Philmont also became an important training center for volunteer and professional Scouters.

Prosperity, peace (of a kind), suburbs full of young families, cars and highways—these all combined to create a kind of "perfect storm" that lifted Boy Scouting into its greatest period of popularity and prominence on the American scene.

PROGRAM CHANGES

For the BSA, the 1950s began with a bang—the first national jamboree since 1937. The event was held at Valley Forge,

Pennsylvania, where George Washington and his Continental Army endured the brutal winter of 1778–1779 during the struggle for American independence. President Harry Truman addressed the 47,000 Scouts who attended:

As honorary president of the Boy Scouts of America, I am proud to open this Scout jamboree. I understand that there are nearly 50,000 Scouts in this encampment. I am glad to see such evidence of the strength of the Scout movement. And I think it most appropriate in times like these that you have chosen to hold your jamboree at this historic shrine of Valley Forge.

From 1950 until 1964, national jamborees were held at Irvine Ranch, California (1953); Valley Forge again (1957); Colorado Springs, Colorado (1960); and Valley Forge for a third time (1964). All told, nearly 200,000 American Scouts and Scouters—plus contingents of international Scouts—took part in the fun and fellowship of these first four postwar jamborees.

ABOVE Sprawling campsite of the second postwar national jamboree, held at Irvine Ranch, California, 1953.

ON THIS PAGE (clockwise, starting from top right) Lyndon Baines Johnson, thirty-sixth president of the United States, speaks at the 1964 Valley Forge jamboree; congregating at the Valley Forge jamboree; Scouts perform assigned tasks at the jamboree; Scouts arriving at the 1964 National Scout Jamboree in Valley Forge, Pennsylvania.

A lot of the Scouts who arrived at Valley Forge in 1950 probably carried copies of the newest (1948—the fifth edition, edited by Ted Pettit) version of the *Handbook for Boys*. And on their heads they wore the new soft cap patterned after the "fore-and-aft" or "overseas" cap issued to World War II GIs. The

new topper wasn't very popular, though; it didn't look as jaunty as the old "Smokey the Bear" hat, and it didn't do much to protect the wearer from sun, rain, or snow.

As the BSA approached and passed its fortieth birthday in 1950, the organization made some changes that went far beyond handbook revisions and headgear, especially at its upper and lower age ranges.

In 1949, Cub Scout membership hit the million mark—a number that would more than double by 1955 as baby boom boys reached the age of admission. There was concern, however, that not enough Cub Scouts were staying in Cub Scouting long enough to make the transition to Boy Scouting—perhaps because older Cub Scouts still did the same activities as their younger pack and den brothers. As a result, in 1954, Cub Scouts over the age of ten-and-a-half who had achieved Lion rank were placed in a separate Webelos den, and the BSA's Cub Scout Division introduced special activities for Webelos Scouts. It wouldn't be until the late 1960s, however, that the Webelos Scouts got their own advancement program.

The mid-1950s saw the start of an activity that proved a big hit with all Cub Scouts: the pinewood derby. In 1953, Don Murphy, Cubmaster of Pack 280C in Manhattan Beach, California,

ABOVE (top left) Scouts at the 1960 jamboree in Colorado Springs, Colorado, go for a wagon ride. (top right) An Explorer tries his hand at some funny business at the jamboree, 1953. (bottom) The fifth edition of the *Handbook for Boys*, 1948.

decided to (in his words) "[Devise] a wholesome, constructive activity that would foster a closer father-son relationship and promote craftsmanship and good sportsmanship through competition." Murphy was an avid model-maker and hit on the idea having his Cub Scouts race miniature cars that they would build with their fathers.

became an official Cub Scout activity. The annual pinewood derby remains one of the highlights of every Cub Scout's year.

At the upper end of the age range, the BSA introduced a sweeping change. Starting in 1949, when the BSA phased out the Senior Scouting program (the BSA's previous designation for older Scouts) in favor of Exploring, all Boy Scouts over age fourteen

The mid-1950s saw the start of an activity that provided a big hit with all Cub Scouts: the pinewood derby.

Fifty-five Cub Scouts from Pack 280C took part in the very first pinewood derby, cheering their little homemade cars on as they raced along a 31-foot-long track. The idea quickly spread throughout the Los Angeles area, and before long Cub Scouting's national director, O. W. "Bud" Bennett, heard about it. "We believe you have an excellent idea, and we are most anxious to make your material available to the Cub Scouts of America," Bennett wrote Murphy. The following year *Boys' Life* published plans for cars, and in 1955 the pinewood derby

were automatically registered as Explorers. They had the choice of remaining within their troop as part of an Explorer crew or joining a separate Explorer post. (The Boy Scouts' established older-boy programs—Sea Scouting and Air Scouting—had their names changed to Sea Exploring and Air Exploring, but they basically remained the same.) From 1945 to 1949, Exploring had its own advancement program based on four ranks—Apprentice, Woodsman, Frontiersman, and Ranger—but the ranks were later replaced by Bronze, Gold, and Silver awards.

ABOVE (left) Fathers and Cub Scouts at the finish line of a pinewood derby race in Iowa, 1955. (right) The cover of the original pinewood derby rulebook.

DON MURPHY ENTERPRISES
Paintings-Prints
3030 Merrill Dr., Suite 43
TORRANCE, CA 90503
(310) 320-4343

21 April 1996

Mr. J. Warren Young, Publisher
Scouting Magazine
1325 W. Walnut Hill Lane
P.O. Box 152079
Irvine, Texas
75015-2079

Dear Mr. Young,

I was referred to you by my nephew, Pierce C. Weir, BSA Executive Board Member, West LA Area County Council, Van Nuys, CA.

I am Art Director, retired from North American Rockwell and continue to pursue the arts. In the twilight of my years at 78, I was reviewing my accomplishments through the years. In my library, I came across the "Pinewood Derby" launched 43 years ago. My most outstanding accomplishment was when in 1953, I originated the "Pinewood Derby".

When my son became of Cub Scout age, I joined scouting with him and the job of Cub Scout Master of a failing pack. I organized the pack of 45 cubs into 5 dens headed by Den Chiefs. Since I was employed at North American Aviation and a member of the Management Club, I interested the Club into sponsoring my Cub Pack 280-C of Manhattan Beach, CA.

My idea of the "Pinewood Derby" actually was a sequel to the Soap Box Derby which the Management Club also sponsored, except, that it would be miniature model cars racing down a 32 foot indoor track where parents could view the race from both sides.

I wanted this to be a father and son event, to bring them together in one common interest and to promote craftsmanship and sportsmanship through competition.

Yes, this was one of my greatest accomplishments and I had as much fun participating in this Derby as did the Cubs. To this day I hear from individuals who were members of Pack 280-C. They are now in their 50's and their fathers who helped in this event are now in their 70's.

I have saved this material over the years which I will share with you. I will supply you with reproducible copies of your choice since the enclosed data is not suitable for reproduction. I have enclosed the one and only <u>original</u> Pinewood Derby Official Rule Book which is reproducible and may be released for scouting purposes.

More than ever, this country needs to somehow get back to strengthening family values and that the "Pinewood Derby" will continue to be apart of this growing up family need.

I would appreciate it if you would see that this original data gets to the right Scouting people and I believe this story would be of interest to your readers.

I have one son, Donn, who teaches at West Valley College, Saratoga, Ca. and I reside with my wife, Anne, in Torrance, Ca.

Sincerely,

Donald W. Murphy

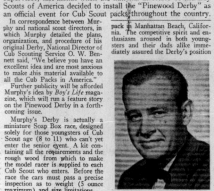

LEFT (front and back) Letter from Don Murphy, father of the pinewood derby®, to Warren Young of *Scouting* magazine, enclosing the original pinewood derby rulebook. **BELOW** News clipping on the BSA approving Murphy's pinewood derby.

T CLUB NEWS   NOVEMBER 30, 1953

Don Murphy's 'Pinewood Derby' Gets National Approval by BSA

Nationwide acceptance of his Cub Scout group participation activity was awarded to Don Murphy, Field Service general supervisor, last month when the national directors of the Boy Scouts of America decided to install the "Pinewood Derby" as an official event for Cub Scout packs throughout the country.

In correspondence between Murphy and national scout directors, in which Murphy detailed the plans, organization, and procedure of his original Derby, National Director of Cub Scouting Service O. W. Bennett said, "We believe you have an excellent idea and are most anxious to make this material available to all the Cub Packs in America."

Further publicity will be afforded Murphy's idea by *Boy's Life* magazine, which will run a feature story on the Pinewood Derby in a forthcoming issue.

Murphy's Derby is actually a miniature Soap Box race, designed solely for those youngsters of Cub Scout age (8 to 11) who can't yet enter the senior event. A kit containing all the requirements and the rough wood from which to make the model racer is supplied to each Cub Scout who enters. Before the race the cars must pass a precise inspection as to weight (5 ounce maximum) and size limitations.

Explaining his intent in originating the activity, Murphy said, "The Pinewood Derby is a father and son event. Its purpose is to bring father and son together in one common interest in promoting craftsmanship and good sportsmanship through competition."

The original Pinewood Derby (named from the wood used to make the model racers) was held last May by Murphy's Cub Scout

pack in Manhattan Beach, California. The competitive spirit and enthusiasm aroused in both youngsters and their dads alike immediately assured the Derby's position

IDEA TAKES HOLD—Don Murphy originator of the "Pinewood Derby", Cub Scout competitive event that will be adopted as official activity for Cub Scout packs throughout the nation. Magazine *Boy's Life* will publicize the derby in feature article soon.

as an annual event, and promise national recognition to an idea generated within North American Management Club sponsorship.

Exploring had a mixed reception at first. Some older Scouts did welcome the chance to take part in activities that were too hard, physically, for younger boys, like long canoe trips or hikes in rough country. Others couldn't quite see the point of the new program. Some troops evidently ignored the Scout/Explorer distinction entirely. In other troops, the Explorer crew simply functioned as junior leaders. Also, Explorer crews within troops had their own adult leaders, called Advisors, and sometimes Advisors and Scoutmasters didn't always see eye-to-eye. In the words of one Explorer Advisor of the time, "If one was stronger than the other or they weren't cooperating, you had conflicting interests."

In 1954, as part of its overall effort to solve the older-boy problem, the BSA commissioned the University of Michigan to undertake a nationwide survey of boys aged fourteen to sixteen to find out what they really wanted in a youth organization. It found that four-fifths of the boys surveyed wanted to take part in a program that would prepare them for adult careers. Around the same time, an executive at California's Irvine Corporation, William H. Spurgeon III, began to promote what would become known as special-interest Exploring, based on posts sponsored by businesses, trade unions, professional associations, and the like. The aim would be to give older boys real-world, hands-on experience in the career fields they wanted to enter as adults.

The University of Michigan survey and Spurgeon's advocacy of special-interest Exploring led the BSA to revamp the entire Exploring program in 1959. Explorer crews in troops were disbanded; boys fourteen and older who wanted to continue in Exploring joined separate posts. Boys in the same age group in troops became Boy Scouts again, officially, although they were

ABOVE Explorers engaging in various activities. RIGHT Document describing uniform and insignia for Exploring.

NATIONAL COUNCIL   BOY SCOUTS OF AMERICA

UNIFORM AND INSIGNIA FOR THE NEW EXPLORING PROGRAM

EXPLORERS AND LEADERS

The use of the Explorer apparel is encouraged for those registered in that program. Scouters not associated with Explorer units and members of all executive staffs may wear the appropriate Explorer garb only when attending functions that are exclusively Exploring.

GREEN OUTFIT

Cap. Green with brown piping. Explorer emblem embroidered on a green background on left side in front. Worn tilted to the right, two fingers width above right eyebrow.

Shirt. Green with "EXPLORER" strip in brown over right pocket. Long sleeves.

Trousers. Green, with no cuffs.

Belt. White web, with Explorer emblem on brass buckle. Belt hooks will only be worn when necessary for carrying equipment.

Necktie. Plain brown without stripe or figure, four-in-hand. Official Explorer tie holder may be worn.

Shoes. Plain brown or black leather.

Socks. Plain brown or black to match shoes, without stripe or figure.

Leggings. (optional) White canvas. Worn only by vote of post members.

INSIGNIA FOR POST EXPLORERS

COMMUNITY STRIP, LOCAL COUNCIL SHOULDER PATCH, STATE STRIP, POST NUMERAL, VETERAN UNIT BAR

Worn as prescribed in current Exploring insignia and uniform regulations.

By that time, America and its allies in Western Europe and Asia were locked in a tense standoff with the Soviet Union and the People's Republic of China. Fears of Communist expansion overseas and Communist spies at home led to sad episodes like Senator Joseph McCarthy's "witch hunt" against alleged Communists in the early 1950s. But the challenges of the Cold War also made Americans keenly aware of the need to support liberty and democracy both at home and abroad.

In short, the two decades following the end of World War II were a time of intense patriotism in America, and the Boy Scouts—now firmly established in the public mind as embodying the best of American values—were expected to do

> "The two decades following the end of World War II were a time of intense patriotism in America, and the Boy Scouts—now firmly established in the public mind as embodying the best of American values—were expected to do their part in the new struggle."

classified as Senior Boy Scouts for some years afterward. The designation carried no real weight, though; it just meant that a boy could wear a "Senior" patch on his uniform once he'd passed his fourteenth birthday.

COLD WAR SCOUTING

World War II devastated Scouting in many countries. Even before the war's end, the BSA committed itself to helping revive Scouting overseas. In late 1944, the BSA established the World Friendship Fund, which provided money, equipment, and training to national Scout associations struggling to overcome the effects of the war and its aftermath. The BSA also joined the United Nations' relief efforts with a clothing drive in 1950–1951. Scouts collected some 2 million pounds of used clothing; some went to needy Americans, but much of the haul was sent overseas for the hundreds of thousands of refugees who still languished in "displaced persons" camps in Europe. The Cub Scouts got into the act, too, contributing 2,889 pennies for Scouts in war-ravaged South Korea in 1953.

their part in the new struggle, as they had in previous crises like the Depression and the world wars. As President Dwight Eisenhower put it in a birthday address to the Boy Scouts on February 8, 1953: "I urge you all to live up to the high ideals for which Scouting stands—your duties as patriotic citizens. If you will follow the Scout Oath, America will be better able to meet its full responsibility in cooperation with other nations in maintaining peace on earth."

The Boy Scouts were already rising to the challenge well before Eisenhower's speech. In 1949, the BSA announced a three-year program called "the Crusade to Strengthen the Arm of Liberty" in a ceremony held at the Statue of Liberty in New York Harbor. The program included distributing 200 "Little Sisters of Liberty"—8-foot-4-inch copper replicas of

ABOVE Scouts spreading patriotism with Lady Liberty, Florala, Alabama, 1949.

ABOUT FIRE EXTINGUISHERS

Many houses and public buildings have fire extinguishers. They will be as useful as ever in putting out fires caused by an incendiary bomb. For putting out the bomb itself, the extinguisher may not be suitable.

Read the label. If it says that the contents include CARBON TETRACHLORIDE, it cannot under any circumstances be used on a magnesium bomb. It is not only ineffective, it may cause dangerous gas to be generated. After the bomb is burnt out, use it on any remaining fire.

All water-type extinguishers are suitable. If the label says SODA-ACID, that's simply a means of creating pressure in the extinguisher. Turn it upside down, use it. You can get a spray effect by putting the thumb over the nozzle, use the jet on surrounding fires. However, *one extinguisher is not enough to burn out a magnesium bomb.* And you cannot refill the extinguisher.

It is best to have sand or pump-bucket equipment handy, use them on the bomb, and save the extinguishers for resulting fires.

A foam extinguisher will also help to control a bomb, but one extinguisher load will not finish the job.

See that the extinguishers you know about are ready for use.

31

A Handbook for

MESSENGERS

United States
OFFICE OF CIVILIAN DEFENSE
Washington, D. C.

ON THIS PAGE (top left) The *Handbook for Fire Watchers*. Using fire extinguishers to neutralize an incendiary bomb. (bottom right) How to dispose of an incendiary bomb with sand. (bottom left) A handbook from the Office of Civilian Defense instructs Scouts how to help other citizens in the event of nuclear attack.

CONTROLLING WITH SAND

APPROACH THE BOMB IN A CROUCHING OR CRAWLING POSITION. PLACE THE SAND BUCKET, UPSET, TO ALLOW A FULL-ARM SWING TOWARD THE BOMB

TRY TO COVER THE BOMB WITH DRY SAND, TO CONFINE IT'S ACTION, SO THAT YOU CAN GET NEAR ENOUGH TO SCOOP IT UP ON THE SHOVEL

WHEN THE BOMB IS UNDER FAIR CONTROL, SCOOP IT UP ON THE SHOVEL, FIRST RIGHTING THE BUCKET, BUT LEAVING SOME SAND IN THE BOTTOM...

...IF THE BOMB CAN BE DROPPED FROM A WINDOW TO SOME PLACE WHERE IT CAN BURN OUT WITHOUT HARM — GET RID OF IT THAT WAY!

...OTHERWISE, PUT IT IN THE BUCKET ON TOP OF SAND, COVER IT WITH MORE SAND...

...THEN, HOLDING THE BUCKET ON THE SHOVEL, CARRY IT OUT OF THE HOUSE...

"It was because of the darkening world situation that we initiated the Crusade to Strengthen the Arm of Liberty, and it was because of increasingly serious world developments that the National Board voted to extend that Crusade through 1951. . . . With an ever more devoted leadership, with a constantly improving program, and a membership which becomes larger and stronger hour by hour, we can and will do our best to serve our country well in this time of great need."

CHIEF SCOUT EXECUTIVE ARTHUR SCHUCK, 1951

the original statue—to communities in thirty-nine states and several overseas territories.

In the presidential election year of 1952, the BSA oversaw a national "Get Out the Vote" campaign. More than 1 million Scouts draped front doors across the country with no fewer than 30 million "Liberty Bell" doorknob hangers and distributed more than 1 million posters to businesses. They repeated the feat in 1956; this time the tally was 36 million doorknob hangers and 1.4 million posters.

With the threat of nuclear war ever-present in these years, the Boy Scouts also cooperated with civil-defense authorities to prepare the public for that terrible possibility. Civil defense was the theme of a National Good Turn in 1958. Scouts delivered 40 million emergency handbooks and 50,000 posters prepared by the federal Office of Civil Defense Management.

IT'S A *BOYS' LIFE*

In 1962, *Boys' Life* marked its fiftieth anniversary as the BSA's

ABOVE Chief Scout Executive Arthur A. Schuck speaks with a Strengthen the Arm of Liberty banner behind him.

official magazine for its youth members. In 1954, the magazine had broken the million-subscriber mark for the first time; that figure doubled within a decade, and in the 1960s *Boys' Life* was ranked in the top twenty magazines published in the United States. In keeping with its motto—"for all boys"—*Boys' Life* appealed not only to Scouts; by the early 1960s, it had several hundred thousand non-Scout subscribers.

Boys' Life owed its success to several factors. There was little competition, as most of the other magazines aimed at boys had folded in the 1940s and 1950s. And of course, it benefited from the surge of boys into Scouting after World War II. Promoting the magazine was also a big priority for Chief Scout Executive Arthur A. Schuck, who served from 1948 to 1960. In the words of Bob Hood, who started at the magazine as an editorial assistant in 1953 and became its editor a decade later, "In those days,

ABOVE (top) BSA fiftieth anniversary postcard, with Norman Rockwell–designed stamp. (bottom) Arthur A. Schuck at his desk with a Scout.

FEBRUARY 1960 • 25c

Boys' Life
FOR ALL BOYS

19

1960

BOYS' LIFE for FEBRUARY, 1960

50TH
ANNIVERSARY
ACHIEVEMENT
AWARD!

FIFTIETH ANNIVERSARY
ACHIEVEMENT AWARD

THERE ARE GOING TO BE BIG DOINGS IN 1960...AND YOU
WILL WANT TO WEAR THIS PERMANENT ACHIEVEMENT
AWARD PRIZE ABOVE THE SERVICE STARS OVER THE
LEFT BREAST POCKET OF YOUR UNIFORM. HERE IS
HOW YOU CAN EARN THE RIGHT TO WEAR IT...

CUB SCOUTS

1. SECURE ONE BOY TO JOIN YOUR PACK, OR ANOTHER PACK DURING 1960.
2. ADVANCE ONE RANK OR EARN AN ARROW POINT.
3. LEARN TO SWIM. IF YOU CAN ALREADY, EARN A CREDIT POINT IN SPORTS OR SWIMMING ELECTIVE.
4. PARTICIPATE WITH YOUR DEN OR PACK IN SOME PLAN OF CONSERVATION PROJECT TO HELP OTHERS, LIKE YOUR CHURCH, SCHOOL, OR NEIGHBORHOOD. ASSIST IN THE GET-OUT-THE-VOTE CAMPAIGN IF CALLED ON TO DO SO BY YOUR CUBMASTER.

BOY SCOUTS

1. RECRUIT A NEW BOY.
2. ADVANCE AT LEAST ONE RANK OR EARN THREE MERIT BADGES.
3. EARN THE PERSONAL FITNESS BADGE. (IF YOU HAVE ALREADY EARNED THIS BADGE, YOU MAY EARN ANY ONE OF THE FOLLOWING AS A SUBSTITUTE: ATHLETICS, SWIMMING, HIKING, CYCLING, ROWING.)
4. WITH YOUR PATROL OR TROOP, RENDER SOME GOOD TURN SERVICE OR PARTICIPATE IN A CONSERVATION PROJECT FOR YOUR CHURCH, SCHOOL, OR COMMUNITY. TAKE PART IN THE GET-OUT-THE-VOTE CAMPAIGN.

EXPLORERS

1. SECURE AT LEAST ONE NEW MEMBER FOR YOUR EXPLORER POST AND PERSONALLY INTRODUCE HIM TO THE OFFICERS AND MEMBERS.
2. CARRY TO A SUCCESSFUL CONCLUSION YOUR RESPONSIBILITIES AS AN OFFICER OF YOUR POST, OR AS A MEMBER OF AN ACTIVITY COMMITTEE.
3. COMPETE IN AN ATHLETIC OR FIELD SPORT FOR AT LEAST EIGHT GAMES OR CONTESTS DURING THE YEAR (DUAL OR TEAM COMPETITION) — OR EARN THE PERSONAL FITNESS BADGE.
4. HELP YOUR POST SUCCESSFULLY COMPLETE A SPECIFIC SERVICE OR CONSERVATION PROJECT FOR THE SPONSORING ORGANIZATION, COMMUNITY OR SCOUTING UNIT. TAKE PART IN THE GET-OUT-THE-VOTE CAMPAIGN.

JUBILEE
FOR GOD AND COUNTRY
1910 • 1960
50 YEARS OF SERVICE
CAMPOREE

From Our Scout Album

AN astronomical total of memories has been built up by the 31,500,000 people who have been members of the Boy Scouts of America during the past fifty years. Poets and painters, the Edgar A. Guests and the Norman Rockwells, have captured with prose and poetry, oil and water color, the romance of Scouting. However, it has remained for the lensmen, the snap-shot shutterbug and the professional photographer, to record the Scout as a citizen — the Explorer fighting the big floods of tragedy and the small floods of erosion, the Boy Scout at work in a nation twice at war, and the Scouts who travel across this land or across that ocean to a jamboree with thousands of his brother Scouts. From the monumental unbound album of Scouting photos come the shots on this page, token of the limitless activities in which you might have found a Boy Scout any day for the past fifty years.

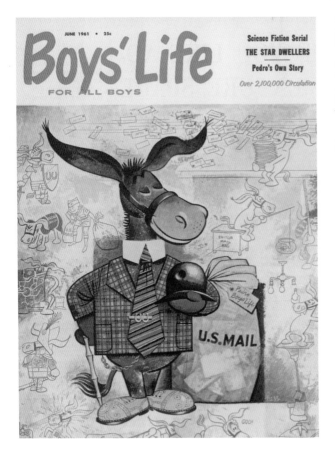

Dr. Schuck never made a speech without praising *Boys' Life* and its vital role in the success of Scouting."

But the real key to *Boys' Life*'s success was its appealing blend of information and entertainment on a broad spectrum of topics. Besides "how-to" articles on Scoutcraft and tales of outdoor adventure, there were stories about sports and science, plus a slew of regular features like "Think and Grin" (jokes and riddles—usually corny ones); "Scouts in Action"—illustrated accounts of Scouts who'd performed brave deeds to help people and animals in danger; "The Hitchin' Rack," a reader mail section "edited" by the magazine's mascot, Pedro the Mailburro; and cartoons featuring the adventures of Boy Scout Pee Wee Harris and a pair of Cub Scouts, the Tracy Twins. In addition, *Boys' Life* also encouraged "audience participation" by running regular contests—inviting readers to send in their designs for neckerchief slides, for example.

A typical issue of this era—March 1956—included, among much else, no fewer than four illustrated short stories; an article titled "Who Makes the Majors?" by baseball great Hank Greenberg; a biographical profile of Booker T. Washington; the winning entries in a photo contest; and how-to's on having a clambake, raising parakeets, and assembling a survival kit.

During these years, an in-house staff of writers, editors, and artists contributed most of *Boys' Life*'s content. It was a dynamic group, including many World War II veterans, and they weren't content to stay at their desks. Instead, many traveled around the country constantly in search of fresh material. In addition to the staff's contributions, *Boys' Life* began to publish articles by well-known writers—or writers who would become well known. The great science-fiction writer Robert A. Heinlein, for example, had his early young-adult novel *Farmer in the Sky* serialized in the magazine in 1950 under the title *Satellite Scout*. (Heinlein

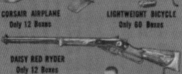

ON THIS PAGE *Boys' Life* readers could earn prizes for selling greeting cards.

The Hitchin' Rack

PEDRO WAS UNUSUALLY *efficient. All his mail was sorted and delivered without a booboo, and the day was nearly over before the boss figured out why the bustling burro was on the ball.*

Then he, the boss, remembered, "Pedro's going to catch the big happy birthday television show this evening. Well, we can't invent anything to keep him here late, since the rest of us want to see the program, too. Anybody got an idea?"

Somebody did. They figured the hoggish hayburner could never resist a free feed. So, some of the gang left the office early and hauled two bales of hay and a bushel of carrots to old flopears' barn apartment. They set the hay right in front of the burro's easy chair, where it would cut off his view of the television screen.

"That ought to do it," said the boss. "He will be too lazy to move that hay, except for moving it into his jaws, and the noise he'll make chomping on those carrots will drown out the TV sound."

When old Dragalong came home and saw the free feed, he chuckled. Before he sat down he went to his closet and dug out a periscope and set of headphones. He plugged the headphones into the television set, then sat down to munch and crunch while he watched and listened. He rested his hoofs comfortably on the lower hay bale, imprinting it with his mark—∪∪

Dear Pedro:
Where is "North Canada" besides being on your November 1959 cover?—*H. Charles Mishkoff, Scarsdale, N.Y.*
● **Oddly enough, scores of BL readers who probably see a globe every school day, asked a similar question. If you look closer you will see that the word "North" is the same size type as the word "America" seen down in the U.S. portion of the map. This is standard with globes, and though it never causes confusion on an actual globe, being reduced and illustrated partially on our cover, the word "North" appeared to apply to the word "Canada" immediately below it. Actually, "Canada" is in smaller type.—∪∪**

Dear Burro:
Is that an eye under the magnifying glass on the November cover?—*John Gwiazda, Rahway, N.J.*
● **That's a reflection of the eye which is above (and off the cover itself) and looking into the glass.—∪∪**

Dear Flopears:
In October, BL announced a contest with the top prize a trip to Switzerland. Last year you did the same thing and I didn't see how the results came out. Would you please let us know how this one comes out?—*Billy Cargill, Eddy, Texas.*
● **The winners of the first contest were announced on page 50 of April, 1959, BOYS' LIFE. Winners of the current contest will be announced in the April, 1960, issue. Incidentally, the grand prize winner of the 1959 Contest is David Wendt, and his story is scheduled to appear in May BOYS' LIFE.—∪∪**

Dear Martian Misfit:
In December Think and Grin, that joke about the octopus has only seven "pows." An octopus has eight legs.—*George Burdge, Farmingdale, N.J.*
● **That octopus is too smart to be caught without one good leg to stand on.—∪∪**

Dear Pedro:
The BSA was founded on February 8, 1910. Is February 8 the first or the last day of Boy Scout Week?—*Harold Levine, Skokie, Ill.*
● **Boy Scout Week is February Sixth through and including the Twelfth.—∪∪**

Dear Balmy Burro:
Among your fishing contest winners in December you list William Bowser for catching a dolphin. That isn't even a fish; it's a mammal.—*Jerry P. Dunham, Indianapolis, Ind.*
● **The mammal you refer to is the *Tursiops Truncatus* or bottle-nosed dolphin, more commonly called porpoise. William Bowser won his prize for catching a *Coryphaena Hippurus*, more commonly called dolphin.—∪∪**

Dear Donkus:
Your "Scouts in Action" in December reports on an incident which happened on April 24, 1958, but you illustrate a 1959 Pontiac. Who's goof?—*Gary Dillenbeck, Delavon, Wisc.*
● **Ouch!—∪∪**

Dear Don Pedro:
Mr. Stewart's article, "How Girls Rate Boys" was wonderful. All my gal pals say the same. We like boys to be polite about little things, but not to over do it. Sloppy Joe and Bully Bill rate strictly "0." — *Annette DeVito, Clifton, N.J.*

returned to the pages of *Boys' Life* in 1958 with another serial, *Tenderfoot in Space*.) *Boys' Life*'s fiction editor in this era was a woman—Frances Smith.

Two regular contributors to *Boys' Life* deserve special attention: Norman Rockwell and William "Green Bar Bill" Hillcourt.

NORMAN ROCKWELL

As an illustrator, Norman Rockwell was celebrated for his depictions of small-town American life, but he was born in the heart of Manhattan in 1894 and grew up in the city and its suburbs. At sixteen Rockwell enrolled in New York's Art Students League. When he graduated two years later, in 1912, he needed a job, and one of his professors at the League suggested he pay a call at the office of a new magazine called *Boys' Life*,

ABOVE (left) Pedro the Mailburro's letters to the editor column. (right) *Boys' Life* cover illustrating its feature story, August 1950, and the opening page of "Satellite Scout," by Robert A. Heinlein. **RIGHT** (top) *Handbook for Boys* covers with painting by Norman Rockwell. (bottom) *Boy Scout Handbook* front and back covers with paintings by Norman Rockwell.

HANDBOOK FOR BOYS

NORMAN ROCKWELL

BOY SCOUTS OF AMERICA

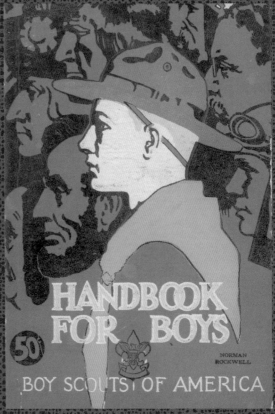

HANDBOOK FOR BOYS

50

NORMAN ROCKWELL

BOY SCOUTS OF AMERICA

BOY SCOUT HANDBOOK

Norman Rockwell

BOY SCOUTS OF AMERICA

BE PREPARED

which had just been acquired by the BSA. The gangly eighteen-year-old presented himself to Edward Cave, the magazine's art director, who hired him to do some charcoal sketches to accompany a story in the January 1913 issue.

Rockwell's illustrations were a hit and he soon found himself with plenty of work from *Boys' Life*, plus a commission to provide illustrations for *The Boy Scout Hike Book*. The following year he joined the magazine's staff at a salary of $50 a week, tasked with producing covers and illustrations for one story per issue. Before long, he was promoted to art director.

In 1916, Rockwell decided to go freelance. (His stint with the early *Boys' Life* was, in fact, his only salaried position in a career that spanned six decades.) Over the next few decades he became one of the country's most sought-after illustrators, contributing covers and illustrations to popular periodicals like *The Saturday Evening Post*. Rockwell's subjects were usually scenes of ordinary American life, which he portrayed in a style that was natural, simple, and often humorous. In his words,

"The commonplaces of America to me are the richest subjects in art: Boys batting flies on vacant lots; girls playing jacks on front steps; old men plodding home at twilight—all these arouse feelings in me."

Rockwell's patriotism and his belief in the promises and possibilities of America were an important element of his work, expressed most vividly in the series of posters he produced in World War II on the "Four Freedoms" proclaimed by President Franklin Roosevelt. Later in life Rockwell's artwork also tackled serious subjects such as racial segregation and strife in the Middle East.

When World War I (in which Rockwell served in the navy as a military artist) ended, the American Red Cross decided to honor the BSA's wartime service with four paintings by Rockwell in the Red Cross magazine. The illustrations caught the eye of Brown & Bigelow, the country's biggest calendar publisher, which had entered into an arrangement with the BSA to produce an annual Scout-themed calendar. Brown & Bigelow hired Rockwell to provide the calendar's illustrations.

NOTABLE SCOUTS

SAM WALTON
EAGLE SCOUT, FOUNDER OF WAL-MART

THE MAN WHO CHANGED THE WAY AMERICA SHOPS was born in Kingfisher, Oklahoma, in 1918. The Walton family moved around frequently during Sam's childhood, eventually settling in Missouri, where Sam joined the Scouts. In 1931, he attained Eagle Scout rank—just thirteen, he was the youngest Eagle Scout in Missouri's history.

Named "Most Versatile Boy" in his high school graduating class, Walton worked his way through the University of Missouri before taking a job as a trainee manager at a J.C. Penney store. After returning from military service in 1945, Walton used his savings and a loan from his father-in-law to open a store of his own—a franchise of the Butler Brothers department-store chain. Astute, ambitious, and extremely hardworking, Walton decided that the era of the old-fashioned department store was coming to a close. He believed that discount stores—which could offer customers lower prices by buying goods in high volume directly from wholesalers—were the wave of the future for consumers. Soon Walton put his ideas into practice with a small chain of "Walton's Five and Dime" stores, which led to the opening of the first Wal-Mart store in Bentonville, Arkansas.

Over the next four decades, the Wal-Mart empire expanded to more than 5,700 stores in the U.S. and overseas. By the early 2000s, Wal-Mart was the world's second-largest corporation and its largest private employer, with more than 1.2 million employees in the U.S. alone. The huge success of Wal-Mart made Walton the richest American for several years running in the 1980s, but he lived a modest lifestyle and remained a "hands-on" manager—often showing up unannounced at one of his stores to see if it was up to his exacting standards. Walton also insisted that "Each Wal-Mart store should reflect the values of its customers and support the vision they hold for their community," a philosophy expressed through programs like college scholarships for local high school students. Walton—a recipient of the National Eagle Scout Association's Distinguished Eagle Scout Award—died of cancer in 1992.

Sam Walton was one of many great entrepreneurs and executives with a Scouting background. Others include H. Ross Perot, founder of Electronic Data Systems (EDS) in 1962 and independent presidential candidate in 1992 and 1996, and Rex Tillerson, CEO of ExxonMobil Corporation.

For all but two years, from 1925 to 1976, Rockwell illustrated the calendar, which was often the best-selling calendar in the country. As a "good turn" to the BSA in gratitude for giving him his professional start, Rockwell didn't accept a fee for his calendar work. And Rockwell continued to contribute covers to *Boys' Life*—more than fifty in all, the last one in 1965.

Besides his calendars and covers, Rockwell's Scouting-related work included the painting *A Scout Is Brave*, commissioned by the BSA in 1932 to commemorate the 200th anniversary of George Washington's birth; a U.S. Postal Service stamp celebrating the BSA's fortieth birthday in 1950; and the covers for three editions of the *Boy Scout Handbook* and one edition of the *Handbook for Scoutmasters*.

The BSA honored Rockwell with the Silver Buffalo Award in 1939. For his seventy-fifth birthday in 1969, the BSA bestowed a singular honor on him—a request to make that year's calendar painting be a self-portrait. Rockwell responded with *At the Easel*, in which he showed himself doing an outdoor painting surrounded by curious Scouts.

Rockwell died in his home in Stockbridge, Massachusetts, in 1978. Rockwell's illustrations were loved by millions of Americans, but both the man and his work occupy a special place in the hearts of Scouts and Scouters. In the course of his long career, Rockwell became (in Scouting historian Robert W. Peterson's phrase) a "visual spokesman" for the Boy Scouts. In a 1994 essay, Susan Kay Crawford and Mark Hunt—the curator of

ABOVE Norman Rockwell's self-portrait, *At the Easel*, painted in 1969.

collections and the director of the National Scouting Museum, respectively—summed up Rockwell's legacy:

> Scouting fit well with Rockwell's view of American life. These illustrations captured important moments in the life of a Scout, his family, and his friends, reflecting a youthful nobility of spirit exemplified by the Scout Oath and Law. The images share with his other work an affirmation of basic human values and exhibit the same warmth, sense of humor, and pathos.

GREEN BAR BILL

For decades, every issue of *Boys' Life* included a column by William Hillcourt, and often an article or feature, too. Hillcourt's work for the magazine, though, was just one of his great contributions to both American and worldwide Scouting—contributions that would win him the accolades "Scoutmaster to the World" and "Mr. Boy Scout."

Hillcourt was born Vilhelm Bjerregaard Jensen in a suburb of Copenhagen, Denmark, in 1900. His introduction to Scouting, when he was ten years old, was a Danish translation of Baden-Powell's *Scouting for Boys* he received as a Christmas present. He joined the newly founded Danish Boy Scouts, rose to Knight Scout—the equivalent of Eagle Scout—attended the first world jamboree in London in 1920, and even published a novel about Scouting at the age of twenty-three. At the second world Scout jamboree, held in Emelunden, Denmark, in 1924, Hillcourt befriended William Wessel, an American Scouter. (Wessel later became a director of Cub Scouting.)

In 1926, Hillcourt arrived in New York City as a foreign correspondent for a Danish newspaper. Through his friendship with Wessel, Hillcourt got involved with local Scouting—on one occasion, the young Dane found himself teaching American Indian dances to a troop of Scouts from Brooklyn. Before long, Hillcourt had a job in the BSA's Supply Service.

Later that year, Hillcourt broke his leg in an accident at the BSA's warehouse. He described what happened next in an autobiographical sketch:

ABOVE William Hillcourt and Robert Baden-Powell, July 15, 1935.

©1972 BOY SCOUTS OF AMERICA

MORTIMER L. SCHIFF SCOUT RESERVATION
NATIONAL EDUCATION CENTER
BOY SCOUTS OF AMERICA

BADEN-POWELL
THE TWO LIVES OF A HERO
By WILLIAM HILLCOURT
with OLAVE, LADY BADEN-POWELL

A week after my accident I hobbled into the national office on my crutches to pick up my mail. I was walking to the elevator when an astonishing coincidence changed my life completely. Someone else was on his way to the same elevator: James E. West, the dynamic Chief Scout Executive of the Boy Scouts of America. He knew of my accident. He stopped to greet me, then said, "Well, my young man, what do you think of American Scouting?" The elevator came. We went down together, chatting.

His words may have been just a casual remark. But I took them seriously. I wrote an eighteen-page report and sent it to him. It was complimentary in spots, critical in others. But for each criticism I offered a suggestion for remedying the situation.

Within a week, he had me in his office. "While I don't agree with everything in your report, I am interested in what you say about the Boy Scouts of America not using the patrol method effectively. You suggest that we should have a Handbook for Patrol Leaders. What should it contain?"

Despite worries that his English "wasn't so good," Hillcourt set about writing the book. In fact he mastered the language beautifully, and the first edition of the BSA's *Handbook for Patrol Leaders*, published in 1927, was a resounding success. Now firmly established in the U.S., he Americanized his name—"Hillcourt" is a translation of "Bjerregaard." His nickname—Green Bar Bill—came from the BSA's insignia for patrol leaders at the time.

Hillcourt's output was prodigious, including three editions of the *Handbook for Patrol Leaders*, and his *Boys' Life* contributions—including a regular column, "Green Bar Bill's Patrol Corner"—ran continuously from 1932 to 1965. He also authored two editions of the *Boy Scout Handbook*, two editions of the *Handbook for Scoutmasters*, and (with James E. West) the first edition of the *Boy Scout Fieldbook* in 1948. Hillcourt's other books include *Baden-Powell: The Two Lives of a Hero* (1964), the

ABOVE (top) Brochure for the Mortimer L. Schiff Scout Reservation. (bottom) Cover of William Hillcourt's laudatory book on Baden-Powell.

first authorized biography of Scouting's founder, which he wrote in collaboration with B-P's widow, Olave Baden-Powell, and the text for *Norman Rockwell's World of Scouting* (1980).

In 1934, Hillcourt and his wife, Grace Brown Hillcourt (formerly James E. West's secretary), moved into a renovated barn on grounds of the Mortimer L. Schiff Scout Reservation in Mendham, New Jersey. The 500-acre facility had opened the

in many *Boys' Life* articles, the first *Fieldbook*, and a variety of training materials, including movies made in a studio donated by the family of Thomas J. Watson Sr., founder of the IBM Corporation. Hillcourt later remarked that the boys of Troop 1 were probably the most photographed Scouts in history.

Thanks to its status as a kind of "national troop," Troop 1 got to attend the BSA's first national jamboree in 1937 as a

"We strive to create an environment where people are valued as individuals and are treated with respect, dignity, and fairness."

FROM *WOOD BADGE FOR THE 21ST CENTURY* (2001)

year before as the BSA's first National Training Center, on land donated to the BSA by Mrs. Jacob Schiff in honor of her son, one of the organization's early leaders, who died just a month after taking office as BSA president in 1931.

Schiff provided Hillcourt with a living laboratory for Scouting. In 1935—on the BSA's twenty-fifth birthday—Hillcourt officially formed Troop 1 with boys from Mendham Township. The troop was unique in that it was chartered to the BSA's National Council rather than the local council. Over the next fifteen years, Hillcourt used Troop 1 to test his ideas about leadership and Scoutcraft. Their activities were documented

complete unit. Two years later the troop also participated in the World's Fair in New York City. The boys evidently enjoyed both the attention and the company of Green Bar Bill. Ernie Maw, who rose to Eagle Scout in Troop 1 during these years, recalled how "We had it made . . . it was a wonderful experience to know Bill Hillcourt. We had the run of the Schiff Reservation. He was an unbelievable leader."

At Schiff, the Hillcourts also hosted Baden-Powell and his wife, Olave, on a 1935 visit. Hillcourt already knew Baden-Powell from world Scout jamborees, but over the course of the visit the couples formed a close friendship.

ABOVE The first ever Wood Badge course, held in Gilwell, England, in July 1919.

SCHIFF'S MISSION

Responsible to the Boy Scouts of America through the Professional Training Division, the national education center's primary mission is professional training. Within the total program, four types of experiences are offered:

1. Professional Scouter education through the National Executive Institute and specialized training seminars, courses, and conferences. These vary in length from a few days to approximately a month. Over 4,500 full-time professional employees of the Boy Scouts of America participate in an ongoing development program.

East Hall

HISTORY

The area surrounding Schiff Scout Reservation is rich in the history of colonial America. The Jockey Hollow Trail leading to George Washington's Morristown headquarters traverses the property. It was heavily traveled by Washington's troops during 1779 and 1780. While using areas within our present boundaries as outposts, Washington camped frequently in nearby Jockey Hollow, now a national historical park.

The area within Schiff's boundaries was accumulated from parcels of land sold originally by the group of East Jersey Proprietors.

The Schiff outdoor training areas carry names honoring early Scouters — James E. West camps are named for the first Chief Scout Executive; Dan Beard camps honor the first National Scout Commissioner.

In 1963 a 28-acre tract of land on the eastern boundary was purchased bringing Schiff's present area to 508 acres.

3

Old Colonial Road follows Jockey Hollow Trail

ABOVE Map of the Schiff reservation. **RIGHT AND BELOW** Pages from inside the Mortimer L. Schiff Scout Reservation brochure.

Schiff Hall

MEN OF SCHIFF

MEN OF SCHIFF TOGETHER
TAKING TO THE WORLD,
SCOUTING WAYS FOREVER
WITH FLAGS AND BANNERS
MIGHTILY UNFURLED.
TO OUR OATH AND SCOUT LAW
TRUE WE'LL ALWAYS BE,
WITH EVERY COUNCIL
EVERY REGION
BOUND TOGETHER IN OUR LEGION
MEN OF SCHIFF ARE WE.

AQUATICS

In support of the overall program, Schiff maintains aquatic facilities for both recreational and instructional uses. These uses include swimming, boating, and canoeing in addition to formal aquatic training as a part of National Camping Schools. When scheduling permits, these lake facilities are made available to other Scouting and non-Scouting groups for supervised programs. Lake Therese, shown above, is used for these purposes. Named in honor of Mrs. Jacob Schiff, it encompasses 16 acres and is located near the entrance to the reservation.

6   7

At Baden-Powell's urging, Hillcourt brought Wood Badge—a course of advanced training for Scout leaders, introduced by Baden-Powell at Gilwell Park, England, in 1919—to America. With the help of British Scouters, Hillcourt led an experimental Wood Badge course at Schiff in 1936. This first course mostly followed the British program, but in 1948, Hillcourt served as Scoutmaster for the first course tailored to the BSA's needs, conducted at Schiff in July and August. The next U.S. course took place at Philmont Scout Ranch that October. It was an event that passed into Scouting legend—unseasonable weather cut off food deliveries, and the thirty-five participants also had to cope with bitter cold and snow.

Wood Badge arrived in America just in time to provide Scouters with the skills they would need to deal with the huge wave of boys entering Scouting in the 1950s. Graduates of the Wood Badge course traditionally receive two wooden beads; in recognition of Hillcourt's role in leading the program in America, he became the first and only recipient of five beads.

In the late 1950s, Hillcourt focused his energies on writing the next edition of the *Boy Scout Handbook*—an effort he called "the most important task of my whole Scouting career"—in time for the BSA's fiftieth birthday. In 1965, he retired after more than a half century in Scouting and nearly forty years of service to the BSA. But his retirement was brief. In the years ahead—a turbulent era both for the country and for the Boy Scouts—Green Bar Bill's great talents would once again be needed.

SCOUTING ON THE NEW FRONTIER

On January 20, 1961, John F. Kennedy took the oath of office as the nation's thirty-fifth president. Kennedy was the first former Scout (he'd risen to Star rank) to win the nation's highest office. His stirring inaugural address called upon Americans to "ask not what your country can do for you—ask what you can do for your country."

Kennedy's inauguration ushered in a spirit of optimism in America. Cold War tensions were still high, it's true, but the possibilities of what he called "the New Frontier"—which would soon extend into outer space—seemed boundless. Much of that optimism would be shattered, though, when Kennedy fell to an assassin's bullet in Dallas less than three years later. America soon found itself contending with racial tensions at home, a controversial war abroad, and the rise of a youth "counterculture" that questioned many of the country's basic values. As young folk musician Bob Dylan put it in a 1964 song, the times were a-changing. And the Boy Scouts would change with them.

NOTABLE SCOUTS

JOHN F. KENNEDY
STAR SCOUT, PRESIDENT OF THE UNITED STATES

THE FIRST SCOUTS TO LIVE IN THE WHITE HOUSE were John Coolidge and Calvin Coolidge Jr.—the sons of President Calvin Coolidge, who succeeded to the presidency after the death of President Warren Harding in 1923. (Tragically, sixteen-year-old Calvin Jr. died of blood poisoning in 1924.) In 1961, John F. Kennedy took office, the first former Boy Scout to win the nation's top job. Kennedy was a member of Bronxville, New York's, Troop 2 from 1929 to 1931, reaching Star Scout rank. (Shortly after joining the troop, Kennedy wrote his father a letter requesting a raise in his allowance from 40 cents to 70 cents per week to "buy Scout things," including "canteens, haversacks, [and] blankets.")

As a U.S. representative and senator from Massachusetts in the 1940s and 1950s, Kennedy took an active role in the affairs of the BSA's Boston Council. In office, JFK often expressed his strong support for Scouting. In a May 1963 speech in West Virginia, Kennedy said, "I can't imagine better training for our younger citizens and I hope that this impressive evidence this morning of their strong patriotic feeling will be an inspiration to thousands of other young boys who, themselves, can become Scouts and demonstrate their desire for citizenship and also their strong love of their country." In another statement, the president noted: "For more than fifty years Scouting has played an important part in the lives of the Boy Scouts of this nation. It has helped to mold character, to form friendships, to provide a worthwhile outlet for the natural energies of growing boys, and to train these boys to become good citizens of the future. In a very real sense, the principles learned and practiced as Boy Scouts add to the strength of America and her ideals."

A plea for a raise
by Jack Kennedy

Dedicated to my
Mr. J. P. Kennedy

Chapter I

My recent allowance is 40¢. This I used for areoplanes and other playthings of childhood but now I am a scout and I put away my childish things. Before I would spend 20¢ of my 40¢ allowance and in five minutes I would have empty pockets and nothing to gain and 20¢ to lose. When I a a scout I have to buy

canteens, haversacks, blankets, searchlights, poncho things that will last for years and I can always use it while I can use a choloate marshmellow sunday with vanilla ice cream and so I put in my plea for a raise of thirty cents for me to buy scout things and pay my own way more around.

Finis

John Fitzgerald Kennedy
Finis

ABOVE In a letter to his father, a young Jack Kennedy asks for an allowance raise to "buy Scout things."

PART FOUR

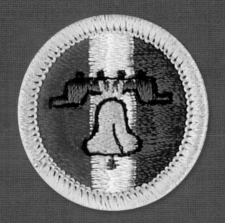

SCOUTING IN A CHANGING SOCIETY

1965 – 1979

In the 1960s, Scouting reached the stars—or at least the moon.

At the time of writing, more than half—180 out of 312—of all U.S. astronauts since NASA's original Mercury program in 1959 through the current space shuttle program have had some involvement in Scouting. Eleven of the twelve Americans to have walked on the moon were former Scouts, and Neil Armstrong—the first human to set foot on the moon—is an Eagle Scout. Among the millions of people who watched on TV as Armstrong (and his fellow astronaut, Edwin "Buzz" Aldrin—another former Scout) planted the Stars and Stripes on the moon on July 20, 1969, were the 35,000 Scouts and Scouters attending the national jamboree at Idaho's Farragut State Park.

Americans took justifiable pride in the nation's achievements in space exploration. But more earthly concerns dominated Scouting in the 1960s and 1970s.

THE INNER-CITY RURAL PROGRAM

The movement to the suburbs that powered Scouting's growth after World War II had a downside: the phenomenon dubbed "white flight." By the 1960s, and especially in the 1970s, many American cities were declining in population, and their residents were increasingly African American, Hispanic, and members of other minority groups. The migration of the middle class—combined with a decline in the industries that had provided city dwellers with the chance to earn at least a living wage—plunged many of the nation's urban areas into crisis. Widespread unemployment and the declining quality of public education and municipal services created conditions that led to a huge rise in crime rates (especially gang crimes), drug use, and the breakdown of traditional family structures.

At the same time, rural America was also experiencing a crisis. The population movement from the countryside to the cities, and then to the suburbs—plus the fact that agriculture was now an increasingly mechanized, corporate enterprise, leading many family farms to go bankrupt—left some rural areas (especially in the Appalachian region and on American Indian reservations) isolated from the American mainstream

ABOVE The Inner-City Rural Program brought Scouting to many underserved boys in urban areas.

NEIL ARMSTRONG
EAGLE SCOUT, ASTRONAUT

"THAT'S ONE SMALL STEP FOR MAN . . . one giant leap for mankind." Those words, crackling with static from a distance of almost 240,000 miles, signaled that astronaut Neil Armstrong had stepped from *Apollo 11*'s lunar module onto the surface of the moon—and that an Eagle Scout had taken the first steps on Earth's satellite.

Born in Wapakoneta, Ohio, in 1930, Armstrong joined Troop 25 in Upper Sandusky, Ohio, after his family moved there in 1941. When the Armstrongs returned to Wapakoneta in 1944, Neil continued in that town's Troop 14. Fascinated by aviation from an early age, one of Armstrong's favorite Scouting activities during the World War II years was making models of enemy warplanes to help civil-defense authorities in aircraft recognition. He reached Eagle Scout rank in 1947.

After two years at Purdue University, Armstrong entered the U.S. Navy, went through flight training, and ultimately flew seventy-eight combat missions as a fighter pilot in the Korean War—including a mission in which he had to eject from his jet after it was hit by anti-aircraft fire and lost part of a wing. After finishing his degree at Purdue, Armstrong became a test pilot. Flying mostly out of Edwards Air Force Base in California, he made more than 900 test flights in a variety of cutting-edge aircraft, taking some of them beyond the sound barrier and to the edge of space. He also volunteered as an adult leader with a local troop.

In 1962, he passed NASA's rigorous selection process and became an astronaut. He was the command pilot on the *Gemini 8* mission in 1966—a mission that saw the first docking between two spacecraft in Earth orbit. Three years later he blasted off into history aboard *Apollo 11*. Armstrong returned to Earth as one of the planet's most famous men, but after leaving active service in the U.S. space program in 1971 he chose to stay out of the limelight, spending his post-NASA years teaching at the University of Cincinnati (1971–1979), working on his Lebanon, Ohio, farm, and serving as a spokesman for and board member of various corporations. Armstrong's courage, coolness under pressure, and modesty have made him a hero to all Americans—and especially to Boy Scouts.

ABOVE (left) Neil Armstrong's boyhood Scout troop, with Neil standing at the far right. (right) Armstrong grew up to become an astronaut, and brought the distinction of a former Eagle Scout to the moon.

and plagued with the same problems of poverty, drugs, and crime that had begun to ravage the inner cities.

To combat these trends, the BSA's National Council launched one of its most ambitious initiatives—the Inner-City Rural Program—in 1965. Scouting's leaders wanted to show that the organization was not just a mostly white, middle-class movement, as some still saw it. Far more important, the program aimed to provide guidance and leadership to the boys who were the most "at risk" in American society.

The program was an outgrowth of the BSA's establishment of the Urban Relationship Service in 1961, which replaced the Inter-Racial Service founded in 1927. While the Urban Relationship Service was set up to serve boys of all races,

the Inner-City component of the Inner-City Rural Program focused its efforts on African American boys in the major cities of the Northeast, the Midwest, and the West Coast. This was in recognition of the fact that much of the nation's African American population, once centered in the rural South, had migrated to urban areas.

The Inner-City Rural Program kicked off with intensive efforts in eighteen urban and rural areas in which organizers—professional Scouters and local volunteers—explored new ways to bring Scouting to underserved boys. The traditional local Scouting structure of sponsorship by schools, churches, and other institutions didn't work in poor communities where residents couldn't spare a dollar, so the program's organizers experimented.

ABOVE African American Scouts marching on an inner-city street draw the attention of a young boy.

In Philadelphia, for example, the program achieved success with "Block Scouting"—recruiting boys in particular neighborhoods, often after a street-cleaning campaign that gained goodwill from local residents. The troops that sprang from these efforts met in private houses and storefronts instead of in the usual church basements or school gymnasiums. And in 1971, a *Time* magazine article described how "In Cincinnati, a Scoutmobile [van] threads its way through the ghetto, serving as a troop meeting place, a recruitment office and a library."

The devotion and bravery of the Inner-City Rural Program's organizers—and the boys they brought into Scouting—can't be praised enough. Boy Scouts have risked taunts and teasing when they appeared in uniform in public from the movement's

beginnings. But on the mean streets of the inner cities of the 1960s and 1970s, Scouts and Scouters risked getting beaten up—or worse. This was especially true in neighborhoods controlled by gangs, who saw Scout troops as intruders on their turf.

Still, in places, the Boy Scouts did indeed make serious inroads against the appeal of street gangs. In Philadelphia, for example, Clarence Phillips managed to organize two Cub Scout packs, two Scout troops, and an Explorer post in one of the city's housing projects—in the teeth of intimidation that included having his car trashed by gang members. As he put it, "After all, a Scout troop is nothing but a gang—a gang under proper supervision . . . a gang with direction." Taking the comparison even further, a 1975 *New York Times* article about Scouting's

ABOVE Boys brought into Scouting by the Inner-City Rural Program stand with Alden G. Barber (center, brown suit), Chief Scout Executive.

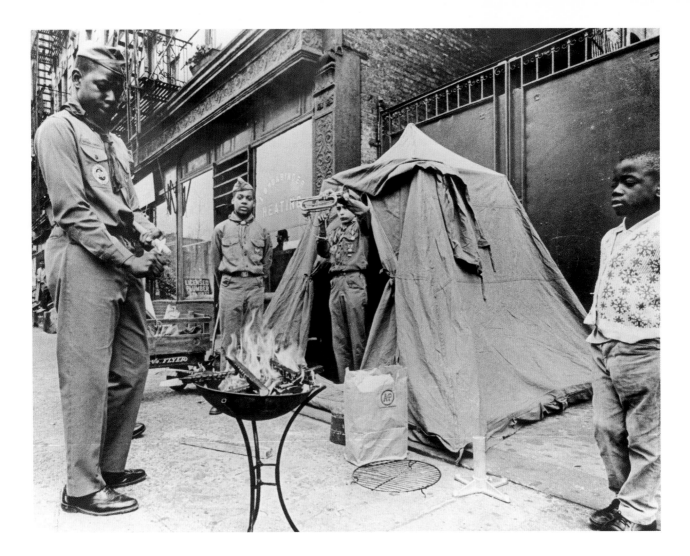

efforts in the city's poorer neighborhoods was headlined (referencing a change to the BSA's official headgear) "Gangs in Red Berets." Around the same time, New York's subway riders saw a poster that portrayed two African American Scouts and a Hispanic Scout, with a caption reading "JOIN OUR GANG . . . In this town, you better be prepared . . . New York is a tough place to grow up."

The Inner-City Rural Program also sought ways to make Scouting more relevant to boys growing up in places where asphalt and concrete were more common than grass. (For example, some inner-city troops expanded first-aid training to cover injuries like rat bites.) In general, this had the approval of the BSA's leadership. In the words of Alden G. Barber, Chief Scout Executive from 1967 to 1976, "The boy in the ghetto had no real basis for many of the things we [the BSA] talked about . . . so we had to make the program acceptable to him."

There was plenty of evidence, though, that what inner-city boys enjoyed most about Scouting were the same activities that had attracted boys to the movement from the start, regardless of their ethnicity, their financial status, or where they lived: camping, hiking, cooking out, and generally learning to enjoy life in the outdoors. The "outdoors" might mean a city park, but financial aid from local councils meant that many of the boys enrolled under the auspices of the Inner-City Rural

LEFT (top) These Scouts are all smiles in their uniforms. (bottom) Preparing for a Good Turn: carrying flowers, plants, and tools with their group leader. **ABOVE** Boys go camping on a city street, with their campfire blazing in a portable grill.

"[We] encourage every troop to offer some kind of outing at least once a month. It can be a day hike, a camping trip, or a conservation project—as long as it's something that gets them outdoors."

DAVID BATES, BSA DIRECTOR OF CAMPING AND CONSERVATION, 2006

Program could also enjoy weekend and summer camp outside the city.

Outdoor skills became a point of pride for many inner-city Scouts. As a thirteen-year-old senior patrol leader from Harlem, New York's, Troop 754 put it in a mid-1970s interview: "OK, say like there are some guys and they call us turkeys. Well, say we took those guys out into the woods. We *know* stuff in the woods, and those guys are going to get lost or, you know, hurt or something. So in the woods what I say is *you're* turkeys."

In overall terms, the Inner-City Rural Program was limited in scope, but its influence on the boys who came into Scouting through it was great. Of course, there was the sheer fun of Scouting, coupled with pride in personal achievement. But for many boys, their Scoutmaster also served as a role model and even as a surrogate father. Plus, participation in Scouting could give a disadvantaged young man an edge in making a better life for himself; a Scouting background carried weight on a job application or a college admission form. Scouting's emphasis

ABOVE Unconventional camping in a city park amid high-rise buildings.

on teamwork and self-discipline could also be an advantage in preparation for a career in the military—a field that many minority youth turned to after President Harry S. Truman ordered the desegregation of the armed forces in 1947.

The Inner-City Rural Program was just the most focused aspect of the BSA's efforts to make the benefits of Scouting readily available to all boys regardless of race. While most troops in the North were integrated by the early 1950s, integration in the South lagged behind—by some accounts there was only one fully integrated troop in the Deep South in the mid-1950s. This was partly due to resistance to integration from local councils and partly due to the fact that many local sponsoring organizations drew the color line and maintained separate (and mostly unequal) troops and packs for white and African American boys.

But now African Americans were gaining in their struggles. The Supreme Court's 1954 *Brown v. Board of Education* decision outlawed racial segregation in public schools. The next year, Rosa Parks's refusal to move to the back of the bus in Montgomery, Alabama, led to a boycott that propelled Dr. Martin Luther King Jr. to the leadership of a burgeoning civil rights movement. The federal Civil Rights Act passed in 1964, and the Voting Rights Act passed in 1965.

Scouting's tradition of racial inclusiveness moved with the pace of the times. In 1968, the BSA refused to charter segregated troops. It would take several more years, though, before full integration was achieved.

THE IMPROVED SCOUTING PROGRAM

In 1969, the BSA's membership stood at a little over 2 million—a

ABOVE Under the Scout Oath, all Scouts band together to help their community—whether they live in the country, the suburbs, or the inner city.

MERIT BADGES: A HISTORY

BESIDES THE CAMPFIRE AND THE UNIFORM, nothing is more emblematic of the Boy Scout experience in the public mind than merit badges—those cloth patches, each recognizing proficiency and knowledge in a specific area, that Scouts proudly display on a sash worn over the shoulder.

To meet a badge's requirements, a Scout meets with a merit badge counselor with expertise in the badge's subject. (Counselors are approved by local councils and districts, and must be registered adults with the BSA.) Besides working with counselors, Scouts can consult an expertly written pamphlet on each merit badge. Most troops maintain libraries of merit badge pamphlets, and many can be found in school and public libraries as well.

Nowadays, Scouts work toward a merit badge under a buddy system. After getting his merit badge application (often called a "blue card") signed by his Scoutmaster, the Scout must meet with the counselor in the presence of another person. According to the BSA's Advancement Guidelines, the buddy can be "another Scout, your parents or guardian, a brother or sister, a relative, or a friend." Once the Scout has fulfilled the merit badge's requirements to the counselor's satisfaction, the counselor signs the application, noting completion, which the Scout returns to his Scoutmaster. (And the Scout must do all that's required for the badge—there are no shortcuts or substitutes.) Typically, the Scout will receive his merit badge patch at his troop's next court of honor.

Most merit badges are "elective," but some are required for rank advancement, and the number of badges needed to advance, and which badges are required for a particular rank, has changed over time. In the BSA's early days, in fact, only Scouts who'd reached First Class rank were eligible to earn merit badges at all. Today's Scouts can start earning merit badges as soon as they join the troop, and achieving Star rank, for example, requires earning six merit badges, including four from the required list for Eagle Scout.

Merit badge subjects have changed with the times, too. The first crop of fifty or so badges introduced in the BSA's early years included subjects like Beekeeping and Blacksmithing that were later discontinued when they were no longer relevant to most Scouts' lives. Other merit badge subjects have been renamed—First Aid to Animals (1911) became Veterinary Science (1972) and then Veterinary Medicine (1995). Separate badges on related subjects have also been "folded" into single badges, too—Corn Farming, Cotton Farming, Food Crops, and other agriculture-themed badges were combined under the heading of Plant Science in the 1970s. The technological progress of the postwar period saw the introduction of badges like Electronics (1963), Space Exploration (1965), and Computers (1967). The BSA's emphasis on promoting multicultural awareness and dealing with pressing social concerns has led to a spate of new badges over the last three or so decades, including American Cultures (1979), Family Life (1991), Disabilities Awareness (1993), and Crime Prevention (1996). As of this writing, Scouts can earn 119 merit badges—a list that begins with American Business and ends with Woodwork. The most recent badge, Composite Materials, joined the list in 2006.

The physical form of the merit badge patch has changed over time, too. Originally, patches were squares of cloth embroidered with a circular design. The circular patch, still in use today, was introduced in 1934; patches had crimped edges until the early 1960s.

LEFT Old and current merit badges for Bee Keeping, Atomic Energy, Veterinary Science, and Law. **ABOVE** A sampling of the many Merit badges offered, including badges for Cooking, Pioneering, Bird Study, and American Business (top row, left to right).

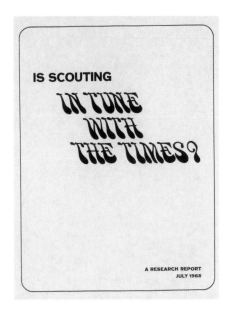

drop of about 65,000 from the previous year. That decline might seem insignificant, but it was the first dip in enrollment in many years. And it was a sign of things to come.

Slowing growth in the 1960s and 1970s was partly a simple matter of demographics. The baby boom ended around 1964, so the number of potential Scouts inevitably became smaller. Plus, Scouting continued to compete with other youth activities.

But there were more worrying trends at work. The optimism of the Kennedy years had been shattered by the president's

American frustration over poverty and lack of opportunity sparked riots in many American cities. The feminist movement sought equal rights for women, and many other groups—from Hispanics to American Indians—demanded bigger places at the American table. Music, television, movies, and literature—everything seemed to be in flux.

The 1960s also saw the rise of a youth counterculture as many baby boomers rejected—or at least questioned—the values they'd been raised with. They preached distrust of the

The BSA's national leadership was concerned not only for the organization's public image, but—much more important— it worried that the organization was no longer serving the needs of individual boys, and the nation as a whole, as best it could.

assassination in 1963, and further undermined by the murder of other leaders, including Robert Kennedy and Martin Luther King Jr. later in the decade. America found itself embroiled in a war in Vietnam—a conflict that became increasingly controversial and divisive as the 1960s wore on. Despite the civil rights advances in the early years of the decade, African

government, organized religion, and traditional values in sexuality and relationships, and they championed maximum freedom for the individual—including the freedom to take illegal drugs, which became a major national problem in these years.

To those on the younger side of what was now called "the generation gap," the Boy Scouts seemed like an old-fashioned

ABOVE (left) Investigative research report on the effects and merits of Scouting, from July 1968. (middle) Scoutmaster with Scouts wearing the new red berets. (right) A version of the newly titled *Scout Handbook* cover, with painting by Joseph Csatari, eighth edition, 1972. RIGHT Front of an announcement about the Improved Scouting Program, responding to a growing perception that Scouting was outdated.

IMPROVED SCOUTING PROGRAM

Improvements
: The improved Scouting program will be launched in early September 1972 to provide a relevant, educational plan that is sensitive to the real needs of youth wherever they may live. For boys from 11 years (or graduated from the fifth grade) through 17 years, the Scouting program will help provide the skills, attitudes, and knowledge required for tomorrow's citizens.

Background
: Since 1968 the Boy Scouting Committee of the Boy Scouts of America has supervised research projects, experiments, and evaluations to provide for boys an effective program designed to build desirable qualities of character, to train in the responsibilities of participating citizenship, and to develop in them personal fitness. The improved Scouting program was approved by the Executive Board in May 1971, and literature and other materials will be available in the fall of 1972.

In the (name) Council, there are (number) troops and (number) Scouts participating in the Scouting program in (number) partner organizations.

Objectives
: The three objectives to be achieved through the improved Scouting program are:

1. Citizenship - growth experiences and participation in the community by which a Scout learns his responsibility and makes a practical application of group skills.

2. Character - growth experiences by which a Scout will acquire desirable personality traits.

3. Personal Fitness - opportunities for a Scout to develop and improve himself in the areas of physical, mental, moral, and emotional fitness.

Aims
: The improvements identify Scouting's traditional strengths and provide ways of making these more effective. Among these are: (1) the patrol method; (2) the boy-man relationship with the Scoutmaster acting as a coach and counselor to boy leaders; (3) the adventure provided by introducing boys to the world around them and helping them to find their place in it, both through outdoor and indoor experiences; (4) the use of Scouting ideals as a personal challenge to boys.

All of these familiar elements of the Scouting program are retained, and there is a return to some original concepts of Scouting. Major thrusts of the Scouting improvements relate to relevant advancement, leadership development, greater boy involvement, and a program for older boys in the troop.

OVER

Advancement   The advancement program, which in the (name) Council is under the direction of (full name, business title), chairman of the council advancement committee, is one of the vital methods that aid in a boy's growth. Optional routes encourage a Scout to accomplish a progressive series of learning experiences concerned with the development of character and improved personal fitness. Three new ingredients in the improved advancement plan are:

1. Skill Awards - fundamental skills a Scout needs to enjoy the program. They provide earlier recognition, retain a strong outdoor emphasis, provide essential skills for everyday living, and give Scouts options and place them in a position to make decisions. The 12 skill awards, which generally combine the present Second and First Class skills plus a number of new skills, are: Camping, Citizenship, Communications, Community Living, Conservation, Cooking, Environment, Family Living, First Aid, Hiking, Physical Fitness, and Swimming.

2. Merit Badge Program - offered to new Scouts so they can become acquainted at an early stage in Scouting with one of the major parts of the advancement plan. New merit badges will include Emergency Preparedness, Personal Management, Sports, Environmental Science, General Science and Citizenship in the World.

3. Personal Growth Agreement - an appraisal by the Scout of his abilities after which he agrees to set personal goals for accomplishment.

Tenderfoot, Second Class, and First Class progress awards require Scout participation, Scout spirit, basic skill awards, merit badges, and the personal growth agreement. Star, Life, and Eagle progress awards require Scout participation, Scout spirit, merit badges, the personal growth agreement, service projects, and service as a patrol or troop leader.

Boy Involvement   One of the major aims of the Scouting improvements is to provide many opportunities for a boy to make decisions and to develop a sense of responsibility for his own growth development. While recognizing the limitations of boys in making decisions, it was felt the present Scouting program has many restrictions that prevent boys from exercising their judgment. In the patrol and troop organization, boys will have more opportunities to make decisions and to help significantly in running the troop. Throughout the advancement plan, the boy will choose a route that he may follow and a skill that he may acquire. Most important, he takes a look at himself and decides on areas of personal development which he can concentrate on in order to grow.

Leadership Corps   Recognizing that in Scouting there is a strength in the number of older boys who want to stay in the troop, there will be an optional program called the "leadership corps." Its primary objectives will be to complete the training of boys in leadership skills and enable them to practice these skills by helping young boys. There will also be greater opportunity to serve the community through participation in more mature activities, and there will be a continued fellowship in activities that are challenging and beneficial to their future.

January 1972

and increasingly irrelevant movement. In an echo of the controversies of the organization's early years, some Americans again saw the Boy Scouts—with its uniforms and structured leadership and advancement—as militaristic, at a time when the military was in disrepute over Vietnam. Scoutmasters and other adult leaders began to be stereotyped as overgrown bullies. And what was the point, some asked, of having boys run around in the woods trying to make fire by rubbing two sticks together (another stereotype) when the nation's inner cities were burning, when pollution threatened the quality of the country's air, water, and other natural resources, and when American society as a whole was undergoing profound changes?

In 1971, a change to a line of the Cub Scout Promise underscored the growing problems Scouting faced. Instead of promising to "be square," Cub Scouts now pledged "to help other people." For decades, to "be square" meant to be fair and honest; but now it was a derisive slang term used to describe someone who wasn't "hip" or "cool."

The BSA's national leadership was concerned not only for the organization's public image, but—much more important—it worried that the organization was no longer serving the needs of individual boys, and the nation as a whole, as best it could.

In 1969, the BSA's National Executive Board commissioned a wide-ranging study from the market-research firm Daniel Yankelovich, Inc. The study found that many boys (especially at the upper end of the age range) did describe Scouting as "too organized" and "kind of out of date."

The Yankelovich study led to the introduction of the Improved Scouting Program in September 1972, which ushered in the most profound—and controversial—changes in the BSA's sixty-two-year history.

LEFT Back of an announcement about the Improved Scouting Program. **ABOVE** A boy from the Improved Scouting Program era shakes hands with his Scoutmaster.

MERIT BADGE REQUIREMENTS

TO GIVE AN IDEA OF WHAT MERIT BADGE requirements are like, here are recent requirements for the Camping merit badge:

· Show that you know first aid for and how to prevent injuries or illnesses that could occur while camping, including hypothermia, frostbite, heat reactions, dehydration, altitude sickness, insect stings, tick bites, snakebite, blisters, and hyperventilation.

· Learn the Leave No Trace principles and the Outdoor Code and explain what they mean. Write a personal plan for implementing these principles on your next outing.

· Make a written plan for an overnight trek and show how to get to your camping spot using a topographical map and compass OR a topographical map and a GPS receiver. If no GPS receiver unit is available, explain how to use one to get to your camping spot.

· Make a duty roster showing how your patrol is organized for an actual overnight campout. List assignments for each member.

· Help a Scout patrol or a Webelos Scout unit in your area prepare for an actual campout, including creating the duty roster, menu planning, equipment needs, general planning, and setting up camp.

· Prepare a list of clothing you would need for overnight campouts in both warm and cold weather. Explain the term "layering."

· Discuss footwear for different kinds of weather and how the right footwear is important for protecting your feet.

· Explain the proper care and storage of camping equipment (clothing, footwear, bedding).

· List the outdoor essentials necessary for any campout, and explain why each item is needed.

· Present yourself to your Scoutmaster with your pack for inspection. Be correctly clothed and equipped for an overnight campout.

· Describe the features of four types of tents, when and where they could be used, and how to care for tents. Working with another Scout, pitch a tent.

· Discuss the importance of camp sanitation and tell why water treatment is essential. Then demonstrate two ways to treat water.

· Describe the factors to be considered in deciding where to pitch your tent.

· Tell the difference between internal- and external-frame packs. Discuss the advantages and disadvantages of each.

· Discuss the types of sleeping bags and what kind would be suitable for different conditions. Explain the proper care of your sleeping bag and how to keep it dry. Make a comfortable ground bed.

Prepare for an overnight campout with your patrol:

· Make a checklist of personal and patrol gear that will be needed.

· Pack your own gear and your share of the patrol equipment and food for proper carrying. Show that your pack is right for quickly getting what is needed first, and that it has been assembled properly for comfort, weight, balance, size, and neatness.

· Explain the safety procedures for using a propane or butane/propane stove, using a liquid fuel stove, and proper storage of extra fuel

· Discuss the advantages and disadvantages of different types of lightweight cooking stoves.

· Prepare a camp menu. Explain how the menu would differ from a menu for a backpacking or float trip. Give recipes and make a food list for your patrol. Plan two breakfasts, three lunches, and two suppers. Discuss how to protect your food against bad weather, animals, and contamination.

· Cook at least one breakfast, one lunch, and one dinner for your patrol from the meals you have planned . . . At least one of those meals must be a trail meal requiring the use of a lightweight stove.

Show experience in camping:

· Camp a total of at least 20 days and 20 nights. Sleep each night under the sky or in a tent you have pitched. The 20 days and 20 nights must be at a designated Scouting activity or event. You may use a week of long-term camp toward this requirement. If the camp provides a tent that has already been pitched, you need not pitch your own tent.

· On any of these camping experiences, you must do TWO of the following, only with proper preparation and under qualified supervision: hike up a mountain, gaining at least 1,000 vertical feet; backpack, snowshoe, or cross-country ski for at least four miles; take a bike trip of at least fifteen miles or at least four hours; plan and carry out a float trip of at least four hours; plan and carry out an overnight snow camping experience; rappel down a rappel route of thirty feet or more; perform a conservation project approved by the landowner or land managing agency.

· Discuss how the things you did to earn this badge have taught you about personal health and safety, survival, public health, conservation, and good citizenship. In your discussion, tell how Scout spirit and the Scout Oath and Law apply to camping and outdoor ethics.

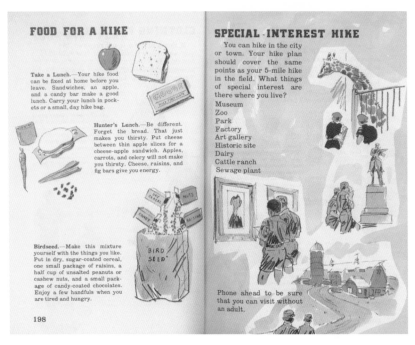

One of the major goals of the new program was to make Scouting relevant to all boys, whether they lived in the country, the suburbs, or the inner city. In fact, the Improved Scouting Program was inspired by parts of the Inner-City Rural Program.

This could be seen in the eighth edition (1972) of the *Scout Handbook*. It was a radical departure from earlier editions. The cover itself made a statement. The covers of most previous

the *Boy Scout Handbook*. As the British Scout Association had done in the mid-1960s, the BSA had decided to de-emphasize the word *boy*. In part this was to avoid any negative associations with the word. It was also recognition of the growing number of girls and women taking part in the movement.

But the changes to the cover and the title were minor in comparison to the changes inside the new *Handbook*. As one writer later put it, "Gone were signaling, map-making, canoeing,

One of the major goals of the new [Improved Scouting Program] was to make Scouting relevant to all boys, whether they lived in the country, the suburbs, or the inner city.

handbooks had shown Scouts having fun outdoors. The new handbook featured a group of Scouts (wearing the new red beret) peering at the moon through a telescope. There was nothing to indicate whether the scene was set in a campsite or a classroom.

The title was a departure, too. Although the words *Boy Scouts of America* appeared on the cover, it was the *Scout Handbook*, not

tracking, and fire by friction. In their place were sections on drug abuse, family finances, child care, community problems, and current events." In the drive for relevance, especially to boys in an urban environment, the eighth edition scrapped much of the information about outdoor skills that had been a mainstay of the *Handbook* from its first edition in 1911. The section on hiking, for example, was geared as much to city streets as to

ABOVE A sample of the *Scout Handbook*, eighth edition. The cover embraces America's new obsession with space exploration and has removed the word *boy* from the title, both to make a statement on the BSA's relevence.

HOME INSPECTION

Knowing the most common kinds of accidents will help in your home inspection. Especially if you know what causes them. Remember, finding the danger is only the first step. It won't do any good unless the things you find are changed.

Here are the major problem areas:

Falls. — Slippery bathtubs and showers. Cluttered stairways. Broken or weak stair railings. Loose throw rugs. Toys like skates and marbles underfoot. Improperly lighted areas.

Wounds. — Using or storing knives and tools wrong. Guns loaded and not locked up. Broken glass and tin cans. Falls against sharp things. Bumping into clear-glass doors. Animal bites.

Fires. — Matches where children can reach them. Trash near stoves and heaters. Oily rags. Overfused and overloaded electrical circuits. Wrong use of extension cords. Frayed electric wires. Ashtrays emptied wrong. Grease fires in kitchens.

Poisons. — Medicine, pesticides, and cleaning items where children can get them. Leaded paint used where children can eat it. Unvented gas or oil heaters. Cars run in closed garages.

RESCUES

Never try a swimming rescue if you can do it a better way. And a better way is always without risk to your own life. These better ways are reaching, throwing, or going with support. Don't try a swimming rescue unless you have been trained in lifesaving.

Throwing. — When the person is too far to reach and you have a ring buoy or a rope, throw it. Keep hold of one end so you can pull the person in. If you don't have a buoy, a rope coil can be thrown quite far.

Going With Support. — For longer distances, use a boat, surfboard, or something else that floats. Keep your eye on the person you are going to help.

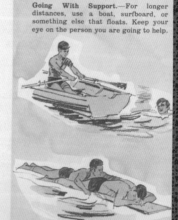

Reaching. — You stay in touch with shore or a dock or pier. You reach with a pole, an oar, a shirt, or even yourself to the person in trouble. But you always hold on to your base.

backwoods trails; it reminded boys to bring along change for pay toilets and advised them to consult the nearest policeman if they got lost.

The Improved Scouting Program also changed the role of Scoutmasters and junior leaders. Older boys in troops—who'd been designated as Senior Scouts since the late 1950s—became members of a troop "Leadership Corps," with their own separate activities and their own forest-green uniforms. (Scouts aged fourteen and fifteen were considered part of the Leadership Corps; older Scouts were supposed to move up to junior assistant Scoutmaster status or transfer to the Explorers.) A program called TLD (Troop Leader Development) was introduced for youth leaders.

Scoutmasters were now expected to be "managers of learning," and to hold "personal growth agreement conferences" with Scouts before they moved up in rank, and they were encouraged to master a "Cornerstone" leadership program based on eleven "competencies." Many Scoutmasters felt that they hadn't volunteered to become "counselors" instead of leaders, and they weren't comfortable with their new responsibilities.

But the single biggest change introduced by the program was to advancement. Previously, Scouts had to master a long list of skills—cooking, camping, swimming, first aid, etc.—until they reached First Class rank. Only then could they begin earning merit badges. Under the new system, however, even Tenderfoot Scouts could earn merit badges. Also, previously, Scouts had to wait for some time between fulfilling the requirements for a merit badge and receiving the actual cloth patch to sew on their merit badge sashes. Now, Scouts who earned merit badges got their patches immediately, and their achievement was acknowledged at a troop ceremony—the court of honor, which also recognized Scouts who'd moved up in rank.

The system didn't do away with skill requirements in important subjects, but these were now recognized in a new way—by a dozen "skill awards" (Camping, Citizenship, Communications, Community Living, Conservation, Cooking, Environment, Family Living, First Aid, Hiking, Physical Fitness, Swimming). Some were "elective"; others were required to move up the advancement trail from Tenderfoot to First Class Scout.

The skill awards were physically distinct from merit badges, being a painted brass loop worn on the Scout's uniform belt.

The idea behind the skill-award system was to give boys immediate recognition for achievement and motivate them to advance further. Some Scouters, however, noted that the new system made it possible for boys to advance without really mastering the basic elements of Scoutcraft that had anchored the program from its beginning. In the words of Scouting historian Robert W. Peterson, "[It] was possible to become a First Class Scout without ever going hiking or camping or cooking over an open fire." (The BSA would ultimately phase out skill awards in 1989.)

Even worse to many Scout leaders was the fact that under the Improved Scouting Program, several of the merit badges previously required for advancement to Eagle Scout rank became optional. In the words of a Buffalo, New York, Scoutmaster: "[Eagle] rank, respected throughout the country as a top-notch achievement for youth, has been cheapened drastically. By the elimination of Camping, Cooking, Nature and other [merit] badges heretofore required, a Scout may become an Eagle virtually without ever setting foot past his city line."

LEFT Pages from a Scout Handbook, eighth edition. **ABOVE** Display case of the twelve skill awards that Scouts could wear on their belts as reproduced in a 1990s collector set.

The Improved Scouting Program caused controversy from the start, at every level of the organization. Some Scoutmasters welcomed the changes and noted that their Scouts thrived under the new system. Certainly, Improved Scouting was a laudable attempt to meet new social challenges and to extend Scouting's range into underserved areas—something that had concerned the BSA from its inception. The new emphasis on personal growth and on helping one's family and community was also a praiseworthy effort. But from early on in the Improved Scouting era, there were plenty of critics who believed that the BSA was diluting the very things that attracted boys to Scouting to begin with. As "Green Bar Bill" Hillcourt—who would soon be called upon to deal with the fallout from the program—later said: "In 1969 we [the BSA] came out with some research with the title, 'Is Scouting in tune with the times?' Scouting has never been in tune with the times! Even in 1908 it was idiotic to suggest that you should go out and do camping because everybody knew

that the night air was bad for you—you could get malaria, for heaven's sake."

Membership in Scouting continued to decline in the 1970s, with enrollment down by as much as one-third over previous decades. Again, a lot of this had to do with demographics (the baby boom had turned into the baby bust) and with popular culture (many boys and young men now loathed the idea of wearing a uniform, and preferred going to a rock concert over camping out). If the period from roughly 1945 to 1970 was the "golden age" of American Scouting, the 1970s was, to a certain extent, its dark age.

The fall in membership wasn't limited to youth. The vast pool of adult volunteers who'd been so important to Scouting's growth after World War II began to dry up in the 1970s. Here, economics played a big part. After nearly three decades of postwar prosperity, the U.S. economy began to falter in the mid-1970s. Recession, inflation, and rising energy costs led to people working longer hours and having less disposable income; this translated into less time to volunteer for and less money to spend on activities like Scouting. Many of the women who had previously had the time to serve as den mothers and in troop auxiliaries were now working outside the home, whether out of the desire for personal fulfillment or out of the need to support their families.

Still, there were many people—both inside the BSA and outside of it—who blamed the Improved Scouting Program, as least in part, for the movement's woes.

THE OLD—AND THE NEW

While the Boy Scouts had their troubles in the late 1960s and 1970s, the BSA's other programs—Cub Scouting and Exploring—had a somewhat better time of it.

As with the Boy Scouts, the post-1964 baby bust also led to a drop in Cub Scout enrollment during the decade—from a high of 2,486,706 boys in 1972 (when Cub Scouts and their adult leaders represented 51 percent of the BSA's overall membership) to 1,717,905 in 1979—but the program remained strong. And also like the Boy Scouts, Cub Scouting's advancement system got an overhaul during this era.

ABOVE While some criticized aspects of Improved Scouting, such as changes to rank requirements, many Scouts thrived under the changes.

WEBELOS
WE-BE-LO-S
WE'LL BE LOYAL SCOUTS

WELCOME TO THE WEBELOS DEN!
You are now a Webelos Scout and a member of the older boys' den. You must be 10 years old to join this den.

...today to be ...orrow. ...s that We- ...the oldest ...k and that ...s who can ...ball farther ...r than most

...are always ...something ...Scouts are ...d, enthusi-

3

...e an Indian name, doesn't it? (Say ...he name of the Indian tribe where ...s has a secret meaning:

...WE-BE-LO-S
...BE LOYAL SCOUTS

Webelos Scouts wear the Webelos badge colors on the right sleeve with the appropriate den number. You get the Webelos badge colors when you are inducted into the den at a pack meeting. Your Cubmaster or Webelos den leader will give it to you.

Ask your mother to take off your old den number and pin the Webelos badge colors in place. Tell her to look on the inside of the back cover of this book to find out where to put it.

IF YOU HAVE NEVER BEEN A CUB SCOUT BEFORE: You will learn the Cub Scout Promise and Law of the Pack when you are inducted into the Webelos den. To learn these things, and other signs and secrets of Cub Scouting, turn to page 297 in this book.

4

THE WEBELOS DEN MEETING

Your Webelos den will meet in the early evenings or on Saturday each week. At these meetings you will have a chance to work on the requirements of the activity areas you choose.

You will learn new skills and improve your work in skills you already have. Go to all the meetings and get plenty of practice.

Sometimes the Webelos den will go on special outings. All of this is meant to prepare you to become a Boy Scout.

THE PACK MEETING

The Webelos den plays an important part in pack meetings. You may be asked by the Cubmaster to help set up the meeting room or usher parents to their seats. Or you may be asked to show some of the skills you have learned —things the younger boys would not be able to do.

At each pack meeting the Webelos Scouts who have earned badges during the month will receive them in a special ceremony. Your Webelos den leader will be in this ceremony with you and give your badge to you.

5

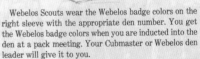

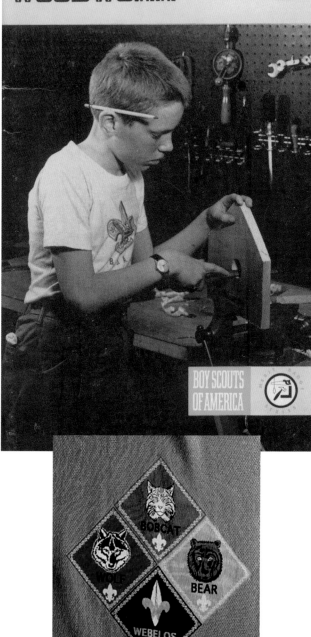

WOODWORK

BOY SCOUTS
OF AMERICA

BOBCAT

WOLF

BEAR

WEBELOS

To emphasize the new Webelos program, the BSA got rid of the Lion rank for Cubs. Instead, Cub Scouts aged ten and up formed their own Webelos dens within packs. These boys were called "Webelos Scouts," instead of just "Webelos." They could choose to wear a Boy Scout–style uniform and earn up to fifteen (later, twenty) special activity badges. (The original badges were Aquanaut, Artist, Athlete, Citizen, Craftsman, Engineer, Forester, Geologist, Naturalist, Outdoorsman, Scholar, Scientist, Showman, Sportsman, and Traveler.)

Cub Scout advancement was further refined in 1975, with the establishment of five ranks: Bobcat, Wolf, Bear, Webelos, and the Arrow of Light. The latter rank honored Webelos Scouts who were eleven years old (or who were ten-and-a-half and had completed the fifth grade) and who had fulfilled the requirements needed to move up to the Boy Scouts.

Cub Scouts also got increased opportunities to camp. As part of the philosophy of keeping Cub Scouting "separate" from Boy Scouting, there wasn't much emphasis on camping in Cub Scouting's first decades. In 1968, though, the BSA approved day camping for Cub Scouts, and in the 1970s many councils set up overnight camping for Cub Scouts as well—often in the form of father-son weekends at the council's summer camp. The BSA also introduced some special educational programs just for Cub Scouts, including the Safe Bicycle Driving Program, Cub Scout Physical Fitness Program (both 1974), and the Learn to Swim Program (1975).

Women continued to be a mainstay of Cub Scout leadership and they were no longer limited to den mother status. From 1976 on, women could serve as Cubmasters and assistant Cubmasters. (By then, the BSA had established a special award for outstanding service by women—the Silver Fawn—but it was discontinued in 1974 when both men and women became eligible for the Silver Beaver Award.)

Exploring was another success story of the 1970s, thanks to the switch to a special-interest and career-based orientation for the movement. By the latter part of the decade, enrollment in Explorer posts was in the 500,000 range annually, with membership gains of around 25 percent per year. And many Explorers were young women; after some experimenting in the

ABOVE (top) Merit badge pamphlet on how to earn the Woodwork merit badge, shown in the lower right corner. (bottom) Emblems of the five ranks of the Cub Scouts. The Arrow of Light, bottom, was added in 1975 to provide a segue into the Boy Scouts. **RIGHT** Pages from the Webelos Scout Book.

You can earn money for your uniform by making and selling handicraft articles, weeding gardens, shoveling snow, mowing lawns, cleaning windows, taking care of a furnace, removing ashes, washing cars, washing dogs, taking care of pets while owners are away, baby-sitting, or running errands.

The distinctive parts of your Webelos Scout uniform tell everyone that you are an older Cub Scout, a member of the Webelos den, and that you expect to become a Boy Scout when you graduate from the pack. Wear your uniform on all Scouting activities—hiking, special service projects, demonstrations, special church services, Boy Scout Week activities, den and pack meetings.

YOUR NECKERCHIEF

A. Roll long edge over upon itself in several narrow flat folds to about 6 inches from tip of neckerchief.
B. Place around neck of V-neck shirt or over collar of official long-sleeved shirt. (The collar of a long-sleeved shirt may be turned under when wearing the neckerchief.)
C. Draw neckerchief slide over ends and adjust to fit snugly. Wear ends loose or tied in a slip knot as preferred by the pack.

ACTIVITY BADGES

To help satisfy your 10-year-old curiosity, a challenging new group of activity badge areas has been developed for you to work on. You can earn as many as 15 of them or as few as none—it depends upon how much ambition you have—how much "get up and go."

AQUANAUT

NATURALIST

CITIZEN

GEOLOGIST

FORESTER

SCHOLAR

SCIENTIST

TRAVELER

SHOWMAN

OUTDOORSMAN

ARTIST

CRAFTSMAN

ENGINEER

ATHLETE

SPORTSMAN

WEBELOS DEN LEADER

Your Webelos den leader is a man who likes and understands boys. He knows all about Boy Scouting and will help you get ready for it.

He will teach you the right way to do lots of interesting things like building a fire and cooking a meal. He will be a good guide on the road to Boy Scouting.

Your den leader knows the importance of "Do Your Best" and will help you improve your skills and learn new ones.

He knows the importance of ideals, he believes in God and the greatness of America. He believes in you and the man you will one day become. That is why he takes the time to lead your Webelos den.

You can say thank-you for what he is doing for you by attending the den meetings and taking part in the special activities.

ASK YOUR FRIENDS TO JOIN

Boys you go to school with or live near may want to become Webelos Scouts, too. Tell them about it; take them to a den meeting. If they are 10 years old, they may join.

IF THEY HAVE NEVER BEEN CUB SCOUTS

The Webelos den leader will ask them to pass the Bobcat requirements just as you did a long time ago. Show them what they will have to do on page 296 of this book if they want to join.

WEBELOS DEN CHIEF

Your Webelos den chief will be a Boy Scout or Explorer who is trained to lead Webelos Scouts. Probably he will be an older Scout than the one who was den chief for the den you were in as a Cub Scout.

WEBELOS DENNER

One of the members of your den —it might be you—will be elected as the Webelos denner to assist the den chief.

YOUR NEW UNIFORM

As the Indian boy became older and wiser in the ways of his people, he gradually changed his boy's clothes for those of a young warrior. So you will add to your uniform the markings of a Webelos Scout.

ON THIS PAGE Webelos Scouts on a canoe adventure.

late 1960s and a lively debate, Exploring became fully co-ed in 1969. Females eventually made up about one-quarter of all Explorers by the 1980s.

Many Explorer posts remained focused on hobbies, sports, and outdoor activities—from bowling to theater. (Athletically inclined Explorers gathered for the first National Explorer Olympics, held in Fort Collins, Colorado, in 1970.) But the real

but all share the purpose of Exploring—the improvement of character, citizenship, and fitness." Exploring also expanded into the nation's public schools, with adult leaders visiting classrooms to conduct seminars, set up in-school programs, and organize field trips.

The Boy Scouts was striving to stay in tune with the times during this era, but in some respects, the times were catching up

Exploring was another success story of the 1970s, thanks to the switch to a special-interest and career-based orientation for the movement.

engine of growth for Exploring was the proliferation of "career awareness" posts sponsored by institutions ranging from local hospitals and police and fire departments to major corporations such as IBM and U.S. Steel.

In the words of Scouting historian Carolyn Soto, "A program in data processing, for example, might be designed by a computer center for its Explorer post. Likewise, an aeronautical firm might design a program for Explorers who have an interest in aviation. . . . The program of each post is developed around the interests and capabilities of the adults in the organization,

to the Scouts. Respect for the environment and taking an active role in conservation of natural resources were a hallmark of the movement from the BSA's founding days. But by the 1970s, the impact of pollution on the environment and the depletion of natural resources were a national concern. The Boy Scouts was in the forefront of the new ecological/environmental movement; it introduced an Environmental Science merit badge in 1972, and it became a required merit badge for Eagle Scout.

The centerpiece of the BSA's involvement was Project SOAR—which stood for "Save Our American Resources."

ABOVE (left) Winners at the first National Explorer Olympics, 1970. (right) The Silver Fawn Award, presented to extraordinary women who led in the Cub Scouts.

GERALD FORD
EAGLE SCOUT, PRESIDENT OF THE UNITED STATES

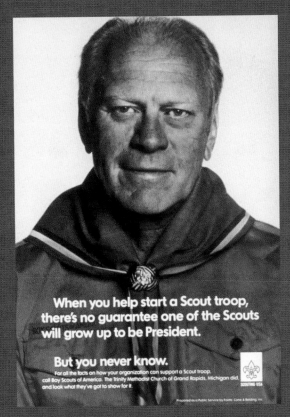

When you help start a Scout troop, there's no guarantee one of the Scouts will grow up to be President.

But you never know.

For all the facts on how your organization can support a Scout troop, call Boy Scouts of America. The Trinity Methodist Church of Grand Rapids, Michigan did, and look what they've got to show for it.

SCOUTING USA

Prepared as a Public Service by Foote, Cone & Belding, Inc.

THE ONLY EAGLE SCOUT (SO FAR) TO ATTAIN THE PRESIDENCY.
Gerald Ford was born Leslie King Jr. in Omaha, Nebraska, in 1913. (His name was changed after his parents' divorce and his mother's remarriage.) Ford grew up in Grand Rapids, Michigan, where he rose to Eagle Scout rank in 1927 as a member of Troop 215. "One of the proudest moments of my life," Ford said more than four decades later, "came in the court of honor when I was awarded the Eagle Scout badge. I still have that badge. It is a treasured possession."

Ford was also an excellent athlete, playing center and linebacker in high school and, later, at the University of Michigan. In fact, Ford was offered professional contracts by the Detroit Lions and the Green Bay Packers, but he turned them down to go on to law school at Yale University. He left his newly established law practice to serve as a naval officer in the Pacific during World War II. After the war, Ford won election to the U.S. House of Representatives as a Republican in 1948, beginning a congressional career that lasted a quarter century, capped by eight years (1965–1973) as House minority leader. In the House, Ford certainly lived up to the Scout Law's point that "A Scout is friendly"; he gained a reputation for getting along with everyone, regardless of party affiliation. As one of his colleagues put it, "What I like about Jerry Ford is that he just doesn't have any enemies."

When Vice President Spiro Agnew resigned in October 1973, Congress confirmed President Nixon's appointment of Ford as vice president. Less than a year later, however, Nixon himself resigned in the wake of the Watergate scandal, and Ford found himself in the White House. He became chief executive at a very troubled time in American history. Watergate and the Vietnam War had shaken America's faith in itself; the economy was flagging, and Americans were still coming to grips with the social upheavals of the 1960s. Ford's calm, genial leadership did much to restore national confidence. He failed to win election in his own right in 1976, but the victor, Jimmy Carter, acknowledged Ford's leadership in his inaugural address: "For myself and for our nation, I want to thank my predecessor for all he has done to heal our land."

Ford died on December 26, 2006, aged ninety-three. At his family's request, Eagle Scouts played a major role in the ceremonies marking Ford's passing. An honor guard of more than 100 Eagle Scouts from the National Capital Area Council assisted at Ford's funeral service at Washington, D.C.'s, National Cathedral on January 2, 2007. Two days later, another honor guard of 400 Eagle Scouts of all ages paid their respects as the former president's body was returned to Grand Rapids for burial. The guard included eight Scouts from Troop 215, Ford's boyhood troop. It was a fitting send-off for the man who had stated that "I can say without hesitation, because of Scouting principles, I know I was a better athlete, I was a better naval officer, I was a better congressman, and I was a better prepared president."

PROJECT

Save Our American Resources

1971 PROJECT **SOAR**
SAVE OUR AMERICAN RESOURCES

BOY SCOUTS OF AMERICA

Begun in 1970, SOAR was envisioned as a new national Good Turn—but one that would be ongoing, instead of just limited to a single year, as had most previous Good Turns. The program also encompassed all of Scouting, including Cub Scout packs and Explorer posts. Some 60,000 units took part in SOAR's first year, doing everything from picking up garbage along highways to planting trees to halt soil erosion in parks and campgrounds. On June 5, 1971, no fewer than 2 million Scouts and Scouters cleaned up an estimated million tons of litter across the country as part of Keep America Beautiful Day. SOAR continued for several years.

The BSA also expanded its long-standing tradition of service to mentally and physically disabled youth. Merit badge pamphlets and other instructional materials, for example, had

LEFT (top) SOAR prompts millions of Scouts to do a Good Turn for Planet Earth, like these boys sorting newspaper at a recycling facility. (bottom) Scoutmasters get in on helping Project SOAR be a success. **ABOVE** (top) Project SOAR debuts in response to the new concern for environmental protection, 1970. (bottom) Project SOAR pamphlet, 1971.

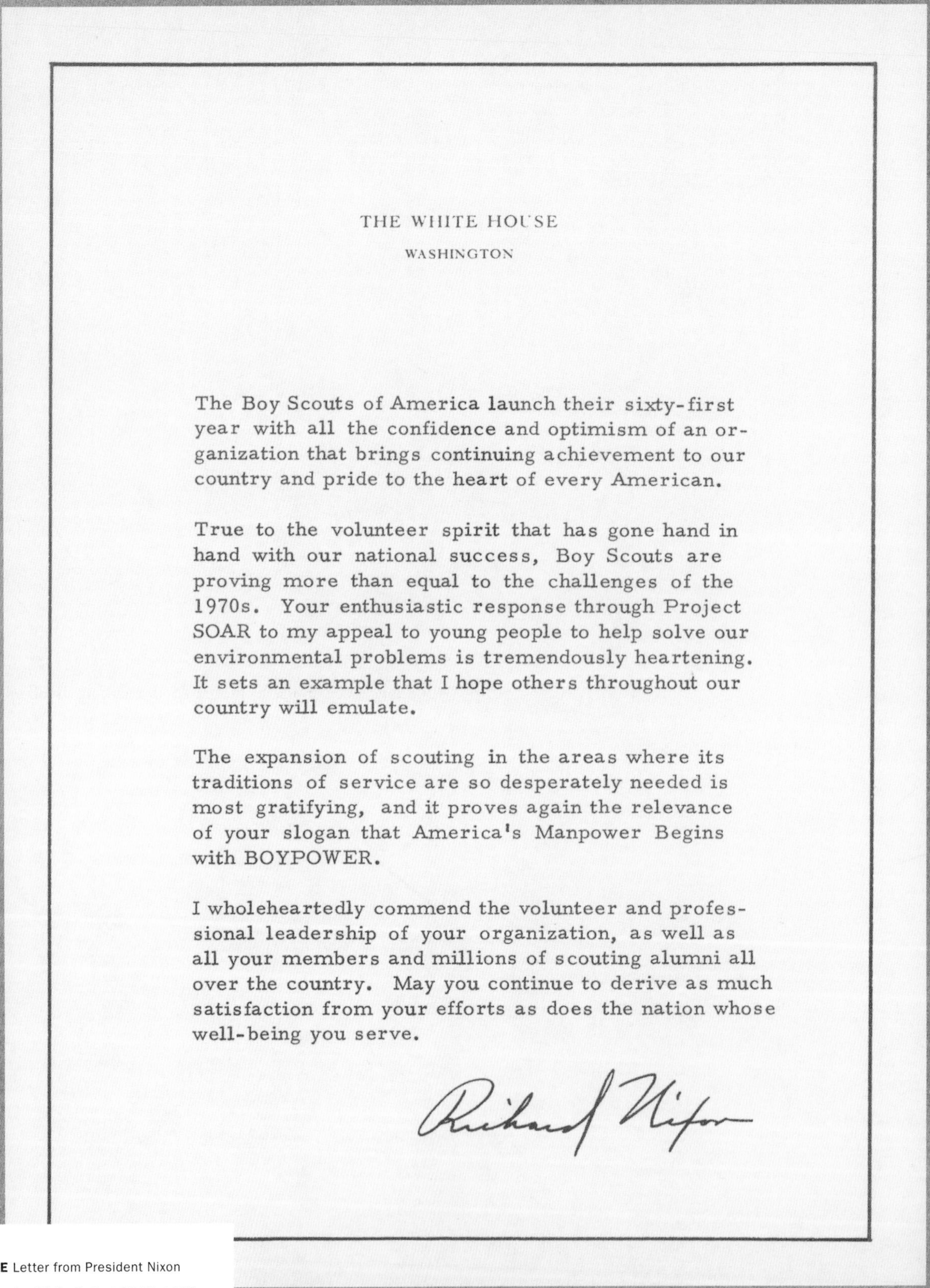

THE WHITE HOUSE

WASHINGTON

The Boy Scouts of America launch their sixty-first
year with all the confidence and optimism of an organization that brings continuing achievement to our
country and pride to the heart of every American.

True to the volunteer spirit that has gone hand in
hand with our national success, Boy Scouts are
proving more than equal to the challenges of the
1970s. Your enthusiastic response through Project
SOAR to my appeal to young people to help solve our
environmental problems is tremendously heartening.
It sets an example that I hope others throughout our
country will emulate.

The expansion of scouting in the areas where its
traditions of service are so desperately needed is
most gratifying, and it proves again the relevance
of your slogan that America's Manpower Begins
with BOYPOWER.

I wholeheartedly commend the volunteer and professional leadership of your organization, as well as
all your members and millions of scouting alumni all
over the country. May you continue to derive as much
satisfaction from your efforts as does the nation whose
well-being you serve.

Richard Nixon

ABOVE Letter from President Nixon
touting the BSA's Project SOAR, 1969.

The Boy Scouts are taking a lot of garbage these days.

Ad #2-37
Available: 2-col, 3-col, 4-col

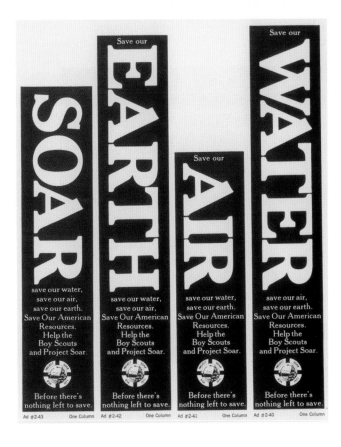

Save our SOAR
save our water,
save our earth.
Save Our American
Resources.
Help the
Boy Scouts
and Project Soar.

Before there's
nothing left to save.
Ad #2-43   One Column

Save our EARTH
save our water,
save our air,
Save Our American
Resources.
Help the
Boy Scouts
and Project Soar.

Before there's
nothing left to save.
Ad #2-42   One Column

Save our AIR
save our water,
save our earth.
Save Our American
Resources.
Help the
Boy Scouts
and Project Soar.

Before there's
nothing left to save.
Ad #2-41   One Column

Save our WATER
save our air,
save our earth.
Save Our American
Resources.
Help the
Boy Scouts
and Project Soar.

Before there's
nothing left to save.
Ad #2-40   One Column

long been available in Braille format for visually impaired Scouts, and now they were joined by cassette tapes and, later, closed-caption videos for the hearing impaired.

In 1965, the BSA relaxed membership-age requirements for the mentally handicapped. In 1978, age restrictions for rank advancement for physically disabled Scouts were lifted as well. The BSA ultimately authorized disabled Scouts to earn alternate merit badges in lieu of required badges that they were incapable of earning so they could move up the advancement trail to Eagle Scout.

Throughout this era, hundreds of local councils formed committees to bring Scouting to the disabled—an effort coordinated after 1974 by NACOSH, the National Advisory Committee on Scouting for the Handicapped. Individual troops welcomed an estimated 150,000 handicapped boys and young men by the end of the 1970s, and about 60,000 other handicapped youths participated in Scouting through special units.

ABOVE (top left and right) Advertising Project SOAR, as well as responding to the flak the BSA had been receiving. (bottom) Scouts sort through recyclables.

HANK AARON
SCOUT, RECORD-BREAKING ATHLETE

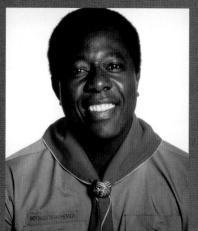

ON THE NIGHT OF APRIL 8, 1974, in the bottom of the fourth inning of a home game against the Los Angeles Dodgers, "Hammerin' Hank" Aaron of the Atlanta Braves connected with a fastball from Dodgers pitcher Al Downing, smacked it over the left-field fence, and shattered one of baseball's longest-standing records, one that many sports fans thought would never be broken: Babe Ruth's 714 career home runs. Aaron had just hit his 715th.

Born in Mobile, Alabama, in 1934, Aaron was a member of Mobile's Troop 235, chartered to the Ebenezer A.M.E. Church. He excelled at both football and baseball in college, but settled on the latter. Aaron began playing pro ball right around the time the major leagues finally accepted African American players. Aged just fifteen, Aaron tried out for the Brooklyn Dodgers, but didn't get a slot in the organization. He spent the first few years of his career in the Negro Leagues before he joined the Boston (later Milwaukee) Braves in 1952. (The Braves moved to Atlanta in 1965.) After a couple of years in the Braves' minor-league system, he got his major-league start in a game against the Cincinnati Reds on April 13, 1954. Over the next twenty-two years, Aaron put fear in the heart of pitchers with his eccentric but effective batting style. Besides exceeding Babe Ruth's record, he won three Golden Glove awards, played in the All-Star Game twenty years in a row, and still holds the major-league record for RBIs.

Aaron retired in 1976 after spending his last two seasons with the Milwaukee Brewers. His final career home-run tally was 755. Aaron was inducted into the Hall of Fame six years later. Since his retirement, Aaron has served in several executive roles in the Braves organization and is an active civic and business leader.

Besides bringing the benefits of Scouting to the disabled, the BSA also sought to make all Scouts aware of what life was like for the handicapped. The first "handicapped awareness trail" was introduced at the 1977 National Scout Jamboree at Moraine State Park in Pennsylvania; it gave some 5,000 Scouts the opportunity to experience what it was like to try to navigate through the woods without sight or in a wheelchair. The handicapped awareness trail concept was soon adopted by many local councils, and a Handicapped Awareness merit badge was introduced four years later.

Along the same lines, Scouting had long emphasized the dangers of alcohol, tobacco, and drugs. The sixth edition of the *Boy Scout Handbook* (1959), for example, included a warning about marijuana—at a time when many Americans were only vaguely aware of the substance. This became all the more important as drugs made serious inroads among young people in the 1960s and 1970s. The eighth edition (1972) of the *Handbook* had an expanded section on drugs, covering LSD and glue-sniffing, among other ways of getting high. In the same year, the BSA launched Operation Reach, a focused anti-drug program for Scouts.

And yet, despite all the changes to American society in general and to the Boy Scouts in particular, some things remained the same. The BSA continued to hold national jamborees every four years: at Farragut State Park in Idaho (1969); a double-header (1973) split between Pennsylvania's Moraine State Park and Idaho's Farragut State Park; and a return to Moraine State Park (1977). In addition, the BSA hosted

RIGHT (top) Scout troop at Michigan School for Deaf. Troops like this one were made possible when the BSA began providing materials for the hearing impaired in the 1970s. (bottom) Scouts onstage at the Skillman Village for Epileptics in New Jersey.

Hallucinogens

These change how you taste, smell, see, hear, feel, and think. The sensations they create are often called "trips." They are like dreams you can't wake up from. These dreams may be like nightmares. You can't tell how a person will react to a dose of hallucinogen, DMT, STP, and MDA. There are many others. Some doctors class THC, a strong ingredient in marijuana, as a hallucinogen.

LSD is one of these drugs. While using it, a person may lose control of himself. He doesn't know what is real. He may get real scared or think he can do strange things like flying. "Flashback" is always possible. This means a person may have a reaction days or months after the last dose.

Stimulants

Any drug that excites or overworks the brain is a stimulant. It can cause convulsions when taken in overdose. Some dangerous stimulants are known as "pep pills."

Abuse of stimulants may cause liver and brain damage. They make your blood pressure much higher. They cause loss of appetite. Users of stimulants often suffer from loss

of weight and have malnutrition. They lose their sense of values and personal identity. They may get emotionally disturbed and act strangely.

Sedatives and Tranquilizers

Sedatives are drugs that when properly prescribed may help bring about sleep. One group of sedatives is called barbiturates, and also known as "goof balls" or "sleepers." An overdose of sedatives can kill. There are many accidental deaths from their abuse.

Tranquilizers calm and relax people. But they have to be properly prescribed by doctors for certain problems. Some of these pills may produce dependency on drugs. They never should be used without the advice and prescription of a doctor.

Narcotics

These drugs have the ability to relieve pain and bring sleep. They include opium and its active ingredient, morphine. They also include heroin, which is a form of morphine. The dangers of narcotic use are extreme. An overdose can kill. The addict can never be sure how strong the narcotic he buys is. Many dis-

eases are caused by using dirty needles for shots. A person on narcotics can't fight diseases such as tuberculosis and pneumonia.

A dependence on narcotics builds and builds in the user. He must have more and more to satisfy his problems. An addict who can no longer get narcotics really suffers. He shakes, sweats, and throws up. His eyes and nose run. His muscles ache and jerk. He has a bad bellyache and diarrhea. He may have hallucinations and delusions.

Other Abusable Substances

Many other chemicals and drugs affect one's mind and body. They are not meant to be used by the human body. They have very bad effects when used that way. Blindness, damage to lungs and kidneys, and even death have been reported from misuse.

Drug Abuse

Why do kids try drugs? Usually just for "kicks," to try to get a little excitement, or maybe out of curiosity. Some try them to go along with the crowd they are in.

Usually those who try drugs are searching for those things they can't find in their regular lives. Those who really know and will level with you say it's better to get those feelings from something real than to try the dangerous way from drugs.

Some kids foolishly use drugs to try to "get out of the dumps." Every

the twelfth world jamboree (1967) at Farragut State Park, and American contingents numbering in the thousands attended world jamborees in Japan (1971) and Norway (1975). A planned world jamboree in Iran in 1979 had to be canceled due to the revolution in that country.

Even as the BSA shifted to a more "urban" focus during these years, outdoor adventures still remained a prime attraction, and New Mexico's Philmont Scout Ranch (augmented by a 10,000-acre addition in 1963) continued to be the jewel in the crown of Scouting's camping empire, as well as serving as an important training center for both junior and adult Scout leaders.

But Philmont soon had competition. The BSA established

ABOVE (top) A boy proudly holds his Operation Reach card and pin. The program was in response to growing numbers of youth using illegal drugs. (bottom) Boy Scouts and Explorers gather around the sign welcoming them to the national jamboree at Farragut State Park in Idaho, 1969.

"Through camping, Scouts are challenged mentally, physically, and emotionally. With these challenges they become stronger leaders, which in turn will benefit them in all facets of life."

EVAN CHAFFEE, 2007 NATIONAL CHIEF, ORDER OF THE ARROW

four "high-adventure bases" during these years: the Charles L. Sommers National High Adventure Base (Northern Tier), near Lake Superior on the Minnesota-Wisconsin border, featured canoeing (1972); the Maine High Adventure program offered whitewater thrills as well as rugged camping (c. 1971); and the Florida National High Adventure Sea Base on lower Matecumbe Key in the Florida Keys featured sailing, swimming, snorkeling, and scuba diving (1975).

The United States celebrated its 200th birthday in 1976, and the BSA helped commemorate the bicentennial with a unique

event. For the entire summer of that year, some 750 Scouts and Scouters camped out on the Mall in Washington, D.C. Like all Scouts, they were proud of the fact that, for the first time, there was an Eagle Scout in the White House—President Gerald Ford. All in all, more than 137,000 Scouting units took part in special activities celebrating America's 200th birthday.

America in the bicentennial years was a country still undergoing great changes, including major population shifts. The BSA began in New York City, and in its first decades the movement was strongest in the East Coast and the Midwest.

ABOVE Aerial shot of the world jamboree in Lillehammer, Norway, 1975. **RIGHT** (top) Boy Scouts and Explorers saddle up at Philmont Scout Ranch. (bottom) Scouts who wear out their hiking boots during a Philmont trek throw them over the entrance sign.

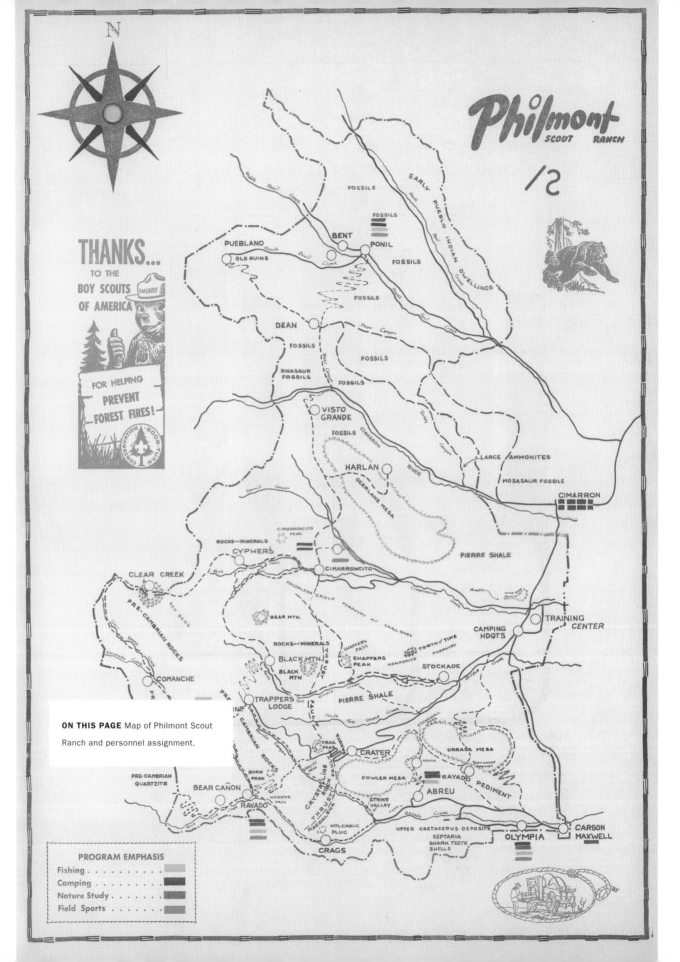

ON THIS PAGE Map of Philmont Scout Ranch and personnel assignment.

PERSONNEL ASSIGNMENT FOR TRAINING AT OLYMPIA

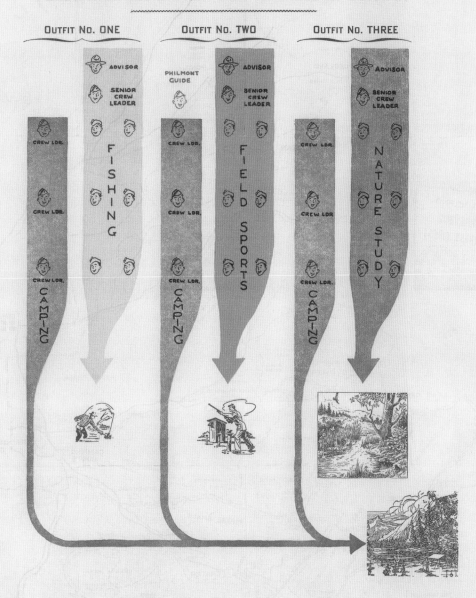

But in a movement that began around World War II and accelerated in the 1970s, more and more Americans began to move away from the so-called Rust Belt to the Sun Belt stretching across the South and Southwest to Southern California. Cities such as Los Angeles, Atlanta, Houston, and Phoenix experienced leaps in population. It was in these communities—and the "edge cities" that sprang up outside them—that Scouting would find most of its new members in the years to come.

As the nation's center of gravity moved westward, so did the BSA. In 1979—after twenty-five years in New Jersey, preceded by thirty-three years in New York City—the BSA moved its national headquarters to Irving, Texas.

LEFT (top) Venturers return from their adventure on the sea at the Florida Sea Base. (bottom) Venturing programs such as this one attracted both boys and girls. **ABOVE** (left) Scuba training at the Florida Sea Base, a unique opportunity for Scouts. (right) Scouts meet in a cabin at the Charles L. Sommers National High Adventure Base in Minnesota.

PART FIVE

BACK TO BASICS

1979—1999

Declining membership and the controversies over aspects of the Improved Scouting Program led the BSA to change direction as the end of the 1970s approached. While still committed to promoting personal development and spreading Scouting's reach as widely as possible, the movement now harked back to its historic roots in search of revival—by putting the "boy" back in "Boy Scouts" and putting the "outing" back in "Scouting."

In 1978, for example, advancement requirements were again to include outdoor skills as mandatory elements. The time-tested skills of camping, hiking, first aid, and cooking would once again be integral to every Scout's experience.

The really big change came in 1979 with publication of the ninth edition of the *Official Boy Scout Handbook* written by William "Green Bar Bill" Hillcourt. The new edition was widely received as a powerful, positive step in implementing the important changes being made to the BSA's overall program. In the words of the BSA, "This edition places greater emphasis on fun and adventure and uses Scout skills as a method to achieve the aims of Scouting. Strengthening the family and broadening the outdoor experience also are major objectives of the new handbook." A Scout of that era said of the new handbook's return to traditions, "Being outside with your friends, and doing the stuff we always do is what makes being a Scout fun."

Even those who had done their best to help foster inner city and urban troops embraced the change. Though the new Hillcourt edition reflected the necessity for an evolved handbook in a changing world, it was created with deference to the extreme importance of traditional Scoutcraft as forming the foundations for Scouting's survival in a new era.

The return to traditional values was also reflected in the BSA's Annual Report for 1979: "The out of doors looms large in the eyes of a Scout. By learning outdoor skills, Scouts find that they have improved their self-reliance, ability to work with others, and personal fitness. The outdoor skills of hiking, camping, cooking, conservation, swimming, and environment are supplemented by skills related to citizenship, first aid, family, community living, communications, and physical fitness."

A NEW DECADE

American values were changing as the eighties began. A more conservative, patriotic culture emerged with the election of President Ronald Reagan. The Cub Scouts turned fifty in 1980, and the organization as a whole was reenergized for a decade of positive advancement.

The recent return to basics didn't mean the Scouts stopped targeting hard-to-reach boys; in fact, important lessons were learned from the programs of the seventies that would remain a solid part of the BSA. Traditionally, Scoutmasters were chosen by the troop committee from among the troop members' fathers or other men from the community, but times had changed. In many urban communities, there simply were no fathers who were willing to participate in Scouting in that way. Often inner-city troops would spring up, only to slowly fall apart due to the lack of available support from among the adults around the Scouts.

ABOVE Cover of the ninth edition of the *Official Boy Scout Handbook*, with *boy* returning to the title and the outdoors returning to the cover.

BOY SCOUTS OF AMERICA ANNUAL REPORT TO CONGRESS 1979

Report to the
96th Congress, 2d Session

ON THIS PAGE (left) BSA Report to Congress that reaffirmed the original belief in giving boys an outdoor education. (below) Letter to the speaker of the House from Chief Scout Executive J. L. Tarr.

LETTER OF TRANSMITTAL

A program for Cub Scouts, Boy Scouts, and Explorers

National Office
BOY SCOUTS OF AMERICA

1325 Walnut Hill Lane, Irving, Texas
P.O. Box 61030, Dallas/Fort Worth Airport, Texas 75261
Telephone: 214 659-2000

SCOUTING/USA

The Honorable Thomas P. O'Neill, Jr.
Speaker of the House of Representatives
Washington, D.C. 20510

Dear Mr. Speaker:

As the Boy Scouts of America nears its 70th anniversary of service to the youth of our nation, we respectfully submit the 1979 Annual Report to Congress in accordance with our Federal Charter.

Since its founding in February 1910, the Boy Scouts of America has provided a unique, educational program for young people that has successfully used the methods of an outdoor program, an advancement plan, the teaching of Scouting skills, and the practice of Scouting ideals.

The strength of our program is stated in the Congressional action in 1916 which called for us "to promote, through organization, and cooperation with other agencies, the ability of boys to do things for themselves and others, to train them in Scoutcraft, and to teach them patriotism, courage, self-reliance, and kindred virtues."

We are most appreciative of the support and interest that has been given to Scouting by the Congress. You can be sure that the more than 1 million men and women who volunteer their service for youth will continue to prepare young people for their responsibilities as participating citizens.

Respectfully,

J. L. Tarr

J. L. Tarr
Chief Scout Executive

Enclosure

ns

2

CUB SCOUTING LOOKS FORWARD

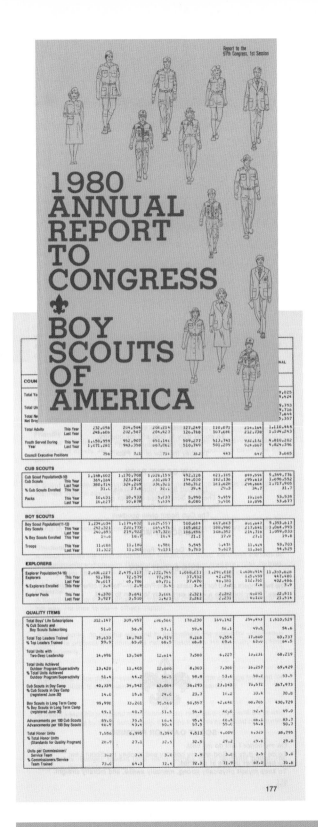

The solution came from a surprising place: corporate America. The hope and expectation were that young executives with strong values would be interested in mentoring youth in a new way.

One example of this new leadership drive took place in Cleveland in 1980. Faced with a total lack of interest from the community in supporting local Scout troops, the local council went directly to various corporations and asked for this innovative form of help. Rather than go directly to the younger managers and executives, the council went straight to the top.

> ### "The out of doors looms large in the eyes of a Scout. By learning outdoor skills, Scouts find that they have improved their self-reliance, ability to work with others, and personal fitness."
>
> **1979 BSA ANNUAL REPORT**

Appropriate CEOs were targeted and asked to aid in finding suitable executives from among their company's ranks to become "executive style" Scoutmasters. Many of the young executives were African American, simply because most of the Scouts were also African American. It was thought that providing a positive role model for these young Scouts was paramount.

In this way and others, the Boy Scouts continued to revive. In 1980, for the first time since 1972, the downward trend in enrollment was reversed. There were 4,326,082 youth members and adult volunteers active in Scouting in 129,753 Cub Scout packs, Boy Scout troops, and Explorer posts. More than 50 percent of local councils saw an increase in membership, making 1980 the best growth year on record.

The Boy Scouts also proved their mettle as record-*keepers*, becoming an integral part of the 1980 U.S. Census, the most comprehensive census to date. Millions of Cub Scouts, Boy Scouts, and Explorers from every state passed out reminders to American citizens in their homes, parking lots, apartments, and farms in an effort to encourage participation. History shows that it was one of the most comprehensive accountings of

LEFT "Cub Scouting Looks Forward," the cover of the organization's fiftieth anniversary pamphlet. **ABOVE** (foreground) BSA report to Congress from 1980, a year of great growth for the Scouts. (background) Page from the report showing 1980's enrollment increase.

FORT A.P. HILL: JAMBOREE CENTRAL

THANKS TO A 1978 ARRANGEMENT with the Department of Defense, the BSA got a new home for its national jamborees: the U.S. Army base at Fort A.P. Hill, just outside the town of Bowling Green, Virginia.

In return for paying for capital improvements like new roads and water supplies, the BSA received permission to hold a jamboree at the facility every four years. (In addition, the Department of Defense considers the gatherings to be a valuable training opportunity for its personnel—the presence of tens of thousands of Scouts living outdoors is a realistic simulation of, say, an overseas refugee emergency or a major military forward deployment.)

The first national jamboree at Fort A.P. Hill took place in 1981. Some 27,000 Scouts and Scouters participated—among them Chief Scout Executive J. L. Tarr, who had attended the very first national jamboree forty-four years before.

The theme of the 1981 jamboree was "Reunion With History," and one of the special features was an interactive "Heritage Trail," with activities based on America's frontier heritage. One such activity involved having each troop carry a 240-pound log through an obstacle course. In the words of a "trail boss," "If the boys expect [just] a history course, they're in for a shock."

As usual, though, the BSA looked to the future as well as the past: The 1981 jamboree was the first to be planned using computer technology, with each troop receiving a printout listing scheduled activities upon arrival.

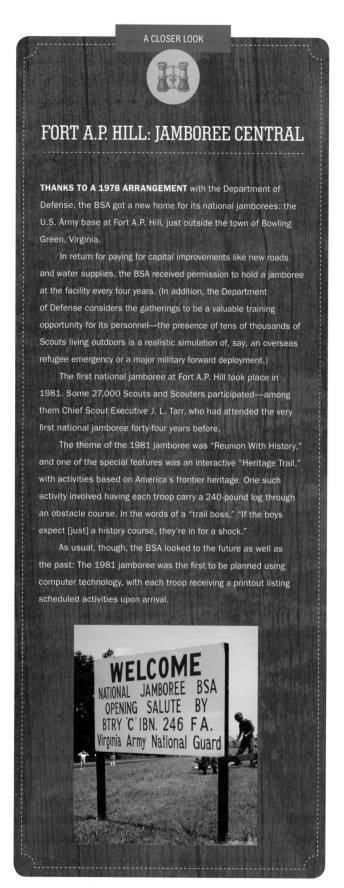

WELCOME
NATIONAL JAMBOREE BSA
OPENING SALUTE BY
BTRY "C" IBN. 246 F.A.
Virginia Army National Guard

American life of all time, and many point to the efforts of the BSA as part of the reason for its success.

TIGER CUBS AND CUB SCOUTS

At its National Annual Meeting in Atlanta, Georgia, in 1982, the BSA announced the start of an entirely new program for younger boys: Tiger Cubs, open to all boys aged seven.

Tiger Cubs was largely the brainchild of Robert Untch, who became the national Cub Scouting director in 1971. In 1978, Untch initiated a research program called "Foundations for Growth." It involved mailing out 20,000 questionnaires to Cub Scout leaders, as well as interviews with Scouters across the country and the use of focus groups. Analysis of the results concluded that "a simple and fun program for first-grade boys and their families" was needed; while such a program would serve as a "bridge" to the Cub Scouts, it would be largely separate from the established Cub Scout program.

At first, there were no formal Tiger Cub units; each boy and an adult family member would gather regularly with neighboring Tiger Cub families for activities and, twice a year, with the local Cub Scout pack. (These two occasions were the annual blue-and-gold banquet celebrating Scouting's anniversary, and a pack meeting—usually in late spring—when Tiger Cubs were eligible to move up to the Cub Scouts.)

ABOVE Robert Untch, the man who created the Tiger Cubs.
RIGHT (top) Tiger Cubs and their parents, all dressed in tiger orange, enjoy an outdoor picnic, with a tiger mascot serving up burgers. (bottom) A fireman directs a Tiger Cub and his father on how to spray a firehose for a promotional photo shoot.

"Go See It!"

THEME FOR MONTHLY TIGER CUB OUTINGS

The only uniform required was a Tiger Cub T-shirt, and initially there was no formal system of advancement; instead, the Tiger program focused on a list of "big ideas," including Family Entertainment, Know Your Community, and Prepare for Emergencies. The Tiger Cubs got their own motto (Search, Discover, Share) and their own Tiger Cub Promise: "I promise to love God, my family and my country, and to learn about the world." (In 2001, the Cub Scout Promise replaced the Tiger Club Promise.)

Tiger Cubs was an immediate success. By the end of 1982, almost 85,000 boys and parents or guardians had enrolled in the program; membership reached about 200,000 by 1985.

Over time and through feedback from participants, the Tiger Cubs underwent significant changes. In 1986, a more systematic advancement program, Tiger Tracks, was introduced; in 1993, local Cub Scout packs were authorized to include Tiger Cubs; and in 2001, Tiger Cub became an official rank of the Cub Scouts.

Untch's Foundations for Growth did more than just lay the groundwork for the Tiger program; it also targeted opportunities for advancement for the nine-year-old boy participating in Cub Scouts. Cub Scouting had remained largely unchanged for the better part of the twentieth century, but thanks to Foundations for Growth, in 1982 it saw a revamped and easily accessible

ABOVE (left) A boy wearing the simple Tiger Cub T-shirt pets a tiger cub of a different sort. (top right) Tiger Cubs and their parents explore a science museum. (bottom right) A growling pack of Tiger Cubs.

RESEARCH AND BOOKS

ACHIEVEMENT 12

It would be wonderful if all of your wishes came true. You know that some cannot. But you can do more than just dream by reading about things you would like to do but can't. Tell your teacher or librarian some of the things you'd like to do. She can give you some fine books to read about those things.

REQUIREMENTS

☐ 1. Visit a public library with your den, parents, or an adult. Find out what has to be done to get a library card to take out books. Name four kinds of books that interest you, such as fiction, nature, sports, history, adventure, etc.

☐ 2. Pick a book on a subject that you like. Tell your den leader, your family, or the den some things about it.

☐ 3. Books are important. Show that you know how to take care of them—open a new one the right way (so as not to break the binding) and make a paper or plastic cover for one.

Date	Parent signs here	Recorded on den chart

OPEN A NEW BOOK: Hold the closed book in one hand. Rest the back of the book on a desk or table. Let go one cover and then the other. Put the covers down gently. Keep the leaves closed and upright. Now take a few leaves at a time and press them down lightly.

MAKE A PAPER COVER: Use wrapping paper or a grocery bag. Cut the paper at least 3 inches bigger than the book. Make folds at the top and bottom. Make at least a 1-inch fold on the right side. Slip the back cover into the fold. Close the book. Make a fold for the front cover. Open the book and slip the front cover into that fold.

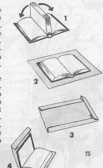

74

75

version of the *Wolf Cub Scout Book*. The book included new ways for Cub Scouts to advance, including twelve new achievements on the way toward Bear rank. In 1984, Cub Scout registration was high at 2,483,950 boys and 805,237 pack leaders. Another major change was the approval of extended camping for Webelos Scouts in 1984, which opened a door for many younger Scouts to experience what was to come when they moved on to the Boy Scouts in a year. Previously, Webelos Scouts had only been allowed to camp overnight or for just a couple of nights; allowing these youngsters to experience longer camping trips was a great way to introduce them to one of the more exciting aspects of being a Cub Scout.

EXPLORERS, VARSITY SCOUTS, AND VENTURERS

Exploring continued to thrive in the 1980s. By 1982, the program boasted more than 600,000 participants. By now about half of all Explorer posts were devoted to specific career areas. With the nation's economy reviving and a new spirit of confidence in the future spreading across the country, more and more young people were interested in preparing for professional careers. Exploring benefited greatly from this trend.

Exploring also encouraged a kind of fluidity among its members. The young male and female participants might come into a post to explore a field or activity that seemed of interest, only to find that it wasn't a match. They might move among several posts before settling in on one that was right. For anyone familiar with the Scouts of Baden-Powell's day, this lack of rigidity would have been a great surprise, but it was effective in its aims. Many participants went on to work in the fields they explored as youths.

As is often the case in Scouting, when non-traditional programs like Exploring gain a foothold, an equally vocal faction calls for a more traditional approach. With Exploring increasingly tied to career preparation, some Scouters felt there was a need to serve older boys who were more interested in Scouting's tried-and-true outdoor activities.

ABOVE Explorers seated in a courtroom consider a future career in law. **RIGHT** (top) Varsity Scouts use teamwork to hoist a giant log. (bottom) One Varsity Scout gets tangled while doing a rope walk between two trees.

THE HISTORY OF THE UNIFORM

THERE ARE FEW UNIFORMS as iconic as that of the Boy Scouts. The shorts, the red neckerchief, the knee-high socks—together these elements are perhaps some of the most recognizable and beloved American emblems. Often cited as "the most distinctly American of uniforms" (alongside that of the Green Berets, the Marines, and the New York City Police), the Boy Scout uniform is more than simply a set of clothing.

It's a symbol of the deeply affectionate place reserved in the American heart for the Boy Scout. Seeing groups of young Scouts doing Good Turns and raising money for their local troops brings feelings of patriotism and cherished values; the uniform is an important part of this experience.

The first uniform design was largely influenced by Baden-Powell's experiences in the South African Constabulary and the British Army. As his friend E. K. Wade wrote, "The uniform of shirt, shorts, scarf, and cowboy hat which Baden-Powell had worn on service became automatically the uniform of Boy Scouts, since it was in that kit that Baden-Powell was known to his hero worshippers." The early British Scout uniform looked very much like the South African Constabulary uniform, with its wide-brimmed hat, socks held up with old-fashioned garters (remember, these were the days before elastic), and a shirt with the sleeves rolled up. The neckerchief, perhaps the most recognizable element in the uniform, even to this day, was present in this early version of the ensemble. Baden-Powell wrote of the uniform: "The correct wearing of the uniform and smartness of turnout of the individual Scout makes him a credit to our Movement. It shows his pride in himself and in his Troop."

The original Boy Scout uniform, designed by the BSA's newly formed Committee on Badges, Awards, and Equipment, consisted of a khaki campaign hat; a five-button, choke-collar tunic; knee breeches; and canvas leggings. By 1917, however, the uniform began to change. The addition of the neckerchief and the removal of the uncomfortable choke-collar tunic were significant in that the uniform took on a more relaxed and less military look. The neckerchief, though part of Baden-Powell's original design, didn't catch on in the U.S. until several years into American Scouting. Loose, khaki shirts that offered better ease of use and movement replaced the high-collared tunics. The khaki shirts were often coupled with four-button coats possessing a more comfortable and breathable collar. The neckerchief was meant to be worn with either.

The khaki shorts so closely associated with Scouting were implemented around 1920. The comfort of shorts while camping and doing vigorous activity made sense for Scouts, even if they were still not entirely fashionable in everyday life. It is said that some Scouts still wore long pants to and from camp, only to change into Bermuda-length shorts in the wilderness.

World War II changed some elements of the uniform, as many GIs either were former Scouts or were related to current Scouts. "Overseas caps" and breeches were part of the WWII uniform and were adopted by Scouts in an effort to emulate their heroes. The uniform remained largely unchanged for the better part of sixty years.

Enter fashion designer Oscar de la Renta. In 1980, recognizing a need for an updated uniform, the Scouts tapped the famed designer to give it an overhaul, changing the long tradition of the Scout's "look." The designer, free of charge, spent two years researching and redesigning the uniforms of the Boy Scouts, Cub Scouts, Explorers, and both men and women adult Scouters.

Boy Scouts now would wear khaki short- or long-sleeved shirts festooned with crimson epaulets, which specifically designated the wearer as a Boy Scout, as opposed to a Cub Scout. Both long pants and shorts were now olive green and had useful utility pockets—a big hit among Scouters of all stripes. The neckerchief was still part of the uniform, but became optional and left up to the discretion of each individual troop. More often than not, the neckerchief is still chosen as part of the uniform.

In 1984, the Webelos Scouts were allowed to wear the Scout uniform, and a blue neckerchief was added to signify the Bear rank. The Tiger Cub uniform was introduced around this same time, consisting of just an orange T-shirt with the bold tiger emblem emblazoned on the chest.

Headgear evolved into three choices: a new baseball-type cap; the red beret that had been introduced in 1972, or—in a nod to the past—a new version of the old "Smoky the Bear"-style campaign hat.

But perhaps one of the most significant changes went largely unseen: the introduction of permanent press fabrics in the 1960s. The early Scout uniforms were largely made of itchy and uncomfortable wool or wrinkle-prone cotton—not the easiest material to keep clean and neat—especially when camping. The new fabrics created breathable, comfortable uniforms that required little or no intervention from an iron or a parent.

This basic design, with minor updates, is still being used today.

ABOVE Oscar de la Renta (right), whose updated designs for Scouting uniforms continue to be used today. **RIGHT** The original Boy Scout uniform resembled military gear. (from top to bottom) Canvas leggings, campaign hat, and choke-collar tunic, with an array of badges on the right sleeve, the red neckerchief commonly associated with Scouting, and the cap that used to be the uniform standard.

This led to the introduction of the Varsity Scouting program in 1980. Designed for boys ages fourteen to seventeen, Varsity Scouts was tailor-made for the older Scout who wanted challenging activities not appropriate for younger Scouts, but who wasn't interested in career-based Exploring. The "Varsity" designation came from the fact that participants represented Scouting's "senior team."

Varsity Scouting centered around five program fields, offering opportunities in Advancement (Varsity Scouts could advance to Eagle Scout by meeting the same requirements as Scouts in traditional troops), High-Adventure Activities, Personal Development, Service, and Special Programs and Events. The High-Adventure component included activities like backpacking, canoe camping, cycling, fishing, freestyle biking, orienteering, rock climbing and rappelling, snow camping, wilderness survival, and white-water canoeing. According to the

teams and squads led by a coach. The older, highest-ranking Scouts were called captains. By 1984, the Varsity program had expanded to include twenty-eight councils around the country. The following year, membership approached the 50,000 mark.

In the late 1990s, the BSA authorized another program for older youth: Venturing, which had previously been called Outdoor Exploring. In a historic 1995 meeting in Long Key, Florida, the Outdoor Exploring Committee chaired by Dr. Dick Miller of Waynesboro, Virginia, met to address the issue of how to maintain the enormous success of the outdoor Scouting programs. It was well known that during the 1990s, Outdoor Exploring had exploded by 94 percent to almost 100,000 members, one of the highest rates of growth in the BSA. The committee decided that it would be beneficial to create a program that was separate from the Exploring program, one that was dedicated to outdoor activities, sports, hobbies, and the arts, with an overall

"It was wrong when the Scouting movement turned away from the outdoors. A Scout learns self-improvement and self-confidence when he's out in the woods, away from home, with his buddies depending upon him. There will be times when he misses the comforts of home, but he won't quit and cry. His ability to prove he's ready takes hold and becomes part of his character."

A PENNSYLVANIA SCOUTMASTER QUOTED IN *TIME* MAGAZINE, 1981

BSA, "[Varsity Scouting] provides options for young men who are looking for rugged high adventure or challenging sporting activities and still want to be a part of a Scouting program that offers the advancement opportunities and values of the Boy Scouts of America."

Contrary to its moniker, Varsity Scouts was not necessarily a sports-oriented program. A Varsity team chooses its program emphasis—which can be either a high-adventure event or a sport. Most choose one theme for three months, then change to another one. The team-like organization was instantly familiar even to those who had never participated in Scouting, and thus was highly effective. The Varsity Scouts were divided into

aim of "[providing] positive experiences to help young people mature and to prepare them to become responsible and caring adults." They decided to form the Venturing program, which would replace the Outdoor Exploring program. Like Exploring, though, Venturing would be open to both sexes. The age range was pegged at fourteen through twenty. Venturing became an official BSA division in 1998.

Venturing was, and continues to be, a great success: even in its first year, Venturing had 188,075 members. The program offers a wide variety of challenging activities like high-altitude rock climbing, white-water rafting, and seasonal activities such as skiing and surfing. Most Venturers today are between sixteen

RIGHT A Varsity Scout makes his way up a cliff face, while another Scout rappels down.

and nineteen years old, and the program actually has more nineteen-year-olds than fourteen-year-olds.

Venturing also has its own awards program, including Bronze, Silver, and Gold awards; the Venturing Ranger Award, recognizing achievement of a "high level of outdoor skills proficiency"; and the TRUST Award, which focuses on religious and community life. The great tradition of Sea Scouting lives on in Venturing, too; the highest achievement in this area is the Quartermaster Award.

At the start of 2007, as Venturing's tenth anniversary approached, the program boasted nearly a quarter-million members. Venturing may be the BSA's newest major program, but its roots stretch back to the very founding of the organization, when the founders recognized that older boys needed their own unique challenges—not just for their own personal growth and prepara-

tion for adulthood, but as a means of giving service to the Scouting movement, local communities, and the nation as a whole.

Venturing has been especially successful in retaining older Scouts who might otherwise have drifted away after attaining Eagle rank, or who might have been distracted from further involvement in Scouting by the many diversions that 21st-century America presents to youth. And the fact that Venturing is open to girls and young women gives it a special significance. Bill Evans, one of Venturing's original associate directors, noted how moving it is to be present when a young woman attains a place within Scouting along with her mom, dad, and brothers.

In addition to making changes to overall Scouting, as the 1980s progressed, the BSA continued to tackle hard-hitting social issues, one of which was organ donation. After careful consideration and years of research, the organization saw a

LEFT (top) A Varsity Scout gets advice from his Scout leaders. (bottom) Two of the young men who took part in the incredibly popular Varsity Scouting program. **ABOVE** Sailing, one of the advanced activities offered to Varsity Scouts.

WHY YOU AND YOUR FAMILY SHOULD DISCUSS ORGAN AND TISSUE DONATION

During your family discussion, you will learn how each person feels about donation and whether they would want to be a donor if the occasion ever arose. With this knowledge, you will be able to ensure that your loved one's wishes are carried out. If they wanted to be donors, you will be able to inform attending medical personnel of their decision. With this knowledge, you will be able to overcome the major impediment to donation today—the failure of medical personnel to ask the question, "Would you consider donating the organs and tissues of your loved one?" This generous caring act on your part and that of your loved one might help to make some sense out of a senseless tragedy by giving the gift of life to others so that they may live.

WHY YOU AND YOUR FAMILY MAY WANT TO SIGN A DONOR CARD

Last year, more than 50,000 people benefited from transplants. Yet thousands still wait for the miracle to happen that will give them the gift of life or significantly improve the quality of their lives. A corneal transplant can return the sight of a blind person. A liver transplant can save a life. A skin transplant can speed the recovery of a burn victim and reduce suffering significantly. A bone transplant can enable a person confined to a wheelchair to walk again. The list goes on. Yet despite the joy that results from successful transplantation, many continue to suffer and die because there are not enough donors to make the miracle happen for them. Because a request for donation is never made.

If enough people express their desire to become donors to their families, the serious shortage of organs and tissues can be alleviated and thousands of people can return to healthy and vital lives.

THE FAMILY DISCUSSION

It is normal to feel uneasy about discussing death. No one likes to deal with his own mortality; but by having a family discussion about organ and tissue donation, you may reduce some of the concern and anxiety your family would face in the event that they were ever asked about your being a donor. In medical emergencies, permission of your next-of-kin is always obtained before any procedure is undertaken. Many families faced with this question have commented that they wished they had known how their loved one felt about donation and what each individual family member would have wanted. By having a family discussion, everyone in the family will know how other family members feel about donation.

The best way to conduct a family discussion about donation is probably the same way that you discuss any matter of importance and concern to your family. The important thing is to do it and do it in a manner that gives everyone the opportunity to express their feelings and views. The objective of the family discussion is to understand the views of each family member before the discussion ends. Those who wish to be donors should complete and sign a donor card and always carry it with them.

Please talk it over. Thank you on behalf of the thousands who wait.

Over 17,000 Americans die each year due to the shortage of human tissue and organ donations. President Reagan has asked The Boy Scouts of America to conduct for him a Presidential Good Turn by raising the public awareness of this tragic shortfall, and what can be done to correct the problem.

The Boy Scouts of America are responding to this request by distributing literature, such as this, and other donor awareness activities.

AMERICAN COUNCIL ON TRANSPLANTATION UNIFORM DONOR CARD

Name _____
Print or type name of donor

In the hope that I may help others, I pledge this gift to take effect upon my death. My wishes are indicated below:

I give: ☐ any needed organs/tissues
or
☐ only the following organs/tissues

Specify the organs and tissues

Limitations or special wishes, if any _____

PLEASE ENCOURAGE OTHERS TO BECOME DONORS

PLEASE DETACH AND GIVE THIS PORTION OF THE CARD TO YOUR FAMILY

This is to inform you that I want to be an organ and tissue donor if the occasion ever arises. Please see that my wishes are carried out by informing attending medical personnel that I am a donor.

Thank You,

THE 1986 ANNUAL REPORT OF THE BOY SCOUTS OF AMERICA

developing need for awareness of this critical issue. Affecting one American out of every twenty-five, organ donations often mean the difference between life and death. Always willing to face pressing social issues, the Scouts organized the nationwide Donor Awareness Good Turn to inform American families of the urgent need for donated human organs and tissue. After working with various donor awareness groups in developing a plan of action and materials to distribute, close to 600,000 youth members distributed 14 million brochures to families, informing them of the need for donated human organs and tissue and urging them to make a commitment to donate.

The following year the Boy Scouts announced a commitment to what it dubbed "the Five Unacceptables": drug abuse, hunger, child abuse, illiteracy, and unemployment. These issues would be at the forefront of the Good Turns program. November of that year showed the world how powerful a motivating force the Scouts could be: Over two days, 72 million containers of food were collected for distribution to the nation's neediest.

ABOVE (top left and right) One of the millions of Donor Awareness brochures distributed by Scouts; the interior suggests a family discussion about becoming organ donors. (bottom) Eagle Scout medal on the cover of the BSA's Annual Report, 1986. **RIGHT** The 1989 Annual Report celebrates the 72 million containers of food that Scouts collected for the needy.

ANNUAL REPORT

BOY SCOUTS OF AMERICA   NINETEEN HUNDRED AND EIGHTY NINE

1989 Scouting for Food National Good Turn
More than 72 million cans of food collected for hungry people...

WHAT WE'RE DOING ABOUT
THE UNACCEPTABLES

The Boy Scouts of America has targeted five unacceptables in American society. They are hunger, drug abuse, child abuse, illiteracy, and youth unemployment. The following pages tell what we're doing to meet these challenges.

Meeting the Challenge of Hunger

ore than 20 million Americans, including 4 million children, go to bed hungry at some time every month—this occurs despite the bounty of our rich land. In the BSA's judgment, this situation is unacceptable.

In an effort to meet this challenge, the BSA conducted nationally the second annual Scouting for Food campaign in November. The harvest was an extraordinary 72 million cans and containers of nonperishable food—20 percent more than we gathered in 1988. It was the largest volunteer collection of foodstuffs in the history of the United States, and it was the most impressive national Good Turn since World War II. Frederick B. Rentschler, president and chief executive officer of Beatrice Company, Chicago, Ill., served as the 1989 Scouting for Food national chairman.

On November 11 BSA local councils sent Cub Scouts, Boy Scouts, Varsity Scouts, and Explorers into the streets to leave food collection bags at households and businesses. One week later they returned to reap the harvest. The donated food was then warehoused locally and distributed to the needy by local food banks. Most of our 407 BSA local councils were involved in this national Good Turn—two of their stories are told here.

The Philadelphia Council had a goal of 70 tons of food when 35,000 Cub Scouts, Boy Scouts, and Explorers took to the streets last November for Scouting for Food. They met that goal and then some, collecting more than 80 tons to be distributed to the needy by the Greater Philadelphia Food Bank. Their harvest was the largest single donation to the food bank during 1989.

With help from scores of local industries, businesses, civic groups, and the National Guard, Philadelphia Scouts did themselves proud. Ted L.

Moore, president of the United Way of Southeastern Pennsylvania, commented, "The Scouting for Food program reminds us annually of the many faces of hunger and prompts us to take action. It's a wonderful program." "Not only is Scouting for Food a boon to the poor," Moore said, "but probably equally important, it introduces the young leaders of tomorrow to the needs of society and gets them involved."

Like most councils around the country, the Ocean County Council in New Jersey made Scouting for Food a community affair. Nearly all of the council's 156 Cub Scout packs, Boy Scout troops, and Explorer posts participated in the event. Similarly, so did several local businesses and community organizations, local media, and even a work crew from the county jail. An estimated 10,000 of Ocean County's 360,000 citizens had a part in it.

Ocean County is not a depressed area, but, like every other region, it has its pockets of poverty. As Senior Patrol Leader Robert Schmid of Manchester's Troop 441 explained, "Everybody knows about the homeless in [other areas], but there are people here who need food, too."

The council's Scouts cheerfully did their best to meet the challenge. The 10-year-old Webelos Scouts of Point Pleasant's Pack 3 were typical. On collection day, they interrupted a campout to come home and gather food. "Duty called," said Webelos Den Leader Robert Phillips. "If you sit down with [the boys] and explain the need, they get pretty excited about it."

By late afternoon, trucks filled with food from 10 collection points arrived at the Ciba-Geigy plant for sorting, packaging, and storing in the company's warehouse. About 400 youth and adult volunteers worked into the night processing 204,000 pounds of food—45 percent more than the Scouts had gathered in the 1988 Scouting for Food campaign. Four local agencies that operate food pantries for the needy will tap the bonanza when needed.

The council's Scouting for Food chairman, John Simas, commented, "To work with these dedicated volunteers throughout the weekend was truly a heartening and rewarding experience. Someone said, 'We couldn't pay people to work as hard as these people worked.' I agree. The effort goes beyond that—it's humanity at its best."

And so it went around the nation in November as our local councils led their communities in a concerted effort to alleviate the problem of hunger in our midst.

86
DONOR
AWARENESS
Presidential Good Turn

ELLISON ONIZUKA
EAGLE SCOUT, ASTRONAUT

ELLISON ONIZUKA OF KEALAKEKUA, Kona, Hawaii, was a decorated Air Force flight test engineer, mission specialist, and, finally, a crew member aboard the ill-fated *Challenger* shuttle disaster of 1986. He was a member of many associations, including the Society of Flight Test Engineers, the Air Force Association, the American Institute of Aeronautics and Astronautics, Tau Beta Pi, Sigma Tau, Arnold Air Society, and Triangle Fraternity. After an illustrious career as an Air Force flight test engineer in the mid-1970s, during which he was awarded the Air Force Commendation Medal, Air Force Meritorious Service Medal, Air Force Organizational Excellence Award, and National Defense Service Medal, Onizuka was selected to become an astronaut in 1978. After training for more than a year, Onizuka participated in his first shuttle mission in 1985 on the shuttle *Discovery*. Onizuka was on his second mission into space on the *Challenger* when it exploded, killing him and the entire crew. He was posthumously awarded the Purple Heart.

It was the largest single volunteer food collection program in the history of the United States.

Scouting's tradition of outreach to all continued with the creation of the Urban Emphasis plan in the early 1990s, which encouraged Cub Scout packs, Boy Scout troops, and Explorer posts to form in low-income and minority communities.

HISPANIC OUTREACH: A NATIONAL AND GRASSROOTS EFFORT

In an effort to promote Scouting among America's fastest-growing minority group, the BSA reached out to Hispanic communities as the 1980s ended. In 1990, armed with a three-year grant from the Kellogg Foundation, the BSA funded training for a number of Hispanic professionals, who were placed with various councils in California and Texas by 1991. Some were later hired into permanent staff positions by the councils in which they had trained. In the words of Ponce Duran, director of BSA professional recruiting, "Many Hispanic families, for example, have no history of Scouting. [The program] will show off the many opportunities available to women and minorities in Scouting." Dubbed "Hispanic Emphasis," the expanded effort soon resulted in the creation of 608 packs, troops, and posts in areas strategically targeted by the organization. In addition to local council support, Hispanic Emphasis also prepared and distributed Spanish-language materials for Scout leaders and parents.

In many documented cases, especially in and around the California farming community of Salinas, Scout troops and Explorer posts worked to keep local youths out of gangs and the cycle of violence associated with them. Salinas's Explorer Post 205, for example, was set up in the early 1990s to serve at-risk Hispanic youth. After just a few short years, the post boasted more than 250 members.

The challenge with implementing Scouting in urban and poor areas had always been the lack of exposure to and understanding of the BSA. Salinas serves as a great example of what one community could do to remedy this problem. Chicago serves as another. One-third of that area's Scouts are members of minority groups or come from economically depressed or disadvantaged communities. Rather than wait for the organizing body of the Scouts to implement a program from the central office, the local Chicago Area Council banded

LEFT (top) Pages from the 1989 Annual Report. (bottom) Donor Awareness Presidential Good Turn card, 1986.

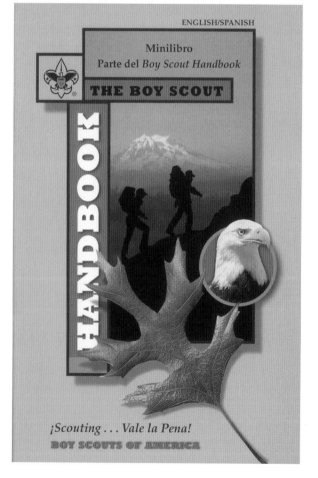

together in the early 1990s to make a strong commitment to minority recruitment "in dollars and philosophy."

The Chicago Area Council created a program that would require about $488,000 per year (about 12 percent of its budget). The program set seven goals for itself during those first few years: to instill a love for school and learning; to create classroom environments that were more stimulating and conducive to learning; to help at-risk youth make choices based on ethics and to do good deeds; to aid in developing future leaders; to provide an alternative to participation in local street gangs; to offer outdoor experiences, including camping, to children who may never have left the urban environment; and to increase the participation of parents both in school and through after-school activities. The sixty special-education students who participated regularly in the program were said to have experienced the most significant change. Many of these underserved youth finally felt included in classroom activities, and later many went on to join local troops.

The goal to aid in developing future leaders was also met, as evidenced by the success of the career-minded Exploring program. Participating students had the opportunity to learn about jobs they may not have otherwise been exposed to, as many Chicago-area companies like IBM, Westinghouse, and local small businesses sent representatives into the schools to give presentations on jobs students might consider when graduating.

Many Chicago-area Hispanics originally had misconceptions about Scouting that kept them from joining the organization. They often thought that Scouting was meant for the rich and upper-middle class, and that a high registration fee would be required. But the recruitment staff of the Chicago council was quick to realize that the values of the Hispanic community and of the Scouts were in fact very similar. Both communities recognize and place importance on religion, patriotism, and strong family values. The staff made huge efforts to emphasize these similar traits and to illustrate that Scouting has always traditionally been for *everybody*, not just the affluent. The efforts worked, and Hispanic youth flocked to the program.

The Chicago council also oversaw the construction of the Hoover Outdoor Education Center, located about an hour west

ABOVE (top) The Dr. Frank "Tick" Coleman National Service Award, given for service to Hispanic American youth. (bottom) Spanish language cover of *The Boy Scout Handbook*. **RIGHT** Spanish language covers of the Webelos manual and the Bear manual.

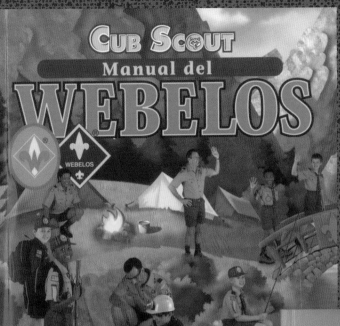

of metropolitan Chicago in Yorkville, Illinois. The $11 million facility, which was completed in 1993, boasted an Olympic-sized swimming pool and a large gymnasium. The camping facilities included tent sites and nature trails. Groups of students have

Sorak National Park for a raucous jamboree that reflected the enormous popularity that Scouting still enjoyed, even as the twentieth century was coming to a close. The jamboree's theme, "Many Lands, One World," introduced international Scouts to

The 1991 World Scout Jamboree set the tone for a decade of renewed brotherhood among Scouts from countries around the world.

since come through the facility by the thousands, including many from local homeless and battered women's facilities.

By all measures, it is this kind of local outreach that has helped the BSA evolve with the changing urban and social dynamics of the American scene.

BOY SCOUTS IN THE WORLD

As the BSA worked to foster the character-building values within the heart of American communities in the 1980s and 1990s, worldwide Scouting saw several major milestones.

In 1991, South Korea hosted the seventeenth World Scout Jamboree. More than 20,000 Scouts and Scouters representing 135 countries and territories gathered in the bucolic Mount

the traditions and culture of the myriad communities represented at the jamboree. Part of the fun that year involved the creation of a replica Brownsea Island camp to celebrate Baden-Powell's first experiment in Scoutcraft. The program was a huge hit with campers from around the world. Though bogged down by torrential rain and flooding, the spirits of the campers, both young and old, couldn't be dampened: "It rained a lot, but we still had fun!" said a Scout from Leeds, England.

The 1991 World Scout Jamboree set the tone for a decade of renewed brotherhood among Scouts from countries around the world. The jamboree marked the first time that Soviet youth participated in a world Scouting event. The troop, which was made up of Scouts and Scout leaders from several former

ABOVE Photographs of the Hoover Outdoor Education Center. **RIGHT** (left) Chief Scout Executive Ben Love (second from left) in Moscow, October 1990. (right) Ben Love (right) shakes hands with a Russian leader.

SCOUTING BEHIND THE IRON CURTAIN

WE SAW IN PART TWO that Scouting was entirely suppressed in Russia not long after that nation became the Soviet Union. When the iron curtain of Soviet domination fell across much of Central and Eastern Europe after World War II, Scouting vanished from those nations as well—a situation that continued through the four decades of the Cold War.

It took the most significant nuclear disaster in history to foster the reemergence of Scouting in the waning days of the Soviet Union. When the Chernobyl nuclear reactor disastrously melted down in 1986, among the many thousands of refugees from the area were children under the age of sixteen. The Soviet government relocated these children to rural areas away from the fallout, but the children remained in want for the most basic of needs. The government appealed to various international humanitarian organizations for assistance in caring for these young nuclear refugees. Among the very first organizations to respond was the World Organization of the Scout Movement. The WOSM called upon its resources to encourage Scout organizations in many countries, including the Boy Scouts of America, to pitch in.

Most incredibly, it was in part the Soviet government itself that made inquiries to the Scouts regarding the reestablishment of Scouting. In a historic mission that took place in October 1990, then Chief Scout Executive Ben Love visited Moscow and met with various government and Scouting leaders. The visit resulted in the creation of Scouting in Russia. By the end of 1991, when the Soviet Union passed into history, there were nearly 7,000 Scouts in units across Russia. By 1994, the number had climbed to more than 25,000.

The BSA was instrumental in further encouraging Russian and former Communist bloc Scouting. The organization funded and sponsored Scout leader training in the United States and sponsored the very first Czechoslovakian and Hungarian youth leaders who took part in the International Camp Staff program. In addition, the BSA hosted a Czechoslovakian Scouting professional for training. And to further solidify its commitment to Eastern European and Russian Scouting, the BSA funded the creation of the new *Russian Scout Handbook* written by Dr. Ludmilla Bondar, an author and psychologist known for writing the World Scouting Bureau's *Scout Leader Handbook*. Though the *Russian Scout Handbook* contains its own unique program, it draws from the traditions of Scout handbooks from around the world—including the Boy Scouts of America.

A WOSM report of the day stated: "The rebirth of Scouting in the USSR is a very complex process, like most things today in that vast mosaic of nations. . . . The potential for Scouting in the USSR is enormous, but its organization had to be built on solid and clear ground. Much patience and understanding, as well as important human and material resources, are and will be necessary to meet such an historical challenge."

Soviet republics, was warmly welcomed into the fold, and many who attended shared the sentiment of one Scout: "They're just like us!"

VALUES OF AMERICAN BOYS—AND MEN

A major factor in whether or not a boy is exposed to Scouting is his home life, and whether he lives in a single-parent or even a no-parent home. At the BSA's 1995 National Annual Meeting, Chicago Archbishop Joseph Cardinal Bernardin addressed that issue, saying, "Immediately after World War II, four out of five children in this country grew up in a two-parent family. Today, one-parent families are no longer the exception; they are rapidly becoming a common experience of our children." By 2000, it was pointed out, the United States would see more single-parent homes than two-parent homes. Most would be single-mother homes. Because the children of these single-

parent households are more likely to get involved in drugs and violent crime and have emotional and behavioral problems, it was very clear that the Scouts could have a strong positive impact on this cycle.

In a 1996 study titled "The Values of Men and Boys in America" undertaken by respected public opinion research firm Louis Harris and Associates (now Harris Interactive), participating researchers studied the prevailing beliefs and attitudes of school-age males and a national cross-section of men, including those with and those without Scouting experience. The results were no surprise to Scouts.

Put simply, Scouting works.

The statistical evidence was undeniable. The study found that boys who participated in Scouting for at least five years "often demonstrate higher ethical standards and moral standards than those who were never in Scouting." Nearly three-quarters

LEFT (top) The world jamboree celebrates the melding of cultures from Scouts worldwide. (bottom) Scouts from around the world gather at the 1991 World Scout Jamboree in South Korea. **ABOVE** Fireworks light up the sky above the jamboree.

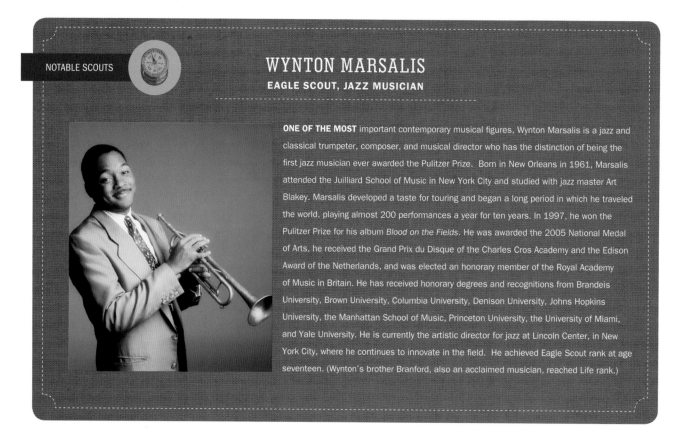

WYNTON MARSALIS
EAGLE SCOUT, JAZZ MUSICIAN

ONE OF THE MOST important contemporary musical figures, Wynton Marsalis is a jazz and classical trumpeter, composer, and musical director who has the distinction of being the first jazz musician ever awarded the Pulitzer Prize. Born in New Orleans in 1961, Marsalis attended the Juilliard School of Music in New York City and studied with jazz master Art Blakey. Marsalis developed a taste for touring and began a long period in which he traveled the world, playing almost 200 performances a year for ten years. In 1997, he won the Pulitzer Prize for his album *Blood on the Fields*. He was awarded the 2005 National Medal of Arts, he received the Grand Prix du Disque of the Charles Cros Academy and the Edison Award of the Netherlands, and was elected an honorary member of the Royal Academy of Music in Britain. He has received honorary degrees and recognitions from Brandeis University, Brown University, Columbia University, Denison University, Johns Hopkins University, the Manhattan School of Music, Princeton University, the University of Miami, and Yale University. He is currently the artistic director for jazz at Lincoln Center, in New York City, where he continues to innovate in the field. He achieved Eagle Scout rank at age seventeen. (Wynton's brother Branford, also an acclaimed musician, reached Life rank.)

of respondents who were former Scouts stated that a person should not do something considered "wrong" even if it meant future success, compared to less than 60 percent of non-Scouts asked the same question. And almost nine out of ten men who were former Scouts agreed that "the values I learned in Scouting continue to be important to me."

The study, later known as the "Harris Study," was the first formal attempt in BSA history to quantify Scouting's impact on the moral code of its young people. The study was a way to measure the impact Scouting could have on the way Scouts view the world, and eventually, how they would interact with that world later in life.

The Harris Study certainly turned up some disturbing data. A shocking 5 percent of the respondents in grades four through twelve said they'd carried a gun to school. Twenty-eight percent of respondents said they had been drunk in their lives. Seventeen percent said they had used drugs. Twenty-four percent said they had shoplifted or stolen items of some kind. Seventy-six percent admitted they had cheated in school.

But those boys who had participated in Scouting were shown to be more likely to be leaders in clubs and school groups, to put the needs of others before their own, to have better self-confidence, and to take better care of the environment (both their immediate environment and the world around them), and were more likely to be honest. The study revealed the importance of character-building programs like the Scouts, and galvanized Scouting to push for further market penetration in the coming 21st century.

CRIME WARS

Given the results of respondents to the Harris Study, it's no surprise that at the end of the twentieth century, the Boy Scouts focused heavily on crime prevention, launching a nationwide "war on crime" in May 1996. Joining forces with other

RIGHT Raising the flag and having fun at summer camp.

SUMMER CAMP: THE ENDURING EXPERIENCE

THERE ARE FEW EXPERIENCES that typify that of being a Boy Scout more than summer camp. It is the place where a lifetime of memories are formed, where friendships are cemented, and the timeless outdoors skills that have been part of the Scouting experience from inception are honed. Plus—apart from bouts with mosquitoes, sunburn, and poison ivy—it's just plain fun.

The first summer camps were an informal affair. As one early Scout remembered it: "The only summer camps were those arranged by Scoutmasters on friendly farmers' lands. Sometimes results had been disastrous because troops knew little of safety or sanitation. To save the movement, Scout executives had set up permanent camps with trained staffs and hired cooks and handy medical help."

In the modern era, summer camp is an integral and thriving part of the Scouting experience; the Boy Scouts is now affiliated with literally thousands of summer camps that are either wholly or partially owned by the BSA's central body or by the local councils themselves. These camps are located in diverse environments, each one offering unique outdoor opportunities along with the traditional hiking, campfires, and swimming.

The BSA Web site said it all: "The greatest adventures of a Scout's life begin at Boy Scout camp. Where but in the great outdoors can a boy hear the midnight hush of the deep woods . . . breathe the sweetness of distant wood-smoke . . . look down in awe at where he's been, and look up in wonder at where he still must go . . . glimpse the deer drinking at first light . . . watch eagles soaring in a cloudless sky . . . feel the warmth of the campfire as it glows orange against the thickening darkness . . . and at the end of a long day, hear the hooting owl under a sky flashing with stars."

These days it's the goal of most camp directors to keep boys interested in coming back next summer. Because many Scouts have already been to camp two summers in a row by the time they enter the eighth grade, camp activities have to be diverse and new to keep them challenged and having fun. At Robert W. Woodruff Scout Reservation in the foothills of north Georgia's mountains, the staff developed an "Ultimate Zone" that includes activities like caving, a ropes course, backpacking, fly-fishing, and white-water rafting on the Nantahala and Ocoee rivers. At the Utah National Parks Council's Entrada High Adventure Base, activities like climbing and rappelling on sandstone cliffs and mountain biking on the Slickrock Trail or Gemini Bridges are just some of the adventurous outdoor choices available. If that isn't enough, Scouts can pan for gold, climb various surrounding mountain peaks, or explore the local Anasazi ruins in one of five camps in different locations in Utah. Scouts who go to the Heritage Reservation in the Laurel Highlands of southwestern Pennsylvania are afforded an opportunity to try their hand at tomahawk throwing, black-powder rifle shooting, canoeing, and climbing a rock wall.

ON THIS PAGE Scouts at Camp Constantine show their exuberance.

organizations like the National Crime Prevention Council, the National Sheriffs' Association, and the International Association of Chiefs of Police, the BSA tackled the issue of juvenile involvement in crime head-on. Problems such as chronic juvenile delinquency, violent youth-on-youth crime, and increasing youth involvement in serious crimes were at the top of the list of issues to combat.

In many ways, the Boy Scouts had been working to prevent juvenile involvement in crime for its entire history. According to a 1993 study by the Office of Juvenile Justice and Delinquency Prevention, "Our children must be taught moral, spiritual and civic values. The decline in inculcating these values has contributed significantly to an increase in delinquent behavior." As the Boy Scouts had advocated these principles all along, it had

undoubtedly influenced unknown numbers of boys who might have otherwise turned to crime.

The BSA's crime prevention program had four main components: family, youth, community, and unit. The Boy Scouts addressed the ways that crime prevention could be incorporated into each facet of a Scout's life, making crime prevention a daily activity. Cub Scouts, Boy Scouts, and Explorers all had the opportunity to work toward a Crime Prevention Award. Youngsters learned how to settle arguments with their words and not their fists, how to spot and report a crime, and how to create programs that helped make neighborhoods safer.

BSA families and communities also worked together to form neighborhood watch groups and hold crime prevention rallies and parents' nights, where local law enforcement

ABOVE Scouts meet to discuss neighborhood partnerships to reduce crime. **RIGHT** Scouts posting a flyer in their effort to stymie crime.

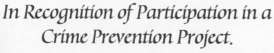

Crime Prevention Award

Is Presented to

In Recognition of Participation in a
Crime Prevention Project.

Given this_____ day of_____, 19____.

As Attested to by:

TAKE A BITE OUT OF
CRIME

Boy Scouts of America

It is evident that as boys get older, their incidence of participating in undesirable behaviors increases substantially. This finding reflects the difficulties our nation's youth are experiencing in today's society. Perhaps more importantly, these findings highlight the importance of reinforcing and rewarding strong moral standards among youth at an early age.

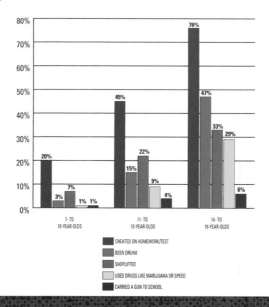

Recent Ethical and Moral Choices
"During the past year, have you..."

Legend:
- CHEATED ON HOMEWORK/TEST
- BEEN DRUNK
- SHOPLIFTED
- USED DRUGS LIKE MARIJUANA OR SPEED
- CARRIED A GUN TO SCHOOL

Behavior	7- to 10-year-olds	11- to 13-year-olds	14- to 19-year-olds
Cheated on homework/test	20%	45%	76%
Been drunk	3%	15%	47%
Shoplifted	7%	22%	33%
Used drugs like marijuana or speed	1%	9%	29%
Carried a gun to school	1%	4%	6%

Your Responsibility to Yourself

An understanding of wholesome sexual behavior can bring lifelong happiness. Irresponsibility or ignorance, however, can cause a lifetime of regret. AIDS and other diseases spread by sexual contact can ruin your health and that of others. An unplanned pregnancy before you are ready could severely limit your chances for education, occupations, and travel.

You owe it to yourself to enter adulthood without extra hurdles to overcome. Learn what is right. Your religious leaders can give you moral guidance. Your parents or guardian or other responsible adults can provide the facts about sex that you must know.

If you have questions about growing up, about relationships, or about sex, **ask**. Talk with your parents, religious lead[...] master. They want what is best for you[...]

officers came to address various ways for young people and parents to keep their neighborhoods safe.

THE SUNSET OF THE CENTURY

The return to basics and the resurgence of the Boy Scouts had begun with William Hillcourt's revised *Boy Scout Handbook*; another edition was published in 1990, and fittingly, at the close of the century, yet another edition was published. Though not a radical change from 1990's tenth edition, the last handbook of the century, released in 1998, does reflect the time in which it was produced. Contemporary references to the Internet, GPS, AIDS, and STDs (though still making it explicitly clear that there should be no sex before marriage) made it an important and modern handbook.

The Chief Scout Executive at the time of the 1990 handbook's printing, Ben Love, said, "I know of no greater piece of literature to reinforce the values of the Boy Scouts of America than this new Handbook. It's our hope and belief that it will serve the needs of Scouts throughout the remainder of this century."

LEFT (top) Crime Prevention Award Certificate. (bottom) Chart from the 1996 Harris Study showing the positive impact of Scouting. **ABOVE** (left) Cover of *The Boy Scout Handbook*, 1998. (top right) Interior page of the 1998 handbook discussing sexual responsibility. (bottom right) Jere Ratcliff, who served as Chief Scout Executive at the time of the 1998 handbook's printing.

THE BOY SCOUT HANDBOOK THROUGH THE DECADES

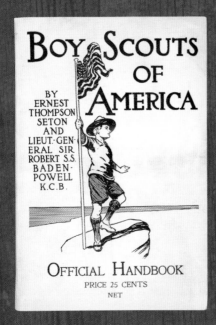

WITH MORE THAN 37 MILLION COPIES in print since 1911, the handbook is the third best-selling copyrighted book in U.S. history—behind the *Guinness Book of World Records* (80 million) and *Dr. Spock's Baby and Child Care* (43 million).

The handbook forms the backbone of the Scout's kit, and is the indispensable guide to all things associated with Scouting. The eleven numbered editions of *The Boy Scout Handbook* (the exact title has varied over the years) is also an invaluable historical record of the first 100 years of Scouting. Like Scouting itself, the handbook has reflected the times in which it was produced and has become a touchstone for those interested in preserving the fundamentals of Scouting, as well as those who seek to help the Boy Scouts of America evolve with changing times.

The handbook traces its lineage back to 1910's *Boy Scouts of America: A Handbook of Woodcraft, Scouting, and Life-Craft* prepared by Ernest Thompson Seton; it incorporated elements from both Seton's own writings and Baden-Powell's *Scouting for Boys*, and is now referred to as the original edition. The official first edition, titled *Handbook for Boys*, hit print at the end of August 1911. Ten further editions were published from 1911 through 1998, generally at eight- or nine-year intervals. At this writing, a twelfth edition is in the works.

A notable feature of the first two editions was an emphasis on conservation of natural resources and respectful treatment of wild animals and plant life—concepts that were unfamiliar to many Americans of the day. These values were also emphasized in the fourth edition (1940), in which the BSA's longtime director of conservation, Ted S. Pettit, wrote of the "web of life" and suggested ways that Scouts might consider their place in the order of nature—at a time when terms like *ecology* and *the environment* had yet to enter the mainstream vocabulary.

In the fifth (1948) edition, writers' bylines were no longer included. This first postwar edition also dropped instructions on how to make things like tents and pack frames—maybe a reflection of the fact that with so much military-surplus gear available, these skills were now redundant. The first handbook for the baby-boom generation arrived in 1959 in the form of the sixth edition. It was also the last edition to carry ads and the first to carry full-color illustrations. The seventh edition (1965) was not much different from the sixth in content, but it's probably the most widely used edition of the handbook, as its publication coincided with the peak years of membership in Scouting.

As discussed in Part Four, the eighth edition (1972) represented a break with the past, de-emphasizing camping and outdoor skills in a well-meaning effort to broaden Scouting's appeal to inner-city boys. The handbook returned to its roots with the ninth edition (1979). Bob Birkby's tenth edition handbook, in use from 1990 to 1998, is notable for its colorful photos and drawings, as well as for its emphasis on low-impact camping.

The most recent version of the handbook, the eleventh edition (1998), the culmination of three or so years of intense research in the field by Birkby, combines Scouting's past, present, and future. Though it makes mention of the Internet and GPS, its tone harks back to the earliest years of the movement. Even on page one, the book invokes Scouting's reinvigorated spirit on the eve of the 21st century: The book opens with "The Adventure Begins," and takes off from there. As the *New York Post* said of the eleventh edition: "The book is simply unassailable; this is a guide for life."

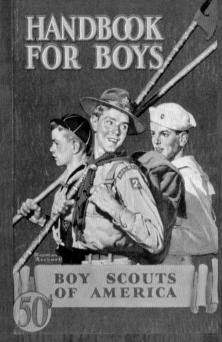

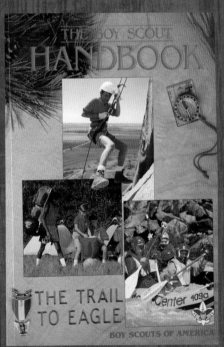

LEFT Handbook cover from Baden-Powell's original edition. **ABOVE** (clockwise, starting from top left) *Boy Scout Handbook* covers from the second edition, a Norman Rockwell painting graced the cover of the fourth edition, the seventh edition, and the tenth edition.

1910

1910 Society

OUT OF THE PAST
INTO THE FUTURE

2000

PART SIX

NATIONAL SCOUT JAMBOREE
STRONG VALUES · STRONG LEADERS
2001

SCOUTING'S SECOND CENTURY
1999—PRESENT

LEFT A tribute to 90 years of Scouting, in a painting by Csatari.

I f the dawn of the new century meant anything to the Boy Scouts, it was that the Scouts' fundamental values and core mission were built on bedrock that proved unshakable. It was in the first years of the 21st century that America remembered that there are few things as distinctly American as a Boy Scout.

On February 8, 2000, the Boy Scouts of America turned ninety years old. The organization marked the anniversary with a look back at nine decades of tradition, and a look forward at Scouting's future. In a yearlong series of celebrations, programs like Salute a Leader and Rekindle the Spirit encouraged present and past Scouts to reflect upon the great place that Scouting held in their lives and in the history of the United States. Incorporated into banquets, fall camporees, and Klondike derbies, the Salute a Leader programs, which took place from November 1, 1999, to February 5, 2000, allowed older Scouters to nominate adult figures who served as childhood role models. The celebration's second phase, from February 6 through June 15, 2000, was called Rekindle the Spirit, and was designed to do just that—remind all Scouts both past and present of the spirit of the BSA. For example, New York State's Rip Van Winkle Council created window displays with Scouting themes. "We thought window displays were a good way to get Scouting's message to the public, and the ninetieth anniversary seemed an ideal time for them," said Scout Executive Jeff Rand. "We had several dozen displays, many of them up for all of February. And we plan to do it again next year."

The celebration year culminated with phase three, which took place from June 16 through October 31. Dubbed the BSA Great Leadership Search, this phase was a nationwide search for exceptional adult leaders who instilled the very best values in young people and who exemplified the principles of the Scout Oath and Law. Winners were recognized in a series of local banquets and received special gifts and certificates of recognition.

RESPONDING TO CRISIS

On the heels of the ninetieth anniversary came a powerful reminder of the Boy Scouts' unique role in critical moments of American history: the events of September 11, 2001—a day that

changed our nation forever. As in virtually every major American disaster, tragedy, and challenge, the Boy Scouts were there. And just as Scouts have during fires and floods, hurricanes and tornadoes, landslides and droughts, Scouts and Scout leaders across the country lost no time in helping. As stated in the BSA's Annual Report for 2001: "'Be Prepared.' 'Do my best to do my duty'. . . 'Help other people at all times' . . . The events of that tragic day drew together Scouts and leaders across the country as a living example that these words that each Scout recites are more than words—they are a way of life."

Those who saw the Scouts walking purposefully through downtown Manhattan on those dark days after September 11 said that seeing them was like seeing the spirit of America piercing through the chaos of the aftermath. "It was like having a slice of pie back home, sitting on the front porch in midsummer, watching fireflies flash through the night air," recounted one observer. "It was like watching America's hope

ABOVE Ground Zero rescue worker shows handwritten thank-you messages written on his hard hat. **RIGHT** Heroes and future heroes in a painting by Joseph Csatari.

return to our streets. When I saw those Scouts, handing out bottles of water and blankets, collecting donations, somehow I knew it was going to be all right."

Troops from Washington, D.C.; to Little Rock, Arkansas; to Provo, Utah; and beyond, organized themselves into patriotic booster groups, holding flag-waving demonstrations in public displays of patriotism and national unity. The National Capital Area Council of metropolitan Washington, D.C., including Cub Scouts, Boy Scouts, Venturers, and leaders, rallied in full uniform in high-traffic locations, waving flags. Numbering in the thousands, these uniformed Scouts helped boost morale and stir up American patriotism.

"Seeing the Scouts waving those flags and standing proudly in their uniforms reminded me of what makes this country so special," said Kelly Steeples, who watched Scouts

from several local troops as they displayed their flags on a D.C. street corner. "It's young people like this who carry the spark of freedom and make all of us proud to be citizens of the United States of America."

"We could hear the crowds and the sirens and all of the people running out of the city when the towers fell," said one young New York area Scout whose local troop swung into action only days after the attack. "We went out and did what we could for the firemen and policemen and for the people who got stuck in the city."

Scouts of Long Island's Suffolk County Council launched a donation drive for liquid refreshments for rescue workers toiling in the wreckage of the towers. More than 153,000 bottles of water, soda, and sports drinks were collected just seventy hours after the first request was made. The donations, which filled six

ABOVE (left) *Boys' Life* page honoring Richard Pearlman, an assistant Scoutmaster who gave his life helping the injured at Ground Zero. (right) Condolence letter from the BSA to Pearlman's mother, Doris Pearlman.

ON THIS PAGE Scouts from the South Florida Council participate in a Ten Commandments Hike, visiting different religions' places of worship to increase their understanding and fellowship, Miami Lakes, Florida, April 2005.

need for resting places for Ground Zero rescue workers, they donated 500 cots.

In addition to collecting canned goods and other supplies, the South Florida Council organized a massive candlelight vigil just seventy-two hours after the towers fell. Scouts in Idaho Falls, Idaho, wanted to bring their community together and demonstrate its deep roots of pride and patriotism. They did so by placing flags in the yards of one house out of every three throughout the town. Long Island's Scouts, not content with their donation of 153,000 bottles of water and other refreshments, placed handwritten messages of appreciation and encouragement in hundreds of hard hats belonging to Ground Zero rescue workers. One young Scout, after seeing a Ground Zero rescue worker showing his worn gloves in a television interview, collected over 300 pairs from family, friends, and neighbors.

Many Scout troops in the greater New York area adopted fire stations during the months following the attack. These troops organized family-style potluck dinners and get-togethers for the firemen and the volunteers, who not only benefited from the homemade meals, but from the kind of spirit that a Boy Scout troop can inspire.

Boy Scouts are one of the most powerful and enduring symbols of American society. As such, the Scouts' participation

"The goodness of a person and of the society he or she lives in often comes down to the very simple things and words founds in the Scout Law. Every society depends on trust and loyalty, on courtesy and kind ness, on bravery and reverence. These are the values of Scouting, and these are the values of Americans."

FORMER PRESIDENT GEORGE W. BUSH

tractor trailers, were trucked to a local distribution warehouse and then sent on to Ground Zero.

Scout troops mobilized elsewhere around the country, collecting donations of canned food, clothing, and supplies to be sent by the truckload to rescue workers at the disaster sites in New York City; Washington, D.C.; and rural Pennsylvania. When the Greater New York Councils learned of an urgent

during times of crisis is imperative on two levels. Their work as volunteers and community leaders is certainly integral to their role, but the Scouts' symbolic power goes beyond mere volunteerism, service, and leadership. The Scouts' participation in the aftermath of September 11 helped remind Americans that while buildings might have fallen, our spirit, embodied in organizations like the Scouts, could not be damaged.

ABOVE Flags fly at half mast at the BSA's national headquarters after September 11.

True to the BSA's deeply rooted tradition of understanding, togetherness, and tolerance, the Boy Scouts did not stop their efforts after that terrible day in September. As part of a long tradition of inclusion, the units in New York's Greater New York Councils participated in programs like the Ten Commandments Hike, on which the boys visited places of worship belonging to Muslim, Jewish, and Christian faiths in an effort to create understanding and brotherhood. The Scouts pledged an ongoing commitment to building a bridge of understanding between cultures and religion, and still maintain many of the programs stemming from their experiences during September 11.

One of the most poignant stories to arise from the tragedy of that day was that of twenty-eight-year-old Shawn E. Bowman Jr., an Eagle Scout and assistant Scoutmaster in Staten Island's Troop 43. Active in Scouting almost two-thirds of his life, Shawn had just taken a job at the Cantor Fitzgerald financial firm as a human-resources specialist. His office was on one of the upper floors of the World Trade Center.

Shocked and saddened by the loss of their fellow Scout, the Greater New York Councils wanted to create a lasting tribute to their fallen friend and fellow Eagle Scout. For months, the troops and Shawn's friends worked together to raise over $30,000, most coming from donations as small as $1, to build a memorial in his honor. Thinking they would create a small memorial, or perhaps rename a campfire area, the group was shocked and touched when more than $150,000 flooded in from outside sources, many of whom didn't know Shawn personally but heard of his friends' efforts.

With the money, the group got together and created an outdoor amphitheater at Shawn's local council campsite, Camp Aquehonga near Narrowsburg, New York.

SCOUTREACH

At the close of 2001, more than 5 million youth participated in Scouting and Scouting-related activities. Part of the credit for this continuing success is attributable to the efforts of the BSA's new Scoutreach Division. An evolution of earlier initiatives like the Inter-Racial Service and the Inner-City Rural Program,

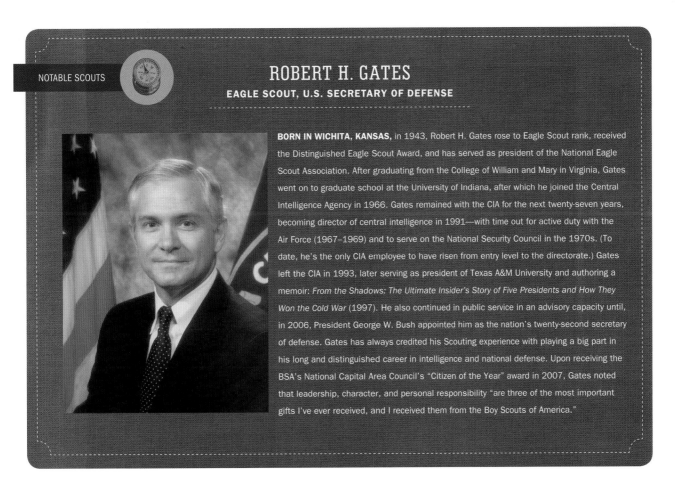

NOTABLE SCOUTS

ROBERT H. GATES
EAGLE SCOUT, U.S. SECRETARY OF DEFENSE

BORN IN WICHITA, KANSAS, in 1943, Robert H. Gates rose to Eagle Scout rank, received the Distinguished Eagle Scout Award, and has served as president of the National Eagle Scout Association. After graduating from the College of William and Mary in Virginia, Gates went on to graduate school at the University of Indiana, after which he joined the Central Intelligence Agency in 1966. Gates remained with the CIA for the next twenty-seven years, becoming director of central intelligence in 1991—with time out for active duty with the Air Force (1967–1969) and to serve on the National Security Council in the 1970s. (To date, he's the only CIA employee to have risen from entry level to the directorate.) Gates left the CIA in 1993, later serving as president of Texas A&M University and authoring a memoir: *From the Shadows: The Ultimate Insider's Story of Five Presidents and How They Won the Cold War* (1997). He also continued in public service in an advisory capacity until, in 2006, President George W. Bush appointed him as the nation's twenty-second secretary of defense. Gates has always credited his Scouting experience with playing a big part in his long and distinguished career in intelligence and national defense. Upon receiving the BSA's National Capital Area Council's "Citizen of the Year" award in 2007, Gates noted that leadership, character, and personal responsibility "are three of the most important gifts I've ever received, and I received them from the Boy Scouts of America."

Scoutreach aimed to foster Scouting in underserved areas. According to the official Scoutreach vision statement: "Scoutreach reflects the diversity of the urban and rural neighborhoods and communities that it serves and uses that strength to enhance customer satisfaction and enrich the Scouting experience." The Hispanic Emphasis of the previous decade was integrated into Scoutreach, but efforts in the Hispanic community remained an important priority.

Asian American participation in Scouting also saw a dramatic increase in the new century, particularly in 2006, and many Scout troops were composed largely of Scouts of Japanese, Chinese, and Vietnamese descent. In San Jose, California, for example, Chinese community life takes place around various Chinese-language schools that form the background to a vibrant and close-knit Asian community; BSA Troop 452 is chartered to the Association of Northern California Chinese Schools. In addition to traditional Scouting activities, the Chinese American Scouts participated in a national Scout jamboree held in Taiwan, and benefited from the many Scouts whose Chinese is good enough to qualify them for the Chinese-language interpreter strip. (An interpreter strip is the patch Scouts wear on their uniforms to show their ability to speak a language other than English.) Troop 452 is highly active not only within San Jose's Chinese American community, but in the larger community as well, through activities like taking part in parades, organizing Good Turn programs, and fund drives.

THE NATIONAL SCOUTING MUSEUM

In many ways, the institution of Scouting reflects the changes of the country itself. It simply made sense, then, that the Boy

ABOVE A Venturer draws a cheerful crowd of fellow Venturers as he strums his guitar. **RIGHT** (top) Young Webelos Scout with his mother, a Webelos leader. (bottom left) Three boys pose in their Cub Scout uniforms. (bottom right) Asian American Venturer.

NORTHEAST REGION HEADQUARTERS
2001 JAMBOREE

ON THIS PAGE In the summer of 2001, 40,000 Scouts converged on Fort A.P. Hill, Virginia, for the national Scout jamboree.

Scouts would create a place where the story of Scouting can come to life. In 2002, the BSA's goal of creating a world-class interactive museum to house its wealth of historical treasures was realized. The National Scouting Museum opened to great fanfare in Irving, Texas, near the BSA's national headquarters. In addition to the museum itself, the 50,000-square-foot campus-like facility is also home to the most extensive archive of Boy Scouts–related material in the world. "This is a museum of the 21st century," said Susan B. Hardin, museum director at the time of the opening. "It's not boring, it's not quiet, it's not dry.

It's designed to provide the typical visitor with three to four hours of unique and exciting activities. Its goal is to present the story, values—and fun—of Scouting in the most entertaining and enlightening way possible."

Anyone who has had the privilege of spending a few hours at the museum has experienced the sense of history, adventure, and high spirits of the Boy Scouts in a wholly new way—from animatronic figures that tell spooky campfire tales, to important works of art by Norman Rockwell, to Boy Scout camps through the ages brought to life in imaginative dioramas.

ABOVE The National Scouting Museum in Irving, Texas.

ON THIS PAGE The theme of the 2001 national Scout jamboree was "Strong Values, Strong Leaders."

"I think that American leadership is vital to peace and prosperity and the advancement of democracy in the world, and that requires having strong leaders. And I don't think there's any organization in the world, certainly not in the United States, that better prepares young men for leadership in this country than the Boy Scouts of America—in teaching leadership skills, in teaching values, in teaching importance of standing up for what's right."

ROBERT H. GATES

Though the Irving museum took the holdings of the Boy Scouts to a whole new level, the BSA has had a fully operational museum since 1960. This first Scouting museum was part of New Jersey's Johnston Historical Museum and held in its collection many of the documents and artifacts now on display at the new Irving, Texas, facility, including important papers of Ernest Thompson Seton and Baden-Powell and the first Eagle Scout medal ever awarded. The New Jersey museum was a popular destination for fans of Scouting, but the space wasn't large enough to do the collection justice. In 1986, the museum was relocated to Murray State University in Kentucky, where it remained in operation until the big move to Irving in 2001.

Though both of the previous museum locations were great facilities for their respective times, the BSA had to make the collections adapt to both locations, not the other way around. When fund-raising and relocation efforts had been successfully completed and it was time for a dedicated building to be designed around the collection, the new museum began to take shape.

LEFT (top) A museum docent shows a young boy gear from an earlier era in Scouting. (bottom) A Cub Scout learns about weather stations. **ABOVE** Scouts are mesmerized by the museum's offerings.

ON THIS PAGE The artist Joseph Csatari (bottom right) captured many iconic moments in Scouting. Many of Csatari's paintings can be found at the National Scouting Museum.

The National Scouting Museum was an instant success. The interactive, hands-on approach proved highly appealing to Scouts and Scouting enthusiasts both young and young at heart. The entryway brings visitors face-to-face with a dramatic engraving of the Scout Oath and Scout Law, flanking the BSA fleur-de-lis emblem. It has been known to cause more than a few older Scouters to tear up in its presence. "Seeing the Scout Oath and Scout Law, looking at that grand Scouting emblem, really made me feel proud to be a part of this great tradition," said one older Scouter visiting the museum for the first time.

The museum also boasts the largest collection of Scouting-related Norman Rockwell paintings anywhere in the world, housed in a special wing along with a life-sized figure of Rockwell and a re-creation of his Stockbridge, Massachusetts, studio. The museum owns the first Scout painting Rockwell created in 1918 when he was an illustrator for *Boys' Life* magazine; it also houses his very last painting, created in 1976. In addition, the museum owns works by other artists relevant to Scouting, including Joseph Csatari and Remington Schuyler, which are on display as part of various rotating exhibits.

ABOVE (top) Two boys explore the museum's expansive gallery. (bottom) The Boy Scout logo is featured prominently in the museum foyer; stone pillars are engraved with the Scout Oath.

STEVE FOSSETT
EAGLE SCOUT, RECORD-BREAKING AVIATOR

"[The] Boy Scouts does very well in making Scouts aware of character and integrity and . . . virtues and incorporates [them] in their lives so that they carry themselves as [those] kind of [people] for the rest of their [lives]."

—STEVE FOSSETT

LONG-DISTANCE BALLOONIST, aviator, and sailor, Steve Fossett was among the most celebrated adventurers of our time. While making his fortune in finance, Fossett set out to break records on land, sea, and air. During the course of his life, Fossett managed to set 116 records in five different sports—76 of which still stand at this writing. He was the first person to circumnavigate the globe alone in a balloon and the first person to successfully fly a nonstop solo and non-refueled flight around the world, making the flight in a single-engine jet airplane. In 2006, he again flew around the world on a non-refueled flight, setting the record for the longest continuous flight of any airplane in history. In 2004, Fossett set the record for the fastest circumnavigation of the globe by sea. In all, he set twenty-three official world records in sailing. Fossett also set a number of records as a glider pilot, including the August 29, 2006, absolute altitude record for a flight into the stratosphere at 50,727 feet. Fossett also set records for the fastest non-supersonic intercontinental flights in a jet. He climbed the highest mountains on six of the world's seven continents, competed in the Iditarod dogsled race and the Ironman Hawaii triathlon, swam the English Channel, and drove the 24 Hours of Le Mans. Fossett became an Eagle Scout at the age of thirteen, and was named a Distinguished Eagle Scout and awarded the Silver Buffalo by the Boy Scouts of America as an adult. He was a member and former president of the National Eagle Scout Association, was one of the first Venturing Committee chairmen, and sat on the National Executive Board of the BSA.

On September 3, 2007, Fossett took off from a small airstrip in the Nevada desert in a small single-engine prop plane. Characteristically, he was in search of yet more adventure and achievement—he was looking for a dry lake bed on which he could attempt to break the speed record for a land vehicle. Fossett never returned, and as of this writing no trace of him or his aircraft has been found. He has been declared deceased.

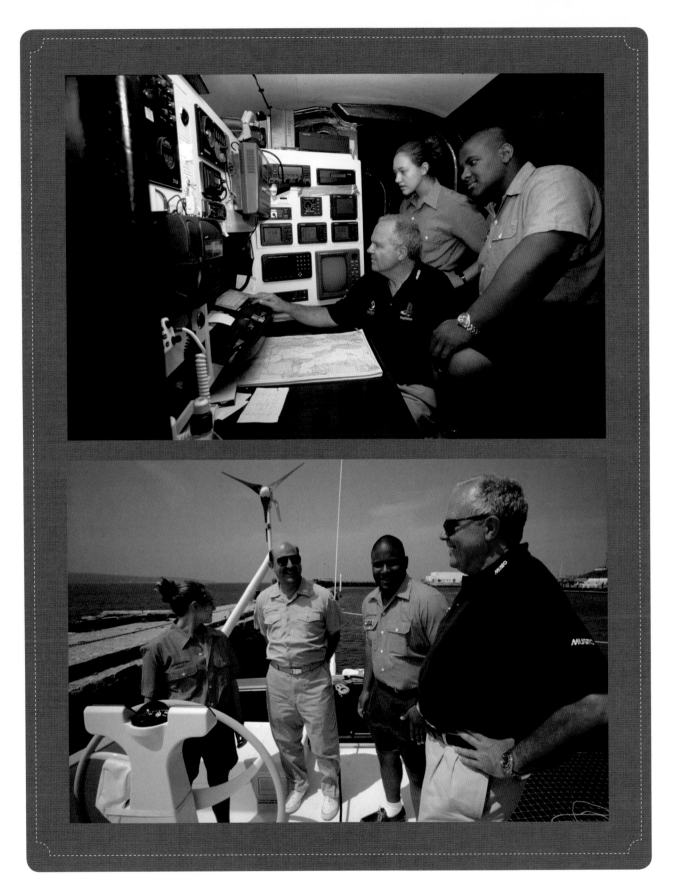

GOOD TURN FOR AMERICA

From W. D. Boyce's encounter with the "Unknown Scout" in 1909, the Good Turn—whether done by an individual Scout, a troop or other unit, or as part of a national initiative—remains at the heart of Scouting's core value of selfless service to others. As we've seen in earlier parts, the BSA conducted a number of National Good Turns in its first half century, from the Safe and Sane Fourth of July campaign in 1912 to the Get Out the Vote efforts of the 1950s.

In 2004, the BSA revived this tradition with the introduction of the Good Turn for America program. This nationwide campaign partnered the BSA with some of America's preeminent service organizations, including the Salvation Army, the American Red Cross, and Habitat for Humanity, as well as thousands of smaller, community-based groups. Actively cooperating with these organizations proved a great way for Scouts to help larger numbers of people and touch more lives. By the end of 2004, Scouts across the nation

ABOVE (top) Scouting for Shelter: Scouts team up with Habitat for Humanity in Atlanta, Georgia. (bottom) The Boy Scouts and Salvation Army team up to collect food donations. RIGHT (top) Willie Iles, director of the Development & Strategic Initiatives Group, speaking at the entry of the National Scouting Museum. (bottom) Iles congratulates a Scout troop's members for their Good Turn for America efforts.

"To people who know about Scouting, the daily Good Turn is one of the finest of our movement. The record of Good Turns, small and large, that have been done by Scouts since the day Scouting was founded is truly impressive."

THE BOY SCOUT HANDBOOK

had devoted over 3 million collective hours of service to the nation's neediest.

The BSA determined that poor health in young people due to lack of access or proper knowledge of medical care, homelessness or near homelessness, and hunger were the issues that were closest to the heart of the organization. So the program focused on the basics: Its three major areas of focus were dubbed Scouting for Food, Scouting for Shelter, and Scouting for Healthy Living.

Scouting for Food tackled hunger in America by partnering with groups like the Salvation Army. Activities in this area ranged from volunteering at local homeless shelters and soup kitchens to helping with food assistance and delivery programs for the elderly and needy.

Scouting for Shelter faced the lack of decent, affordable housing by many of the nation's poorest people. In collaboration with Habitat for Humanity, Scouts helped build thousands of new houses throughout the United States. Cub Scout Pack

ABOVE Youth across America jump into action for Habitat for Humanity. **RIGHT** (top) Scout volunteers get a lesson in electrical wiring while helping to build a house. (bottom) Scouts put a coat of paint on a newly constructed home.

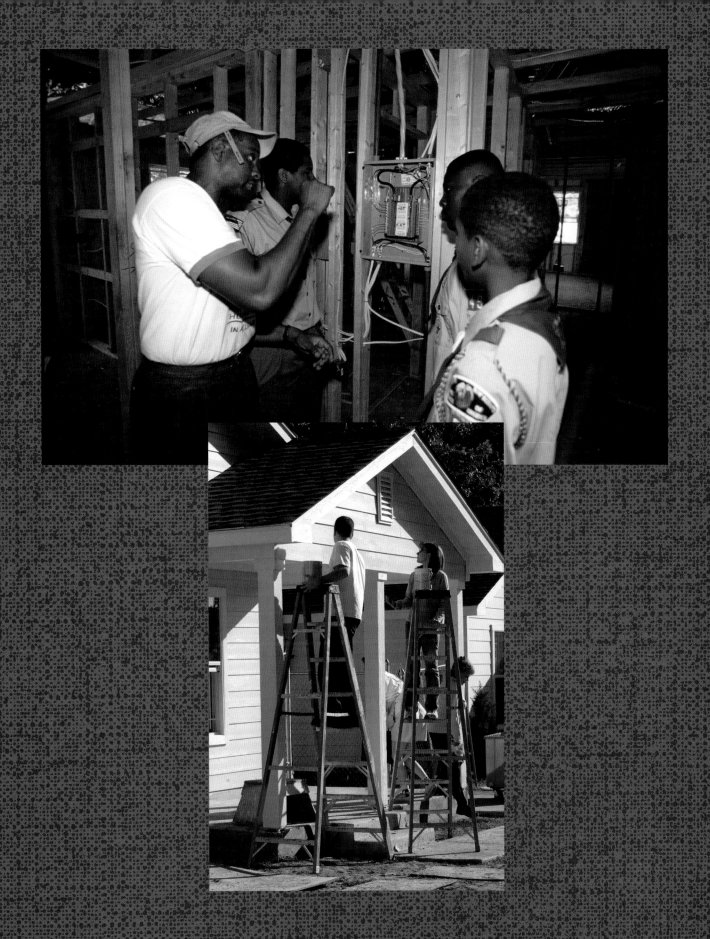

Habitat for Humanity **and the** Boy Scouts of America: **Making a Difference One Family at a Time**

Habitat for Humanity and the Boy Scouts of America are working together to address the problem of inadequate housing in our nation—one house, one community, one family at a time.

Whether you're part of a Habitat affiliate looking for volunteers, or a Scouting leader looking for volunteer opportunities for youth, this brochure tells you what opportunities are available. Depending on their age, Scouts can undertake a wide range of projects. Here are just a few ideas:

Tiger Cubs and Cub Scouts

- Make a welcome basket for the homeowner family, sing a song at the dedication, or perform a flag ceremony.
- Stock the pantry for a new Habitat for Humanity partner family.
- Draw messages or blessings on two-by-fours before the house framing.
- Landscape, learn about the local environment, and plant environmentally friendly trees and gardens.

Boy Scouts and Venturers

- Construct and paint window boxes to be used as housewarming gifts or as fund-raising items.
- Help clear the construction site of debris before or after construction.
- Help fold or stuff newsletters or mailings.
- Design an affiliate Web page or newsletter.
- Register volunteers at the construction site information table.

Boy Scouts of America and Habitat for Humanity

**Building Stronger Communities
ONE House,
ONE Community,
ONE Family at a Time**

Habitat for Humanity® International

Service Opportunities With Habitat for Humanity

Habitat for Humanity International is a nonprofit, ecumenical Christian organization dedicated to eliminating poverty housing worldwide.

Habitat brings together people with resources and people in need to build simple, decent, affordable houses. The houses are sold to those in need at no profit, through no-interest loans. Habitat for Humanity has built and sold more than 150,000 houses, providing shelter for more than 750,000 people worldwide.

Habitat has affiliates in every state of the United States and in 100 countries around the world.

People may volunteer individually or in groups or with organizations such as churches or Scouting units.

Contacting Habitat for Humanity

To find volunteer opportunities where you live, use the affiliate search engine at www.habitat.org.

ON THIS PAGE Brochure for the BSA's Scouting for Shelter collaboration with Habitat for Humanity. A page from the Scouting for Shelter brochure (top background) explains how Scouts of all ages can help build homes for families in need.

157 in Glenshaw, Pennsylvania, spent their Memorial Day weekend working to build new homes in their community. A Scout troop belonging to the W. D. Boyce Council in Peoria, Illinois, collected over 5 million cans to raise money for Habitat for Humanity.

Scouting for Healthy Living partnered with the American Red Cross to tackle problems associated with one of America's leading health issues: obesity. Obesity became a growing problem for American children in the early 21st century, when studies showed that almost one-third of children were overweight and 5 percent were clinically obese, putting them at risk of diabetes, heart disease, and other serious ailments as adults. Scouting for Healthy Living's efforts have focused on educating young people about habits of healthy living.

Good Turn for America's second year, 2005, saw an event that demonstrated the need for the power of volunteerism: Hurricane Katrina, which devastated the Gulf Coast and, especially, the city of New Orleans. As they had after 9/11, Scouts were on the scene quickly.

ABOVE (top) In December 2005, Troop 33 from Dekalb, Illinois, arrived in New Orleans to help after Hurricane Katrina. (bottom) A volunteer checks hundreds of cases of food donated to aid victims of Hurricane Katrina.

Boy Scouts of America

GOOD TURN FOR AMERICA
VOLUNTEER SERVICE PROJECT CHECKLIST

Community First Aid and Safety

First Aid/CPR/AED
☐ Sign up for a Red Cross first aid class.
☐ Take a Red Cross CPR class.
☐ Arrange for a CPR instructor to visit your group.
☐ Become a Red Cross instructor.
☐ _____

Disaster and Emergency Preparedness

Emergency Preparedness
☐ Build a family emergency kit.
☐ Build an emergency supplies kit.
☐ Build and donate kits to a day care facility or nursing home.
☐ _____

Disaster Relief
☐ Make a donation to victims affected by a disaster.
☐ _____

Personal Lifesaving

Blood Donations
☐ Donate blood at a local center.
☐ Organize a blood donation day at your workplace, school, or community center.
☐ _____

Swimming and Water Safety
☐ Take a Red Cross learn-to-swim class; invite a friend to join you.
☐ Attend a water safety presentation.
☐ _____

Lifeguard Programs
☐ Become a Red Cross–trained lifeguard.
☐ _____

02-780

Jamboree Scouts
build character

and a better tomorrow for a
mother and daughter

Learn more>>

FOOD • SHELTER • HEALTHY LIVING

⊠ Tell us about your service project

BOY SCOUTS OF AMERICA®

ON THIS PAGE (background) Good Turn for America checklist for volunteers, published by the BSA and the Red Cross. (foreground) Good Turn for America brochure promotes Scouting for Healthy Living.

Troop 33 of Dekalb, Illinois, for example, had plans to visit China for a Scout-sponsored trip. Instead, they made a trip to the storm-damaged region, bringing donated items—including fifty bicycles—for the victims of the disaster. For days afterward, the Scouts reported the great feeling of seeing people finally able to get around the damaged areas on bikes they had donated. That same troop also aided Animal Rescue New Orleans in saving pets that had become homeless during the storm and its aftermath.

By December 2007, more than 1.5 million Scouts and adult participants had taken part in Good Turn for America, conducting almost 70,000 service projects. Churches, food banks, homeless shelters, and the like gratefully welcomed the many thousands of young Scouts who tirelessly knocked on doors, hammered nails, and braved storms to perform the millions of individual Good Turns that composed the national effort. Besides the direct impact of 3 million hours of volunteer service, Good Turn for America had the welcome effect of strengthening Scouting's ties with service organizations and non-profit groups throughout the country.

2010: WHEN TRADITION MEETS TOMORROW

By the end of 2005, with its centenary just a few years away, the BSA had a youth membership of nearly 3 million youth members and over 1 million adult leaders, organized into 122,582 units. In that year, a total of 49,328 youths earned Eagle Scout rank—the

ABOVE Bicycles collected by Troop 33 in March 2006.

SCOUTING'S HIGHEST HONORS:
THE FOUR LIFESAVING AND MERITORIOUS ACTION AWARDS

THEY ARE PERHAPS the most highly regarded honors in Scouting. Since 1911, brave Scouts have been awarded these prestigious medals for sometimes dangerous, usually heroic, always selfless acts. Presented to Scouters of all ages and backgrounds, from the seasoned Eagle Scout to the green Cub Scout, these medals recognize heroes who have put themselves in the face of danger to intervene in the lives of those in emergency need.

The four medals are the Honor Medal, the Honor Medal With Crossed Palms, the Heroism Award, and the Medal of Merit—all given in recognition for "lifesaving or meritorious action." According to the official BSA charter: The Honor Medal is awarded to a youth or adult leader who demonstrates unusual heroism and skill in attempting to save a life at considerable risk to his own. In cases of exceptional resourcefulness and extreme risk of life, the medal is awarded with "Crossed Palms." The Heroism Award is given to a youth or adult who demonstrates heroism in saving or attempting to save a life at minimum risk to self. The Medal of Merit is awarded to a youth or adult who has performed some outstanding act of service of a rare or exceptional character that reflects an uncommon degree of concern for the well-being of others.

The medals recognition program became one of the rarest and most respected honors in Scouting. Under the direction of the National Court of Honor, the medals were originally differentiated by the type of material used in their creation. Gold, silver, and bronze designations, much like Olympic medals, were used to indicate degrees of risk involved in the act being honored. Gold was reserved for the few who risked death to save a life. The first recipient, Charles Scruggs of Cuero, Texas, received the bronze medal in 1911—although the act he received it for seems lost to history. Nine years later, it was determined by the National Court of Honor that medals should be of one designation due to the subjectivity in determining the degree of risk for lifesaving acts. Acts that did not involve risk would be honored first with a letter of commendation and later a certificate for heroism.

In 1923, National Court of Honor member Belmore Browne designed a new honor medal that he dubbed "The Red Badge of Courage": a medal suspended from a crimson ribbon. This new red badge replaced the old metal badges. It was just a year later that the National Court of Honor designated a special medal with crossed palms, to designate the higher honor and degree of risk for a heroic act.

In 1945, the Meritorious Action Award was added to the medal lineup for "Scouters and Scouts who performed some outstanding act of service not necessarily involving risk of life, but evidencing Scout skills and ideals of an unusually high order." This was first awarded in 1946 to recognize actions that didn't necessarily involve physical risk—quickly administering first aid to an accident victim, for example. In 1977, the Certificate of Merit was turned into a medal and was re-designated as the Heroism Award.

More than 12,000 individuals in Scouting have received these medals. Whether it was an Eagle Scout in Elmhurst, Illinois, saving a boy who had been badly cut after falling through a window; or a group of Scouts saving a man who had been choking in a house fire in Kansas City; or helping car crash victims with shock and bleeding in Utah, recipients nationwide have shown how Scouting skills and training can be used effectively in the world outside of the campground.

The
Boy Scouts of America
upon Recommendation
of the
National Court of Honor
Awards this

National Certificate of Merit

to

In Recognition of
Performance of a
Significant Act of Service

President   Chairman, National Court of Honor   Chief Scout Executive

No. 92-214   1996 Printing

LEFT (from left to right) the Heroism Award, the Medal of Merit, the Honor Medal, the Honor Medal With Crossed Palms.

ABOVE Outstanding Scouts are recognized with the National Certificate of Merit.

largest one-year total in the history of the Scouts. It was also a jamboree year, and this time some 43,000 Scouts, Scouters, and staff converged on Fort A.P. Hill.

As the BSA began to prepare for its next 100 years and beyond, it did what it always has: looked to its past to understand what's worked and what hasn't. The BSA has continually learned from experience and grown and changed with the times, yet the movement has remained faithful to the core values of its founding days. As the organization itself has stated: "Our mission has not changed, nor have the principles of Scouting. However, we realize our methods must adapt to meet the needs of time."

Scouting, which attracts approximately 1 million new youth members per year, continues to be the benchmark for youth-oriented, character-building organizations in the United States. Its mission, to prepare young people to make ethical and moral choices over their lifetimes by instilling in them the values of the Scout Oath and Law, continues to be the foundation upon which the organization is built.

ABOVE (top) President George W. Bush visits the 2005 jamboree. (bottom) Going rafting at the jamboree. **RIGHT** Hot-air balloons fly over the crowd at the 2005 jamboree's closing arena show.

BILL GATES
SCOUT, FOUNDER OF MICROSOFT

ONE OF THE WEALTHIEST MEN IN THE WORLD, with a personal fortune in excess of $50 billion, William "Bill" Henry Gates III is an entrepreneur, philanthropist, and the chairman of the Microsoft Corporation. Gates is widely credited as having played a key role in the early personal computer explosion of the 1970s and 1980s, after having gotten his start writing code for the first small personal computers on the market. After dropping out of Harvard, Gates, along with childhood friend Paul Allen and fellow Harvard student Steve Ballmer, formed an early partnership to produce programs for the Altair 8800. This small enterprise was the beginning of Microsoft, which came to dominate the PC software market with its DOS and Windows operating systems and other programs. Recently, Gates has taken a step back from the day-to-day operation of the company he founded to focus on the Bill and Melinda Gates Foundation, a philanthropic partnership he and his wife formed in 2000. Since its inception, Gates has given away $29 billion in awards, and after a financial commitment from financier Warren Buffett worth up to $1.5 billion per year, the foundation is the richest charitable organization in the world. Gates was an active Boy Scout and achieved the rank of Life Scout.

"I think the character that you learn in Scouting—working together, being honest with each other, being close knit . . . and depending on one another, on our camping trips and doing things—all these things build character in a young man that he takes with him into adulthood and makes him a much better citizen. And that's why Scouting to me has always been an organization I've always wanted to help. I think it's one of the best youth organizations that we . . . have in this country."

JAMES A. LOVELL JR., ADVISORY COUNCIL, BSA, AND *APOLLO 13* ASTRONAUT

In order to meet the challenge of continuing to keep Scouting vibrant and relevant, it established important goals as its centennial approached. First and foremost, every eligible Scout, regardless of geographical location, resources available, and social, cultural, and economic strata, will have the opportunity to take part in a high-quality Scouting experience that is both traditional and meets the needs of the time. Volunteers, the backbone to Scouting's survival, will be actively recruited and retained so each Scout troop they serve will have the opportunity and resources it needs. Professionals from all walks of life will be brought into the organization to add their expertise and energy to the movement.

As a sign of the changing times, the BSA is targeting outreach to younger parents. Noting a marked lack of interest in volunteering for youth organizations, the BSA conducts ongoing research programs to find ways of encouraging younger parents to participate as adult leaders and volunteers. And because most new growth occurs as part of existing relationships with chartered organizations, the BSA will begin a series of outreach programs to organizations like the Knights of Columbus, United Methodist Church, and home school associations.

Like a good parent or a trusted mentor, the BSA has helped form, shape, and guide not only the individual character of tens of millions of young people, but also the character of America itself. The second century of Scouting in America will certainly hold many challenges, but the Scouts will meet them on a time-tested base of values and traditions.

ABOVE Some of the many activities Scouts found at the 2005 National Scout Jamboree at Fort A.P. Hill, Virginia.

It's Our Turn To Make A Difference!

If you are a parent or grandparent, you may recall a time when some adult made a difference in your life. Now, it's your turn to make a difference in the life of a child. Don't miss the opportunity that is in front of you. Invest time in the life of a child. While today's youth may have different needs than you had as a child, one thing remains true: they need time with you.

BOY SCOUTS OF AMERICA

ON THIS PAGE (clockwise from top left) Brochure designed to inspire adult volunteers to participate in a new generation of Scouting; Scouts at the jamboree take part in a 5K run/walk (the U.S. surgeon general also took part); boys spread out badges for trading at the 2005 jamboree.

ON THIS PAGE Aerial shot from the 2005 jamboree.

INSIGNIA AND PATCH COLLECTING

IT'S ONE OF THE MOST REWARDING and enduring aspects of Scouting, and it's been a part of Scouting tradition almost since the birth of the BSA: It's called patch trading, and its history is intimately connected with the history of Scouting itself. When current and former Scouts get together, along with telling tales and having a good laugh, it's the trading of the multitude of patches and insignias produced as part of Scouting's system of organization and awards that often takes center stage. Patches and insignias have been a part of Scouting since the early days of British Scouting, and collecting these pieces of history has been a popular activity since that first badge was placed on that first chest more than 100 years ago.

Before patches and insignias were part of the Scouting tradition, trading among Scouts was limited to collectible items like handmade neckerchief slides, or even the trading of uniforms in their entirety. Once patches and other insignias were introduced, they became the main focus of trading activity. The early days of American trading was on a much smaller scale than today; the only patches available were the rank, merit, and position badges worn on the uniforms at the turn of the century. Trading was most commonly seen at the jamborees, where Scouts from every corner of the country were together in one place.

According to Scouting historian Bruce C. Shelley, the popularity of trading was due in part to the Order of the Arrow. The patches associated with this elite group were relatively rare and carried with them a cache: The OA patches were only awarded to a small number of Scouts and displaying them on a uniform was an indication of a Scout's achievement. A tradition developed among OA lodges, wherein different lodges made alliances with one another and exchanged patches as a symbol of friendship. These Scouts grew into adult supporters of Scouting who maintained an interest in patch collecting and trading. The majority of collectors today, according to Shelley, are former OA members.

It was at the 1937 jamboree, however, that patch collecting was most likely introduced to the larger population of Scouts. Though OA patches were traded here, trading was opened up to patches of all kinds, including those associated with camp, activities, regions, and professional designations. By 1950, different patches existed for most individual councils, and it was these unique examples that became hot items in the trading game. It was in response to this wide variety of patches that historian Dwight Bischel published the first definitive book on the subject in 1952: *Wabaningo Lodge Emblem Handbook*.

Around 1960, Scouting witnessed its first event dedicated solely to the trading mania: the tradeoree. Because jamborees were held every four years, rabid traders were unable to easily trade during the breaks. The tradeorees are now held all over the country, and some play host to more than 300 individual traders, each with his own table dedicated to the hobby.

Most traders focus on one of sixty categories of collectible patches and insignias as recognized officially by the American Scouting Traders Association, the largest of several collectors' groups. According to the ASTA, the most popular items to collect are the Order of the Arrow flaps and council shoulder patches, also called CSPs. These CSP collectors often fall into two camps: those that collect the red-and-white lettered patches that were used up to 1970, and those that collect the colorful, visually striking post-1970 CSPs. Both are highly collectible and equally as fun to hunt down. Some shoulder patches are now worth upward of $10,000!

Though trading started out as a way to cement friendships and forge bonds with Scouts from other regions, patch and insignia trading has become a serious pursuit for some collectors. Though Scouting memorabilia may not be at the level of stamp or baseball card collecting, prices for early and rare patches have increasingly gone up over the years. At an auction in the early 21st century, an Order of the Arrow patch issued in about 1920 by the Ranachqua Lodge No. 4 in the Bronx Council of the Greater New York Councils, went for $24,500—the highest price ever paid for a piece of Scouting history. The patch that sold is the only known example of this rare design, depicting a green owl with the OA symbol serving as the background design.

Patch and insignia collecting is an ever-growing hobby whose popularity seems to increase every year. With new patches and insignias being constantly produced, collectors never cease to find ways to add to their collections.

ABOVE (top left) A Scout wears his Order of the Arrow sash. (top right) The beloved activity of patch trading. (bottom) Rare patches associated with lodges and councils.

"Many fathers who participated in Derbies years ago still have their cars. Today, they watch their sons embark on the same adventure."

CUBMASTER DON MURPHY, 2003

PINEWOOD DERBY® 60TH ANNIVERSARY

On May 15, 1953, a small California Scout House hosted a group of Cub Scouts racing their own miniature, hand-carved pinewood cars along a sloped track. The inspiration for these races had come to Cubmaster Don Murphy on witnessing his son's disappointment at being too young to enter a local soap box derby. The event's success brought it to the attention of the BSA Directors, who thought it worthy of national promotion. Murphy little dreamed that sixty years later, in 2013, the Boy Scouts of America would be celebrating the diamond anniversary of what had become a national Cub Scout event.

Aside from some technical alterations to the cars and tracks, today's Pinewood Derby® is essentially the same as it was on its initial inception. Its mission—to unite fathers and sons in a spirit of craftsmanship and sportsmanship—still lies at the heart of the event. What has changed is its scale: today, over one million youths take part in Pinewood Derbies across the U.S. every year.

The notable anniversary inspired many Cub Scout packs to organize their first derby, while those with established races saw a surge in interest. Some packs chose to make the occasion extra special by awarding trophies designed in a diamond motif to reflect the sixty-year history of this cherished event.

ABOVE Some of the parents and sons who have raced their cars at pinewood derbies over the event's sixty years.

ABOVE Cub Scouts check out their competition before the race.

RIGHT Wolf Cub Scouts proudly display their Pinewood Derby® cars.

BELOW Participants hand-carve and decorate their own cars.

EAGLE SCOUT® CENTENNIAL

Over two million youths have reached the level of Eagle Scout, the highest rank in the Boy Scouts of America program, since Arthur Rose Eldred of New York achieved 21 merit badges to officially become the first Eagle Scout on August 21, 1912. The following one hundred years witnessed a huge evolution in the Boy Scouting program as a whole and the 2012 centennial of the Eagle Scout award marked a celebration of both the history and the modern manifestation of this Boy Scouting honor, and also served as a recognition of the great contribution that its members have made to their communities and to the nation. Eagle Scouts have certainly left an indelible mark on history, with astronauts, U.S. presidents, entrepreneurs, sports stars, and actors numbering among the ranks of Eagle Scouts past— and with less than 5 percent of all Scouts typically achieving this rank, the centennial of such an illustrious award deserved a worthy celebration.

The National Eagle Scout Association commissioned Joseph Csatari—the official artist of the BSA since 1977—to paint a picture in honor of the anniversary. *100 Years of Eagle Scouts* was unveiled at the National Annual Meeting of the Boy Scouts of America in June of the centennial year. In keeping with the occasion, while being a representation of the modern-day Eagle Scout, the painting also succeeds in capturing the spirit of the traditional Norman Rockwell Scouting artwork of the past.

Every young Scout experiences a surge of pride on placing his Eagle badge on his uniform for the first time. As an extra-special honor—and an added incentive—all of those lucky enough to join the Eagle Scouting ranks in 2012 became eligible to wear a special edition of the red, white, and blue badge featuring the words "Eagle Scout Centennial" stitched in silver and the years "1912" and "2012" prominent in gold.

Scouting groups and councils around the country organized their own commemorative centennial celebrations, which saw Eagle Scouts past and present come together for parades and other events and to partake in anniversary dinners and banquets. Eagles of yesteryear were invited to share their Scouting memories with today's Boy Scouts at community gatherings, where stories were swapped and cherished badges admired in a demonstration of the truth of the phrase "Once an Eagle, always an Eagle."

ABOVE (left) The special edition Eagle Scout Centennial merit badge. (right) Anthony Thomas, the two millionth Eagle Scout, proudly wears his merit badge sash.

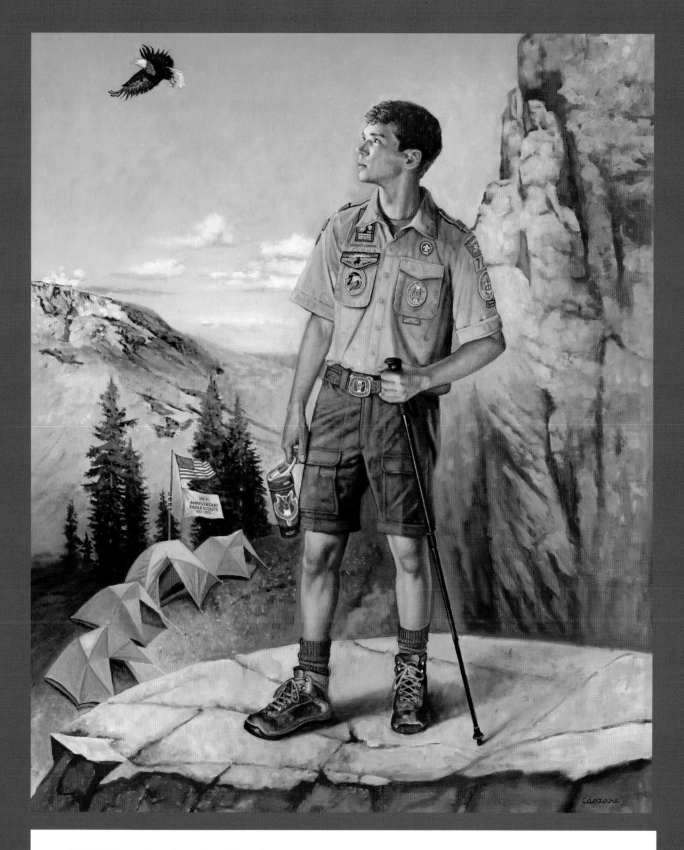

ABOVE *100 Years of Eagle Scouts*, Joseph Csatari's centennial painting, portrays Eagle Scout Matthew Dobromilsky of Jamesburg, New Jersey.

"That [land] represents an ideal of my youth ... Now I want to make it available to other boys."

WAITE PHILLIPS

PHILMONT® 75TH ANNIVERSARY

First established in 1938 when businessman Waite Phillips donated 38,000 acres of New Mexico land to the Scouts as a wilderness camp, the following 75 years saw Philmont® Scout Ranch grow to encompass 137,000 acres, becoming Scouting's largest adventure base. Almost one hundred Scout camps and hundreds of miles of rocky trails are nestled among high hills and mountains, canyons and streams. This rugged terrain, the abundant wildlife, and the marks of Native American history that the land still bears are just some of the elements that make Philmont a jewel in the BSA's crown—and the reason why close to one million adventure seekers have come here since its inaugural season to participate in multi-day treks, training programs, and activities such as mountain climbing, horseback riding, and panning for gold.

The milestone of one of the BSA's best loved locations was marked in several ways: "Celebration Treks" were held at the site in July 2013 and for the duration of that year all who took part in a Philmont trek earned a special 75th-anniversary edition

of its famed arrowhead patch. Philmont also chose this year to launch Campaign4Philmont, a project to upgrade several of its facilities to ensure that the ranch can continue to fully serve the Scouting needs of the future. Seventy-five years after Waite Phillips' original gift of land was given, his legacy lives on.

ABOVE (top) The entrance to Philmont Scout Ranch in the Santo de Cristo mountain range, New Mexico. (right) Climbing is just one of the many outdoor activities enjoyed by Philmont's visiting Scouts.

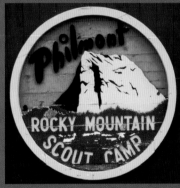

TOP Philmont is loved for its spectacular natural scenery.

ABOVE Almost one hundred Scout camps are located throughout the ranch.

LEFT Thousands of Scout leaders come to Philmont each year to participate in training programs.

"This is a once in a lifetime experience and every Sea Scout deserves an opportunity to participate in a centennial celebration."

JOSH GILLILAND, CHAIR OF THE SEA SCOUT CENTENNIAL TASK FORCE

SEA SCOUT® CENTENNIAL

In 1912, after Arthur Astor Carey organized a Scouts troop aboard his ship, the *Pioneer*, Sea Scouting was officially recognized by the Boy Scouts of America. One hundred years later, celebratory events all around the country were marking the Sea Scout program's centennial—from this single ship had grown a national organization boasting tens of thousands of members.

To qualify as an official centennial event, each activity was required to include the four Ss of Sea Scouting: Scouting, Seamanship, Service, and Social. Baltimore's inner harbour played host to one of the largest celebrations, at which Sea Scouts

from across the nation were treated to a weekend of festivities including a regatta, a cannon salute, and a parade of ships, while in Massachusetts the centennial had particular resonance as it was there that the first troop boarded the *Pioneer*. In recognition of its role in Sea Scouting history, Massachusetts Governor Deval L. Patrick issued a proclamation declaring October 8, 2012 to be Sea Scouts Day in that state, and a commemorative wreath was placed at what had been the *Pioneer*'s docking point during her sailing days. Special centennial lapel pins and temporary patches were also issued to mark the anniversary and to support the Sea Scout program.

ABOVE Sea Scouts and Leaders enjoy frequent boating expeditions.

Commonwealth of Massachusetts

A Proclamation

His Excellency Governor Deval L. Patrick

Whereas Sea Scouts, a specialized program of the Boy Scouts of America traces its roots back to England and Sir Robert Baden-Powell, the Founder of Scouting, whose vision to teach boat management and seamanship as a means of self-development and self-improvement for young men inspired Arthur A. Carey of Massachusetts to begin using the schooner Pioneer as a Boy Scout Training Ship, on the waters of the Massachusetts coast; and

Whereas The Sea Scout program which started in Massachusetts and has since grown into a national coed outdoor program for young adults ages 14 to 20, that promotes knowledge of our nation's maritime heritage and provides young people with positive opportunities through hands-on maritime education, training, and experiences; and

Whereas Sea Scouts has partnered with civic organizations promoting safe boating, environmental conservation and community service; and

Whereas Thousands of Sea Scouts have served in the military and naval forces of this nation and actively defended their country; and

Whereas Fleet Admiral Chester W. Nimitz stated that forty percent of the men under his command in WWII had been Scouts, sixty percent of whom won decorations for valor; and

Whereas This year we celebrate the 100th anniversary of the Sea Scouts and their many contributions to the Commonwealth,

Now, Therefore, I, Deval L. Patrick, Governor of the Commonwealth of Massachusetts, do hereby proclaim October 8th, 2012 to be,

SEA SCOUTS DAY

And urge all the citizens of the Commonwealth to take cognizance of this event and participate fittingly in its observance.

Given at the Executive Chamber in Boston, this twenty-fifth day of September, in the year two thousand and twelve, and of the Independence of the United States of America, the two hundred and thirty-sixth.

By His Excellency

DEVAL L. PATRICK
GOVERNOR OF THE COMMONWEALTH

WILLIAM FRANCIS GALVIN
SECRETARY OF THE COMMONWEALTH

God Save the Commonwealth of Massachusetts

LEFT Governor Deval L. Patrick's official proclamation declaring Sea Scouts Day in Massachusetts.
BELOW Sea Scouts enjoying activities onboard ship.
BELOW LEFT The official Sea Scout Centennial patch was worn on dress uniforms throughout the centennial year.

"The Summit is a place that takes kids to the limits of what they think they can do, and then goes further. The Summit is more than just a place for Scouts; it's Scouting's next step."

BOY SCOUTS OF AMERICA

SUMMIT BECHTEL RESERVE™

In Mount Hope, West Virginia, in an area encompassing over 10,000 acres, lie a Scout Reserve, a High Adventure Base, and a National Center for Scouting Excellence. Here, at Summit Bechtel Reserve, an impressive range of high-tech facilities and innovative programs bring Scouting firmly into the modern era.

One of the Summit's most spectacular sights is the CONSOL Energy Bridge. This marvel of modern engineering is over 700 feet long and crosses a huge gorge at a height of 200 feet. Built with the aim of minimal intrusion on the surrounding environment, the lightweight bridge features several walkways with purpose-built observation points offering stunning views of the valley.

In the summer of 2014, when the Summit is officially opened, the first Scouting groups will begin to arrive to embark on week-long adventures, over the course of which they will have the opportunity to test their skills at climbing, shooting, and biking, as well as facing the challenges of zip-lining and kayaking along the New River Gorge.

In the meantime, the Summit does not lie empty; on July 15, 2013, it welcomed the National Scout Jamboree to its new permanent home. Over 50,000 Scouts and staff, Venturers and volunteers descended on the site for this celebration of all things Scouting, held once every four years. Whether testing their skills or learning new ones, cementing old friendships or making new ones, for the next ten days outdoor adventure was the order of the day, while shows and concerts entertained the masses by night. The success of this event means that the next World Scout Jamboree, which is to be held at Summit Bechtel Reserve in 2019, is much anticipated

ABOVE The steel New River Gorge Bridge stretches over 3,000 feet across the New River Gorge, high above the whitewater river below.

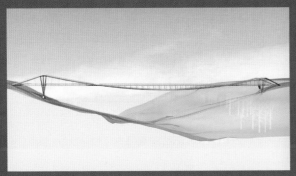

TOP Aerial view of Summit Bechtel Reserve, with the CONSOL Energy Bridge under construction at the center.

ABOVE left and right Digital impressions of the completed bridge structure.

LEFT Map of Summit Bechtel Reserve.

TM

TM

SCOUT STRONG

Over a century's worth of Boy Scouts have pledged the words "to keep myself physically strong" as part of the Scout Oath— and never has an awareness of physical health and fitness been of such prominence as in our health-conscious contemporary society. Recognizing this, the Boy Scouts of America made a formal commitment to promoting wellbeing among its members with the launch of their SCOUTStrong initiative in August 2011. As part of this endeavor, the BSA aligned itself with the President's Council on Fitness, Sports & Nutrition to create the Scout-specific Presidential Active Lifestyle Award (PALA).

Open to current Scouts and their families as well as to all Scouting staff, volunteers, and alumni, earning the PALA award requires that participants undertake to:

• Do 60 minutes of physical activity a day (30 minutes for adults) five days a week for six weeks.

• Implement and maintain a new healthy-eating goal each week.

• Keep a progress log using the online activity tracker or a paper-based personal activity log.

In addition to the health benefits gained, participants will be eligible for a Certificate of Achievement as well as a joint BSA/PALA SCOUTStrong PALA Challenge award patch.

To promote the challenge among their troops and within their community, Scout leaders are encouraged to build awareness via local media and online channels, as well as to organize activities that will help members to meet the physical activity requirement or to endorse existing events as tie-ins to the PALA scheme.

Intended to be a springboard to an entire lifetime of healthy habits—and with the aim of seeing over half a million youngsters achieve the award by 2013— SCOUTStrong is a fitting continuation of Robert Baden-Powell's declaration that "the purpose of the Boy Scout Movement is to build men and women as citizens endowed with the three H's namely, Health, Happiness and Helpfulness."

TOP (left) The official SCOUTStrong logo. (right) The SCOUTStrong PALA patch is available to participants who successfully complete the challenge. ABOVE The SCOUTStrong Achievement Certificate can be downloaded once all the program requirements have been met.

SCOUTStrong™ PALA Activity Log

Participant name _____ Age _____ Date started _____

Council name _____ Date started _____

Verification

I certify that I met the requirements of the Presidential Active Lifestyle Award.

❑ I was physically active for at least five days each week, and I met my healthy eating goals.

❑ I have performed my healthy eating and physical activities for at least six weeks.

Participant signature _____

Supervising adult's signature (if applicable) _____

Note: Submit this paper log to your Scout leader, or keep for your own records. Please do not submit to the President's Challenge office.

	Day	Physical Activities	No. of minutes or pedometer steps
WEEK 1	Mon		
	Tue		
	Wed		
	Thu		
	Fri		
	Sat		
	Sun		

Healthy Eating—Select a goal this week

	Day	Physical Activities	No. of minutes or pedometer steps
WEEK 2	Mon		
	Tue		
	Wed		
	Thu		
	Fri		
	Sat		
	Sun		

Healthy Eating—Circle and continue with last week's goal, and add a new goal.

	Day	Physical Activities	No. of minutes or pedometer steps
WEEK 3	Mon		
	Tue		
	Wed		
	Thu		
	Fri		
	Sat		
	Sun		

Healthy Eating—Circle and continue with last week's goal, and add a new go

	Day	Physical Activities	No. of minutes or pedometer steps
	Mon		
	Tue		
	Wed		
	Thu		
	Fri		
	Sat		
	Sun		

	Day	Physical Activities	No. of pedom
WEEK 5	Mon		
	Tue		
	Wed		
	Thu		
	Fri		
	Sat		
	Sun		

Healthy Eating—Circle and continue with last week's goal, and add a new g

Healthy Eating Goals

I filled my plate with fruits and vegetables.

At least half of the grains that I consumed were whole gr

I chose fat-free or low-fat (1 percent) milk, yogurt, or che

I drank water instead of sugary drinks.

Instructions: **Online**—Create an online account at www.scouting.org/SC
affiliated and complete the registration process. Once you achieve your
track your progress. Once completed, you should self-certify the results

---

Program Overview

SCOUTStrong™ PALA

BOY SCOUTS OF AMERICA®

SCOUTStrong™ PALA Healthy Eating Goals

I will make half my plate fruits and vegetables. All forms count—fresh, frozen, canned (fruit in water or 100 percent juice), dried, or 100 percent juice.

At least half of the grains I consume will be whole grains. Switch from a refined grain food to a whole-grain food that lists a whole-grain ingredient first. Examples include whole wheat, brown rice, oatmeal, or wild rice.

I will choose fat-free or low-fat (1 percent) milk, yogurt, or cheese. Dairy products should be a key part of your diet because they provide calcium, vitamin D, and many other nutrients your bones need.

I will drink water instead of sugary drinks. Regular soda and other sweet drinks, such as fruit drinks and energy drinks, have a lot of added sugar. Add a slice of lemon, lime, or a splash of 100 percent juice to your glass of water if you want some flavor.

I will choose lean sources of protein. Select leaner cuts of beef, turkey breast, or chicken breast. Grill, roast, or boil meat, poultry, or seafood instead of frying. Also include beans or peas in main dishes, like chili or a casserole.

I will compare sodium in foods like soup and frozen meals and choose foods with less sodium. Look for "low sodium," "reduced sodium," and "no salt added" on food packages.

I will eat seafood this week. Seafood has protein, minerals, and heart healthy omega-3 fatty acids. Adults should try to eat at least 8 ounces a week, with children eating smaller portions.

I will pay attention to portion size. At home, become familiar with recommended portion sizes in the plates and glasses you use. When dining out, avoid "supersizing" your meal. Instead, choose small size items or request a "to go" box for half of your meal before you start to eat.

SCOUTStrong™ PALA Recommended Activity List and Pedometer Requirements

- Aerobics
- Foot Bag
- Nintendo Wii (Sports)
- Snowshoeing
- Archery
- Football
- Nordic Walking
- Soccer
- Badminton
- Frisbee
- Orienteering
- Softball
- Baseball
- Gardening
- Paddleball
- Squash
- Basketball
- Golf
- Pedometer
- Stationary Bike

- Baton Twirling
- Gymnastics
- Pilates
- Stretching
- Bicycling
- Handball
- Polo
- Surfing
- Billiards
- Hang Gliding
- Racquetball
- Swimming
- Bowling
- Hiking/ Backpacking
- Rock Climbing
- Table Tennis
- Boxing/ Kickboxing
- Hockey
- Roller Skating

- Tai Chi
- Calisthenics
- Home Repair
- Rope Jumping
- Tennis
- Canoeing
- Horseback Riding
- Rowing
- Track & Field
- Cardio Machines
- Horseshoe Pitching
- Rowing Machine
- Trampoline
- Cardio Tennis
- Household Tasks
- Rugby

- Trap & Skeet
- Cheerleading
- Hunting
- Running
- Unicycling
- Children's Games
- Inline Skating
- Sailing
- Volleyball
- Circuit Training
- Jai Alai
- Scuba Diving
- Walking
- Cricket
- Juggling
- Shuffleboard
- Wallyball
- Croquet
- Kayaking
- Skateboarding

- Water Aerobics
- Cross-Country Skiing
- Lacrosse
- Skating
- Water Jogging
- Curling
- Lawn Bowling
- Ski Jumping
- Water Polo
- Dancing
- Lawn Mowing/ Gardening
- Skimobiling
- Water Skiing
- Darts
- Lifting/Hauling
- Skydiving
- Weight Training
- Diving
- Marching

- Sledding
- Whitewater Rafting
- Downhill Skiing
- Martial Arts
- Snorkeling
- Wrestling
- Fencing
- Motocross
- Snow Shoveling
- Yoga
- Field Hockey
- Mountain Biking
- Snowboarding
- Fishing
- Mountain Climbing
- Snowmobiling

SCOUTStrong™ PALA Pedometer Requirements

Age	Steps
Girls (Ages 6-17)	At least 11,000 steps a day
Boys (Ages 6-17)	At least 13,000 steps a day
Adults (Ages 18-older)	At least 8,500 steps a day

TOP An activity log helps participants to keep track of their progress.

ABOVE RIGHT The structure of the program is outlined in an official brochure.

RIGHT Participants must meet nutrition and exercise requirements.

Kayaking

Search and Rescue

Welding

Game Design

Programming

Sustainability

MERIT BADGES

There are over 130 Merit Badges available for Boy Scouts to earn—but these round patches, each bearing an image representing its theme, belong to an ever-changing list. Every year, the National Council examines the catalog of badges to determine whether changes are needed to ensure that the list suits both the times and the current direction of Scouting.

Recent years have brought several changes to the line-up, with the latest additions reflecting our modernized society:

• Game Design: allows Scouts to use their creative and planning skills to design both computer and non-computer-based games (released March 2013).
• Sustainability: an Eagle-required badge promoting responsible use of the world's resources (July 2013).
• Programming: focuses on the basics of modern technology (July 2013).

Three new Merit Badges were also introduced in 2012:

• Welding: introduces Scouts to the fundamentals of this technique (February 2012).
• Kayaking: an introductory-level flatwater kayaking award (June 2012).

• Search and Rescue: provides skills to track and aid people lost or in difficulty (August 2012).

These six awards, along with the existing line-up, do not comprise an exhaustive list—changes and updates to the Merit Badge roll call are always afoot!

MERIT BADGE SERIES

GAME DESIGN

BOY SCOUTS OF AMERICA

TOP The patch for each new badge bears an image relating to its topic. **ABOVE** A merit badge pamphlet outlines the requirements of each award.

American Business · American Cultures · American Heritage · American Labor · Animal Science

Archaeology · Archery · Architecture · Art · Astronamy

Athletics · Automotive Maintenance · Aviation · Backpacking · Basketry

Bird Study · Bugling · Camping · Canoeing · Chemistry

Chess · Cinemalography · Citizenship in the Community · Citizenship in the Nation · Citizenship in the World

Climbing · Coin Collecting · Collections · Communication · Composite Materials

Computers · Cooking · Crime Prevention · Cycling · Dentistry

Disabilities Awareness · Dog Care · Drafting · Electricity · Electronics

Emergency Preparedness · Energy · Engineering · Entreprenourship · Environmental Science

Family Life · Farm Machanics · Fingerprinting · Fire Safety · First Aid

Fish and Wildlife Management · Fishing · Fly-Fishing · Forestry · Game Design

Gardening · Geneology · Geocaching · Geology · Golf

Graphic Arts · Hiking · Home Repairs · Horsemanship · Indian Lone

Insect Study · Inventing · Journalism · Kayaking · Landscape

Law · Leatherwork · Lifesaving · Mammal Study · Medicine

Metalwork · Model Design and Building · Motorboating · Music · Nature

Nuclear Science · Oceanography · Orienteering · Painting · Personal Fitness

Personal Management · Pets · Photography · Pioneering · Plant Science

Plumbing · Pottery · Programming · Public Health · Public Speaking

Pulp and Paper · Radio · Railroading · Reading · Reptile and Amphibian Study

Rifle Shooting · Robotics · Rowing · Safety · Salesmanship

Scholarship · Scouting Heritage · Scuba Diving · Sculpture · Seach and Rescue

Shotgun Shooting · Skating · Small-Boat Sailing · Snow Sports · Soil and Water Conservation

Space Exploration · Sports · Stamp Collection · Surveying · Sustainability

Swimming · Textiles · Theater · Traffic Safety · Truck Transportation

Veterinary Medicine · Water Sports · Weather · Welding · Whitewater

Wilderness Survival · Wood Carving · Woodwork

LEFT AND ABOVE The current set of merit badges numbers over 130.

Scout Oath

On my honor I will do my best
To do my duty to God and my country
and to obey the Scout Law;
To help other people at all times;
To keep myself physically strong,
mentally awake, and morally straight.

UNIFIED OATH

Oaths of allegiance have been sworn by members of the Boy Scouts of America for over a century; the aim, to instill a lifelong appreciation for the moral, ethical, and community values that are so integral to the Scouting movement. For years, the oath sworn by a Scout was determined by the program to which he belonged: while Boy Scouts said the Scout Oath and Law, Cub Scouts pledged the Cub Scout Promise and the Law of the Pack, and Venturers the Venturing Oath and Code.

October 17, 2012, however, signalled an end to this long-established order with the official approval of a BSA declaration that the Scout Oath be used across all Scouting programs and program-specific pledges phased out. This approval came following a year of consultations and task forces, during which research indicated that Cub Scouts would not experience a significant level of added difficulty at comprehending the Scout Oath than they did the Cub Scout Promise, while it was also determined that Venturers might benefit from a closer identification with the values expressed by the Boy Scouts. The summer of 2015 will mark the end of the Cub Scout Promise as the official pledge of the Cub Scouts, while the Venturing Oath will cease to be sworn as early as the end of 2013 or the beginning of 2014. Venturers will also adopt the three-finger sign and salute used by the Boy Scouts and the existing full-hand Venturing sign and salute will be retired.

Several reasons drove the move: because, as the BSA Resolution recalls, "the Mission of the Boy Scouts of America is to prepare young people to make ethical and moral choices over their lifetimes by instilling in them the values of the Scout Oath and Law," regardless of the program to which they belong, the thinking would indicate that the earlier a youngster is familiar with this oath the greater the success of this "lifelong" aspiration. In addition, since many youths progress from one Scouting program to another as they grow older, a shared pledge would serve to reinforce the link between each program and perhaps support a continuance of membership. The unified oath will help to unite the Boy Scout, Cub Scout, Venturer, Varsity, and Sea Scout programs, which, though separate in name, all share a core mission at heart.

AFTERWORD

MY LIFE IN SCOUTING

THIRTY-FIVE YEARS ON, I can recall my start in Scouting. It was the spring of 1973. I'd just passed my eighth birthday. One afternoon, as the school day ended, I marched up to my third-grade teacher and told her, with great pride, that I was going to my first Cub Scout den meeting.

Scouting for me began that afternoon in the basement rec room of our den mother's suburban Long Island house. I don't remember whether I personally had any interest in becoming a Cub Scout, or whether my parents just signed me up. In any event, I loved it. We had *fun*. We did *interesting* things, like making holiday wreaths from the paper punch cards then used to program IBM computers. (I guess that really dates me.)

Then it was up through the Cub Scout ranks, Webelos, the Arrow of Light . . . and then into a Boy Scout troop. Now there was even more fun—because now we got to go camping.

And therein lies the true genius of Scouting. From its inception, Scouting has taught good citizenship, personal development, physical fitness, spiritual growth, concern for the environment—but Scouting would never have become the world's foremost youth movement without appealing to something fundamental to boys and young men: the sheer enjoyment of getting out in the woods, pitching a tent, making a fire, cooking a meal over it, and settling into a sleeping bag and falling into a satisfied slumber to the sound of crickets and the wind sighing in the trees.

My troop camped out frequently—probably one weekend a month, on average, in the spring and fall, a couple of times in the winter, and then a week of summer camp. The troop spent the latter at Yawgoog Scout Reservation in Rhode Island. My first summer-camp experience came when I was eleven. It literally expanded my horizons. The lights of New York City suck up much of the darkness of the night sky in eastern Long Island. Growing up, I'd seen only the very brightest constellations. Now, away from home for the first time, in the clearer air of the New England countryside, I marveled at a night sky that was ablaze with stars.

There were stars in the day, as well. Like a lot of young Scouts, I admired and envied the teenaged and twenty-something camp staffers. I determined to become one of them.

At fourteen, I spent four weeks as a counselor-in-training at Yawgoog. But when I did get a camp-staff position the following year, it was at my local council's camp—Baiting Hollow, in Wading River, Long Island—where I would ultimately spend five summers on staff in various jobs, from waterfront staff to kitchen worker to director of the archery range.

I got one of the most profound moral lessons of my life during a summer at Baiting Hollow. The staff worked a six-day week. Our only day off was from noon on Saturday until noon on Sunday—the interim between the departure of the preceding week's campers and the arrival of the next week's batch.

Early in the summer, on that day off—a drizzly and unseasonably cold day—I went for a walk. As I wandered along a trail, I heard the sound of hammers. Through the trees, I saw the camp director and the program director setting up platform tents and off-loading cots from the camp truck.

I grasped what was happening. At the end-of-the-week staff meeting the night before we'd learned that an unusually large contingent of troops was due to arrive the following week. We would have to prep a couple of disused campsites to accommodate them. But—without announcing it to the staff—the camp director and program director had taken it upon themselves to do the hard work of getting those campsites ready. They could easily have delegated the job to us younger staffers and spent the day with their families. But they didn't.

We all know the saying that a true leader doesn't ask anyone to do what he or she wouldn't do himself or herself. But it takes it to another level when the leaders go ahead and do what needs to be done themselves, without drawing attention to the effort. It's a lesson that's stayed with me ever since.

A couple of years into Boy Scouting I was inducted into the BSA's "honor camping" fraternity—the Order of the Arrow. The OA would become a cherished part of my Scouting experience. Its American Indian–based ritual had a strong appeal, as did the feeling of true brotherhood among members and its ethos of service.

I eventually worked my way up to Eagle Scout—but truth be told, I was a late-soaring Eagle. I fulfilled the requirements for the rank and passed my Eagle board of review not long before my

LEFT The author at his Eagle Scout court of honor.

eighteenth birthday—after which I would have been ineligible. What I really loved about Scouting was camping, summer-camp staff, and the OA. Earning Eagle just seemed a matter of accumulating merit badges. What did it signify, really?

After I turned seventeen and the deadline started to loom, though, I realized that my attitude toward Eagle was immature and just plain wrong. Earning Eagle was something I owed to my parents, who had faithfully supported me for all those years—driving me to meetings and campouts and other events, paying my troop dues and camping fees, and encouraging my Scouting efforts in every way. It was something I owed to the Scouters who had guided me along the advancement trail and who had gone out of their way to impart the moral and practical lessons of Scouting to me. It was something I owed to the community and nation that had nurtured me. And, finally, I realized at some level that it was something I owed to myself. I had come this far over ten years; now I needed to go the distance.

I earned my last required merit badges and developed a plan for a service project. And that service project was one of the most fun and fulfilling things I've ever done. It involved transplanting beach-grass plants from an island in the Great South Bay of Long Island to the barrier beaches that separate the bay from the Atlantic Ocean in order to stem soil erosion. The local town government contributed a barge to carry the burlap-bagged plants from island to beach.

The main effort took place on a sparkling fall day when the sun danced on the blue waters of the bay. It was hard work digging up the plants, bagging them, loading them on the barge, and then placing them in their new habitat. But I had a great crew of helpers, and the hours flew by amid joking and laughter—and a lot of chilly, salty mud. I was especially happy and proud that the Scouts who turned out to help weren't just members of my troop, but friends from camp staff and the OA—some of whom traveled a considerable distance to pitch in.

And later that year, at my Eagle Scout court of honor, I saw the beaming faces of my family, friends, and fellow Scouts and Scouters, and I knew that I'd done the right thing.

Then it was off to college. I spent one more summer on camp staff. The following year I was inducted into the Vigil Honor of the OA—something that I viewed with almost as much pride as attaining Eagle.

During my active years in Scouting, I'd always had it in my mind that after I "grew up and settled down," I'd return to Scouting as an adult leader—teaching the young 'uns how to tie a bowline knot ("The rabbit goes through the hole . . .") and how to make a "fuzz stick" out of a twig to start a fire—as I'd been taught myself.

It didn't work out that way. I may have grown up but I never really settled down; moving frequently, bouncing between the United Kingdom and the United States, I never put down roots deep enough to regain my footing in Scouting.

But the legacy of the dozen years I spent in Scouting never left me. At my Eagle Scout court of honor, the words of the ceremony informed me that I was now a "marked man"—having attained this status, much would be expected of me as a grown-up. And I found that this was true. When people learned that I was an Eagle Scout, they indeed looked at me a little bit differently. And indeed, they had higher expectations of me.

It would be dishonest of me to say that I've always met those Eagle-Scout expectations—or that I've always lived up to the letter of the Scout Oath and Law. But the lessons I learned in Scouting are still ever-present in my mind, and I still measure myself against the principles that the BSA upholds.

So when the publisher approached me about writing this book, I jumped at the opportunity. I saw the project as a way of finally giving something back to an organization that was such a vital and positive influence in my life.

If you've enjoyed this book—if you've learned something from it—if it motivates you to further involvement in this magnificent movement—then I've done my job.

Yours in Scouting,
CHUCK WILLS
NEW YORK CITY, 2008

RIGHT Scouting prepares boys for a lifetime of adventure.

London, New York, Melbourne,
Munich, and Delhi

BOY SCOUTS OF AMERICA®: A Centennial History is
produced by becker&mayer!, Bellevue, Washington
www.beckermayer.com

DESIGN Ann Cannings, Richard Czapnik, Joanna Price,
EDITORIAL Emer Fitzgerald, Cécile Landau, Jenna Land Free,
Kristin Mehus-Roe, Amelia Riedler,
SENIOR DTP DESIGNER David McDonald
PHOTO EDITOR Shayna Ian
PRODUCTION COORDINATION Diane Ross and Leah Finger
BUSINESS DEVELOPMENT Michael Vaccaro and Brian Saliba
ASSOCIATE PUBLISHER Nigel Duffield

This edition published in 2013
First American edition, 2009

Published in the United States by
DK Publishing
345 Hudson Street
New York, New York 10014

13 14 15 16 17   10 9 8 7 6 5 4 3 2 1
001-175877-Sep/13

A catalog record for this book is available from the Library of Congress.

ISBN: 978-1-4654-1406-9

DK books are available at special discounts when purchased in bulk for sales promotions,
premiums, fund-raising, or educational use. For details, contact: DK Publishing Special Markets,
345 Hudson Street, New York, New York 10014 or SpecialSales@dk.com.

Produced by DK Publishing under license from the Boy Scouts of America.

For more information on the Boy Scouts of America programs, visit www.scouting.org.

Printed and bound in China by South China Printing Co. Ltd.

Discover more at
www.dk.com

BIBLIOGRAPHY

Anderson, H. Allen. *The Chief: Ernest Thompson Seton and the Changing West*. College Station, Texas: Texas A&M University Press, 1986.

Applebome, Peter. *Scout's Honor: A Father's Unlikely Foray into the Woods*. Orlando, Florida: Harcourt Publishing, 2003.

Bezucha, R. D. *The Golden Anniversary Book of Scouting*. New York: Golden Press, 1959.

Birkby, Robert. *The Official Boy Scout Handbook*, 10th edition. Irving, Texas, 1990.

Birkby, Robert, *The Official Boy Scout Handbook*, 11th edition. Irving, Texas, 1998.

Blassingame, Wyatt. *Dan Beard: Scoutmaster of America*. Champaign, Illinois: Garrard Publishing Company, 1972.

Boy Scouts of America. *Annual Report 75th (1984)–97th (2006)*. Washington, D.C.: Government Printing Office, 1984–2006.

Boy Scouts of America. *The Big Bear Cub Scouts Book*. Irving, Texas: Boy Scouts of America Publishing, 1993.

Boy Scouts of America. *Fieldbook*, 4th edition. Irving, Texas, 2004.

Boy Scouts of America. *Handbook for Boys* (facsimile reprint of the 1911 Doubleday, Page & Co. edition). Bedford, Massachusetts: Applewood Books, 1997.

Boy Scouts of America. *Handbook for Boys*. New York City: Boy Scouts of America, 1935.

Cass, William F. *Return to the Summit of Scouting: A Scouter's Midlife Journey Back to Philmont*. Davisburg, Michigan: Wilderness Adventure Press, 1993.

Hillcourt, William. *The Official Boy Scout Handbook*, 9th edition. Irving, Texas, 1979.

Hillcourt, William and Keith Monroe. *The Official Patrol Leader Handbook of the Boy Scouts of America*. Irving, Texas, 1980.

Jeal, Tim. *Baden-Powell: Founder of the Boy Scouts*. New Haven: Yale Nota Bene, 2001.

Mechling, Jay. *On My Honor: Boy Scouts and the Making of American Youth*. Chicago: University of Chicago Press, 2001.

Murray, Williamson D. *The History of the Boy Scouts of America*. New York: Boy Scouts of America, c. 1937.

Oursler, Will. *The Boy Scout Story*. Garden City, New York: Doubleday, c. 1955.

Peterson, Robert W. *The Boy Scouts; An American Adventure*. New York: American Heritage Publishing, 1985.

Petterchak, Janice A. *Lone Scout: W. D. Boyce and American Boy Scouting*. Rochester, Illinois: Legacy Press, 2003.

Rosenthal, Michael. *The Character Factory: Baden-Powell's Boy Scouts and the Imperatives of Empire*. New York: Pantheon Books, 1986.

The Scout Association. *An Official History of Scouting*. London: Hamlyn (a division of Octopus Publishing Group Ltd.), 2006.

Scouting Magazine. January 1984–April 2007. Boy Scouts of America. Irving, Texas.

Soto, Carolyn. *The Boy Scouts*. New York: Exeter Books, 1987.

BOY SCOUTS OF AMERICA®
FIRST EDITION (2009)
ACKNOWLEDGMENTS

Assembling a book the size and scope of *Boy Scouts of America: A Centennial History* is a tremendous undertaking. Untold hours of research and review were devoted to the setting up of the original (first) edition and the Boy Scouts of America would like to acknowledge the following individuals and their contributions.

RESEARCH TEAM

The research team worked closely with the author and publisher to assemble historical documents for reproduction and reviewed information for historical accuracy.

Connie Adams, manager, Records Management/Archives

Tracy Waters, records coordinator

Sarah Walker, records coordinator

Michael Roytek, photo manager

Christy Batchelor, photo technician

Caryl Lombardi, media buyer/digital assets manager

Elizabeth Brantley, curator of collections and exhibits, National Scouting Museum

Amanda Durst, assistant curator, National Scouting Museum

Steven Price, archivist, National Scouting Museum

IMAGE PREPARATION TEAM

The image preparation team assembled and prepared for publication all of the wonderful historical imagery presented in this book.

Kim Garrett, senior graphics specialist

Michael Ruiz, graphics specialist

Mary Hager, senior graphic designer

REVIEW TEAM

The review team read and reviewed the book, from manuscript to finished product, and provided significant input and feedback on the content and accuracy.

James J. Terry, assistant Chief Scout Executive

Wayne Brock, assistant Chief Scout Executive

Michael A. Ashline, director, Supply Group

Willie Iles, director, Development & Strategic Initiatives Group

David K. Park, BSA legal counsel

Norman Burkhalter, director, Strategic Planning/National Events

Jim Wilson, associate publisher, BSA; director, Custom Communication Division

Rick Diles, director, Sales/Planning and Development Division

Larry Knapp, director, Merchandising and Marketing Division

Dan Buckhout, director, Publishing Support, Custom Communication Division

Karen Thompson, senior team leader, Custom Communication Division

Mike Gibson, editor/copy editor, Custom Communication Division

Stephen Medlicott, director, Marketing & Communications Division

Renee Fairrer, associate director, Marketing & Communications Division

Bill Evans, associate director, Venturing Division

Joe Glasscock, director of Boy Scout Program Development

Clyde Mayer, director, Order of the Arrow

Bill Steele, director, Advancement/NESA

Sam Thompson, director, Cub Scout Division

Bob Mersereau, director, 100th Anniversary Project

David L. Harkins, associate director, Business Development, Sales/ Planning and Development Division

Karen Brown, senior buyer, Merchandising and Marketing Division

Paul Claus, associate director, Planning and Development, Sales/ Planning and Development Division

Norman Schaefer, territory manager, Sales/Planning and Development Division

LEAD TEAM

The lead team provided daily coordination and management of the project from inception to the published piece.

Dan Buckhout, director, Publishing Support, Custom Communication Division

David L. Harkins, associate director, Business Development, Sales/ Planning and Development Division

ABOUT THE AUTHOR

Chuck Wills worked as a writer and editor for more than twenty years, serving as an editorial director for DK Publishing, Inc., and international and co-editions editor for Rodale Books International. As a writer, his books include *Destination America*, a history of immigration to the United States (published in 2005 as a companion volume to the PBS series of the same name), *America's Presidents*, and *Lincoln: The Presidential Archives*. He was an Eagle Scout, a Vigil Honor member of the Order of the Arrow, and a veteran of five seasons as a staff member at Baiting Hollow Scout Camp on Long Island, New York. A highly esteemed friend and colleague, Chuck died unexpectedly on April 6 2011.

AUTHOR'S ACKNOWLEDGMENTS

I'd like to thank Brian Saliba at DK for giving me the opportunity to write this book; the staff at the BSA national office for their help and guidance; everyone at becker&mayer!, including Shayna Ian, Joanna Price, Matthew Taylor, Kristin Mehus-Roe, Leah Finger, and Jason Astrop—and Jenna Land Free in particular, for her patience, good humor, and superb editorship; all of the Scouts and Scouters who encouraged and inspired me on my own Scouting trail—especially my fellow staffers at Baiting Hollow Scout Camp and my brothers in Shinnecock Lodge 360 of the OA; and finally, as always, to Rachel, for everything.

This book is dedicated to Rich and Fitz—who now soar with the eagles forever.

IMAGE CREDITS

INDEX

Page numbers in *italic* refer to the illustrations

BOY SCOUTS OF AMERICA
100 YEARS OF SCOUTING

BSA
2010

CELEBRATING THE ADVENTURE
CONTINUING THE JOURNEY